PRENTICE-HALL FOUNDATIONS OF EDUCATION SERIES
Hobert W. Burns, Editor

A Social History of Education	Robert Holmes Beck
Problems in Education and Philosophy	Charles J. Brauner and Hobert W. Burns
Teaching and Learning: A Psychological Perspective	Thomas E. Clayton
Schools, Scholars, and Society	Jean Dresden Grambs
Tradition and Change in Education: A Comparative Study	Andreas M. Kazamias and Byron G. Massialas

JEAN DRESDEN GRAMBS

PRENTICE-HALL, INC., ENGLEWOOD CLIFFS, N. J.

SCHOOLS, SCHOLARS, AND SOCIETY

PRENTICE-HALL INTERNATIONAL, INC., *London*
PRENTICE-HALL OF AUSTRALIA, PTY., LTD., *Sydney*
PRENTICE-HALL OF CANADA, LTD., *Toronto*
PRENTICE-HALL OF INDIA (PRIVATE) LTD., *New Delhi*
PRENTICE-HALL OF JAPAN, INC., *Tokyo*

Second printing..... August, 1965

FOUNDATIONS OF EDUCATION SERIES
SCHOOLS, SCHOLARS, AND SOCIETY
BY JEAN DRESDEN GRAMBS

© COPYRIGHT 1965 BY PRENTICE-HALL, INC.
ENGLEWOOD CLIFFS, N. J.

Library of Congress
Catalog Card No.: 65-11325

PRINTED IN THE UNITED STATES OF AMERICA
C–79386-C   C–79385-P

Public education is the "growth industry" of the nation today. Next to defense, education is the single largest enterprise in our political economy and, unlike even defense, it is the one American activity that in some way or at some time directly involves every single citizen.

If public education is quantitatively important, then the training of teachers is one of the most qualitatively important undertakings of the entire educational enterprise. Indeed, the training of teachers is already the single largest undertaking of American higher education, since more college graduates enter the profession of teaching than any other vocation, and it may well be the most important undertaking of our colleges and universities.

Even so, despite the size of the American educational establishment, it is remarkable how little is understood of the educative process, especially of the intellectual bases of education that support all pedagogy; and of all those who have—in the language of defense rather than education—a "need to know," the prospective teacher has the greatest need.

Prospective teachers need to understand education through the historical perspective of Western culture—and so the series includes a volume in the history of education, a volume that may fairly be called an intellectual history of education, rather than a mere chronology of educationally important dates or historically important pedagogues.

Prospective teachers need to understand that the school, and the children and teachers in it, are social organisms inevitably influenced by the nature of the society in which they exist—and so the series includes a volume in the sociology of education, a volume showing how the public school reflects, for better or worse, the reality rather than the image of contemporary American society.

Prospective teachers need to understand the psychological nature of children and how it limits, if not determines, what schools should or should not do (Is it reasonable to expect, as many teachers do, a six- or seven-year-old to sit quietly and attentively for a major portion of his waking day?)—and so the series includes a volume in the psychology of education, a volume that pays particular attention to the ways in which children grow, develop, mature, learn, and change their behavior.

Prospective teachers need to understand the close functional relationship between philosophy and practice in education and, at the same time, to

v

FOUNDATIONS OF EDUCATION SERIES

see that many of the practical problems they will face as teachers (e.g., How shall I grade? Shall I use drill? Should children be segregated on such bases as talent, color, or religion?) are solvable only in terms of prior philosophic inquiry—and so the series includes a volume in philosophy of education, a volume that views philosophy as dressed in the working clothes of a practical discipline rather than in the formal attire of impractical abstractions.

Prospective teachers need perspective to see the historical, philosophical, social, and psychological foundations of education in a context both different and larger than any one locality, region, or nation affords—and so the series includes a volume in comparative education, a volume designed to help the teacher compare and contrast his experience and educational system with the experiences and systems of other teachers in other nations and cultures.

These things the prospective teacher needs to know; he needs to be well grounded in the foundations of education, for they represent the intellectual tools that can give him scholarly leverage in his profession. But, given the thinness of time and the immensity of need in teacher education curriculums, how is this to be done?

The authors of this series believe that no single volume, be it a large, well-edited book of readings or a long treatise by one scholar, can meet the challenge of offering prospective teachers what they need to know as well as can a series of smaller volumes, each written by a specialist in one particular aspect of the foundations of education. Each volume in this series, by design, can stand alone as an introduction to an intellectual discipline; but when taken together the volumes unite these independent yet related disciplines into a series that offers prospective teachers a fuller, more unified introduction to the subject matters that underlie the profession of teaching.

We are convinced that prospective teachers who study these volumes in the foundations of education, and who discuss the concepts and issues presented with their instructors, will take to their future classrooms a firmer understanding not only of how to do the teaching job at hand but, more significant, of why their teaching job is so surpassingly important.

Hobert W. Burns

Educating the young in and out of school is one of the major activities of any society. Because it pervades so much of life and is typically so close to every parent and growing child, a whole view of the educational process is extremely difficult to achieve. In fact, it is probably impossible ever to feel that one has a certain grasp of the totality of educational experience. The sociologist, however, may lay modest claim at least to making a brave attempt. Sociology, borrowing liberally from sister social science disciplines, provides a vantage point for taking some provocative looks at a most elusive and pervasive institution.

In this brief book, we can only begin to suggest the rich literature that provides insights into the educational process in society. It is hoped that following this introduction, the student of the schools will proceed to look further and, perhaps through his own observations, help fill in some of the blanks or correct some of the biases.

While one attempts to approach objectivity, it is inevitable that one's background, experiences, and predilections will serve as a selective screen. It is hoped that the reader will find ample cause to argue (or agree) with the points made, and that he will seek further data to counter or defend a position. Educated discussion about education is one of the more urgent needs of the times; this volume, hopefully, will contribute much ammunition to the argument. In order to provide additional depth of understanding, a companion volume of related readings is available: *Sociology and Education: a Book of Readings*, James D. Raths and Jean Dresden Grambs, editors, (Englewood Cliffs, N. J.: Prentice-Hall, Inc., 1964). These readings were selected especially to augment the presentation in this volume, as well as to present some material not covered.

The author takes full responsibility for all errors and opinions. However, acknowledgment must be made of the help, advice, and counsel of many colleagues. This book would never have been written had not the author been introduced to the field many years ago by the inspiration of Professor Lawrence G. Thomas, of Stanford University. Dr. Hobert Burns, of Hofstra College, persuaded me to undertake the task of writing this book. Many of my colleagues have read and criticized portions of the manuscript and individual chapters. I wish particularly to thank the following for giving me their reactions to individual chapters and, in some instances, to the whole manuscript: J. Paul Anderson, Glenn O. Blough, Angeline J. Boisen, Katherine Evans, Roger R. Kelsey, John R. Lawson, George L. Marx, Clarence A. Newell, Franklin Patterson, M. Brewster Smith, and Kimball Wiles. Miss Diana Powers, of Prentice-Hall, provided sympathetic, patient, and expert editorial help. Mr. Roger Holloway, editor, Prentice-Hall, has been a staunch friend and supporter throughout the whole enterprise.

I would also like to express special appreciation to Mrs. Ellen Behrens for her assistance in the typing and preparation of the manuscript through its several drafts.

Jean Dresden Grambs

PREFACE

CONTENTS

School . . . what picture does it conjure in your mind? Are your memories pleasant or unpleasant? Do you remember a face, a smell, an event, a crisis? Are your feelings mixed and unclear, or sure and sharp?

"School" has a different meaning to each of us. The teacher will view the school differently from the first grader; the parent from the congressman; the custodian from the adolescent.

One's view of school derives from thousands of experiences. It is influenced by success or failure, by acceptance or rejection in the school environment, by what parents and friends thought and felt about school. As one's role in life changes, so does one's view of school. As school recedes into the background, selective recall provides us with a censored and screened version of what it was like.

Whose view of the school is the true one? To this question there probably never will be a definite answer. A complex institution that touches the life of everyone in one way or another can never be fully known. We would have to know the life experience of all; yet, even this would give us only an accumulation of impressions, not the whole picture.

An approximation of what school is "really" like

THE EYE
OF THE
BEHOLDER

1

is one of the goals of the sociologist when he examines the school. The sociology of the school or the sociology of education (we use these terms interchangeably) is an attempt to organize the many views of the school into some kind of coherent picture. Assuming that no one person's "school" is the same as that of any other person, we can add up these impressions and versions (and there is a good deal of research on aspects of the school which does just this) and see how the various versions and impressions fit.

The sociological view provides objectivity. Because something is familiar, we tend to see it less and less. If you have been away from home on a trip, on your return the old place looks, somehow, different. Scenes recalled from childhood are often terribly disappointing when revisited. The huge mountain is only a meager hill; the fabulous haunted house is an old deserted barn; the pounding surf is only gently rolling waves. Thus, it is with schools. Memory distorts. The familiar or the remote is not clearly seen.

The sociological approach takes one out of the picture, so to speak, so that one gets a new impression by veiwing the familiar in a new and perhaps more accurate perspective and by including in the total picture portions hitherto hidden from sight because of one's own specialized view. The sociological approach may be likened to that of the biologist who studies the ecology of a frog, for example, the kind of pond it lives in, the kind of water in the pond, the insects who inhabit the pond, the weather over a period of days or months, and the effect of these factors upon the nature of the frog's life in the pond.

The sociologist, in approaching the school, is attempting a somewhat similar task, but the school is harder to catch and study than a frog. We need to examine the social setting in which the school—education—occurs: the ecology of the school, so to speak.

School as a social institution has been subject to a remarkable amount of comment, but also to remarkably little organized and systematic study. As the school is one of the most influential institutions in our society, this lack of study is regrettable. *Education about education* is one of the major missing areas in our educational process.

The sociology of education provides a big tent under which can be gathered many kinds of data. Since the school involves people, the social psychology of youths, teachers, parents, and other adults must be considered. Anthropology tells us a good deal about how society molds youth. Sociologists have studied relevant aspects of social interaction both within and without the schools. Social philosophers have considered problems of values that require consideration by educational designers. The dividing lines among and between the social science disciplines are fuzzy at many points, and rarely so tenuous as when we try to outline the area of concern of the educational sociologist. A more accurate term might be the "educational social psychologist."

The history of education is the story of an institution that has responded slowly and erratically to social pressure. In our time, its survival will perhaps be dependent upon whether the educational process can change rapidly, *in the right way*, and in the right direction. The study of the sociology of the schools should enable all who are parts of the educational enterprise to make deliberate improvements in the social arrangements of the institution on the basis of clearly observed need, rather than having change come or be resisted as it has in the past because of pressure, whim, comfort, inertia, or rigidity.

BIBLIOGRAPHY

BELL, ROBERT R., ed., *The Sociology of Education: A Sourcebook*. Homewood, Ill.: The Dorsey Press, Inc., 1962. A well selected book of readings.

BROOKOVER, WILBUR B., *A Sociology of Education*, rev. ed. New York: American Book Company, 1964. A good introduction to educational sociology, with major emphasis on the inner workings of the school system.

CHARTERS, W. W., JR. AND N. L. GAGE, *Readings in the Social Psychology of Education*. Boston: Allyn and Bacon, Inc., 1963. A good balance between psychological and sociological orientation in the readings collected here.

HALSEY, A. H., JEAN FLOUD, AND C. ARNOLD ANDERSON, *Education, Economy and Society, A Reader in the Sociology of Education*. New York: Free Press of Glencoe, Inc., 1961. Includes a number of studies from English experience.

HARRIS, RAYMOND P., *American Education, Facts, Fancies, Folklore*. New York: Random House, 1961. In forthright style, this educator pokes holes in some well-beloved myths about American education.

HAVIGHURST, ROBERT AND BERNICE NEUGARTEN, *School and Society*, rev. ed. Boston: Allyn and Bacon, Inc., 1962. Relates school processes and problems to major issues in society.

HODGKINSON, HAROLD L., *Education in Social and Cultural Perspectives*. Englewood Cliffs, N. J.: Prentice-Hall, Inc., 1962. Covers such topics as school rewards and motivation, social mobility, cultural lag, and human learning.

SPINDLER, GEORGE D., ed., *Education and Culture: Anthropological Approaches*. New York: Holt, Rinehart & Winston, Inc., 1963. These readings present insights into the schools in America and other cultures from the viewpoint of the anthropologist.

WALLER, WILLARD, *The Sociology of Teaching*. New York: John Wiley & Sons, Inc., 1932. This is the classic study of the school as a social institution. It is brilliant, witty, and devastating.

3

To whom does the school belong? The children who attend school could be said to have quite a stake in the institution. The principal speaks of "my school" and "my faculty"; is it then his school? The teacher, too, talks about "my school" and "my children" as though he, too, owned them, but does he really? The parents speak proudly or critically of "our schools." And the taxpayer, whether parent or not, considers that his contribution to the school operation makes him a part owner of the enterprise.

THE INTERRELATEDNESS OF CULTURE AND EDUCATION

It would be hard to argue with the proposition that, in the last analysis, society owns the schools. But then, what is society? Society can be defined as a group of people who share a common culture, which includes the formal and informal social arrangements, the mores and language, the religious institutions and beliefs, and the processes of governing and ordering that envelop a group of similarly socialized persons. Some groups of people have national character and are designated by national identities; for example, French, Italian, or Moroccan, etc. Within

4

WHOSE SCHOOL IS IT?

2

many nations there are subgroupings that may be based on different languages, religious beliefs, food habits, or other differences. Whatever the subgroup, however, those in it are readily identified by other members because of similarity in values, beliefs, etiquettes, dialect, and so forth.

Education is the process whereby each social group or society inducts the young into its own particular style of social relationships. Cultures have various ways of dealing with children; in some they are permitted utter freedom until puberty, when, after successfully passing through severe rites, they are adjudged to be adult and capable of adult tasks and responsibilities. In some cultures, children are viewed as nuisances, to be kept out of the way and out of sight. In others they are loved and pampered and adored. Each way of dealing with a child is an aspect of his education. All of the ways adults respond to him tell him what is right or wrong, what is expected, and what is taboo.

Nonliterate cultures, where there are relatively few roles to be filled, do not have "schools" in our sense of the word. The world of the child is close to that of the adult. The little girl sees her mother, and innumerable aunts and female cousins, performing the tasks that women perform. She is told thousands of times how she will grow up to be similar to them. So with the boy. He observes older boys and men going through their tasks, and is told what the group expects of him as a growing boy. Perhaps most essential in this picture is the fact that the worlds of child and adult are close; children are not segregated from the working members of their group for hours at a time. The societies of which we speak do not usually develop extensive privacy—each family to its own home and each person in the family to his own room. Children learn about social and life processes because these processes are going on around them all the time.

As the social order becomes more complex—and the introduction of written material is one of the first steps toward complexity—the educational process necessarily changes.

First, of course, learning to read becomes a major educational task. Someone must be available who understands how to teach another person to read. Then, having teachers, one has to have schools, places to gather children together so they can be instructed. Thus, we observe the gradual separation of the society of children and youths from the society of adults. The more there is to learn—the more books there are, and the more varied the tasks needed to keep the social order in healthy motion—the longer will be the period of separation. Our culture is a prime example of such separation: having an extraordinarily high degree of technological equipment, we need thousands of different kinds of trained personnel to keep things going. Young people are needed who are highly literate and skilled in many kinds of operations because they will be called upon to perform many roles in life. Children therefore, are kept in school for longer and longer periods. We will examine this phenomenon later. The point here, of course, is that *cultural variations determine the kind of educational process a society establishes.* Every culture, no matter how it may look from the outside, must civilize its young, albeit in its own terms.

5

The amount of time, attention, and money devoted to the education of children reflects to a certain extent the social valuation and the social role of children. Children have always been valued in America, though for different reasons and to differing degrees over the centuries. In early America, children were valued because they were useful and economically necessary. The settler on the edge of the wilderness could not count on any labor except that which he could provide himself; thus, the more children he had, the more free labor was available to him. This was somewhat hard on the women, and as a result many families had successive mothers. A widower could not rear his children alone; consequently, quick remarriage was common. Since many of the children born did not survive the hardships of frontier living, those who did live until a useful age were that much more valued. In the industrial cities and the mining areas, too, children were an economic asset. At a very tender age, children were put to work in the factories and mines.

Such a role for children did not support formal educational processes to a very great extent. Every year taken up by school meant a year less for productive work. It was recognized, however, that a literate apprentice was better than an illiterate one. Also, the Protestant emphasis on being able to read the Bible supported minimal education for all.

Later, as a labor surplus developed and as humanitarian interests disclosed the horrible conditions of child labor, efforts were made to get children out of productive labor and into classrooms. Slowly but surely children were pushed out of the labor market. The only area where children continue to work today is in agriculture, particularly among migrant farm labor groups where enforcement of child labor laws is lax.

Children ceased to be productive in the old sense. But to the immigrant, his children became his investment in the future. *He* could never become a doctor, but if he pushed hard enough, his son could. Having many children became an economic liability, particularly if one were to invest so much in their education. With growing prosperity, the average number of children in American families declined to such a point that in the 1930's, fear was expressed. A population decline can spell economic decline, particularly in an economy based on continual expansion of consumer demands. However, population pessimists were wrong. Since World War II, the American population has increased rapidly.

Again, the role of the child has shifted. Today children are a particular kind of asset. Economically they are expensive; they do not return anything to their parents in the way of income, and their years of dependence are getting longer with each generation. Why, then, do we continue to want more children and to have them at such a rate?

Today the immediate family is the main source of emotional satisfaction. Relatives often live across the continent, and our own roots are apt to be shallow and easily pulled up when jobs change. Also, many people feel there is little reason to save money. Even children can be obtained on credit. There seems less reason to save for old age because inflation may destroy the value of anything saved and the retirement plans of business, industry, and government are almost adequate. There is no longer a tradition of handing down to our children a carefully amassed nest egg; we know that inheritance taxes or inflation will take most of it anyway. The best we can do is to have children of our own to love, and to invest all in them today and now. Children, thus, become the focus of concern for today's adults—they are all parents now have of the future.

This different valuation placed on children, and their new role in the personal and emotional life of parents, has significant implications for the school. At one time it was felt to be psychologically dangerous for a couple to have only one child. They would invest too much of their emotions in a vessel too frail to support such a load. Today, unfortunately, we see the phenomenon of three or four children all burdened by the intense interest and almost undivided attention of their parents. The middle-class suburban mother, in particular, expects and is expected to spend full time on her children. To help her in this task are the endless columns of advice to mothers that appear in nearly every magazine read by women and in many newspapers. TV specials have been devoted to helping mother understand her role and her relations to her children. This is, as Harold Taylor put it, the age of the "Understood Child." He says:

> As a result of this new attitude towards child rearing it is extremely difficult for the child to rebel, since he is understood rather than repressed. This has its consequence in giving him nothing but feather pillows to fight, and in developing an attitude of self-understanding before there is a great deal of self to understand.[1]

7

There has been some petulant comment that a little psychology is a dangerous thing; better that people know nothing about personality than have bits and pieces of information. It is our contention that knowledge is never dangerous or useless, and that what is needed is more and more knowledge. In any event, today's parent is striving mightily to understand what happens to his child, and in the process is often confused, frightened, apprehensive, and laden with guilt feelings. Children who are so entangled in the emotional lives of their parents are a different breed from children who may not have been loved as much, but were let alone more.[2]

Children, then, are one of our most precious possessions. Considering this fact, it is one of the paradoxes of the American scene, which we can describe if not explain, that the public at large will spend more for toys, candy, and clothes than for their children's education.

HISTORY MOLDS THE SCHOOLS

What we see happening in the classrooms of today did not get there by accident. Educational procedures, the skills being taught, and the knowledge being conveyed are the result of the particular history of a particular culture.

[1] "The Understood Child," *Saturday Review*, XLIV (May 20, 1961), 47-49.
[2] Arnold W. Green, "The Middle-Class Male Child and Neuroses," *American Sociological Review*, 11 (Feb. 1946), 31-41.

Education in America is a story of borrowing and innovation. The educational purpose was initially religious and Protestant. The forms and content of education derived from British models. As later settlers came from other countries—Germany, Holland, Sweden—some of their views of education were incorporated into the American version. The religious purpose foundered on the sectarian differences that were also brought here by peoples from many different nations. The efforts to sustain democracy necessitated a minimally educated citizenry, forcing eventual acceptance of a common school. Many non-English speaking immigrants needed Americanizing, and quickly. American educators traveled abroad and read educational treatises of foreign leaders. Since there was no tradition-bound national school structure to act as an inhibiting factor, new ideas could be and were incorporated in one locality and thence spread to others. Add to these factors the pressure of the frontier, the incredible hardships of living in a new and rugged land where all institutions had to be built from scratch. Also add a population boom requiring expedients to deal with more and more and more children all the time. Out of this welter of influences has emerged a school system that is truly unique in many ways:

First, our schools are locally controlled by the lay public. No central federal bureaucracy can tell a local school system what to do, what to teach, whom to hire, how long to keep schools open.

Second, the lay public exercises its control through election (in most places directly) of school-board members, who are themselves lay persons. The public also controls schools by voting upon school finance matters in many places, either directly or indirectly.

Third, the American school is inclusive and comprehensive. The common school for all young people, from first grade through twelfth, is typically a nonselective institution. That is, except in some large cities, students pursuing many different vocational and academic goals are all housed under one roof.

Fourth, the public schools, with few exceptions, are coeducational through university and graduate levels.

Fifth, the schools are nonsectarian, nor can any unit of government in any way appear to be supporting any religious organization of an educational nature. This is a tenet of American belief, but the issues are unclear and the resolution of them is still to come.

There are some other aspects of the American school that appear very different, if not downright odd, to foreign observers. But the preceding are probably those that cut most deeply and characterize most of the educational experiences provided for young people.

THE SCHOOLS AND CHANGE

It has been said that the elementary school is 25 years behind the times, the secondary school 50 years, the college and university several centuries. Ideas for educational innovation, which are being discussed today with high excitement among educators and the public, have actually been in the educational literature for many decades. Until very recently, the schools have been conservative institutions. Although this tendency is understandable, some psychologists state that adequate mental health requires both security and change; too much of either can be prison or chaos, neither of which is desirable. Social institutions provide a strong measure of security. Public buildings are big and expensive, not because they need to be, but because the more massive they are, the more permanent they appear.

There are two formal institutions that are particularly resistent to change: the church and the school. We can readily understand why religious change is difficult, and why individual religious change occurs mainly through the traumatic process of conversion. In fact, probably fewer than 5 per cent of adults change their basic religious identification.[3] Religion helps us deal with the unknowable, and it is thus a fundamental security-giver to individual personalities.

The schools, too, strike close to home. In fact, they are even more generally related to the home than is the church: every child in our society *must* attend school or have his educational needs cared for in some way. The society does not make the same demand for religious affiliation or obligation: only 63 per cent of Americans are church members today.[4] What happens in the school happens at home; the school comes home with the child and he brings his home to the school. Parents who may happily trade in a car for a new model every year are content with a vintage model school because it is familiar and known. Parents by and large will permit just so much tinkering with the educational lives of their children; then, they become upset.

Another reason for the conservative nature of the school resides in the very nature of social institutions. The structure into which teachers move as neophytes is similar in most respects to the school in their own past; therefore, they can more easily adapt to peculiarities of principals, parents, or children. Changing the structure means rearranging many kinds of subtle and gross relationhips. Teachers, like other human beings, tend to repeat what they have done even if they are not fully satisfied with their performance; another approach might be worse. The plea of educational innovators that a change will be for the better does not often appeal to an overwhelming number of teachers or administrators. Our human tendency is to fear and, therefore, to avoid the unknown.

Being unaware of the need for change may be due to either fear or apathy. We may not know that change is needed in our ways of doing things because we are afraid to look at reality. Or we may not know that change is required because we have been too lazy, indifferent, or provincial to notice how things around us have changed. The teacher is in a particularly critical position in relation to change. *He* changes: he grows older, he takes on different home responsibilities. But the children always remain the same age! Every year there is a new crop of nine-year-olds, or a new group of eleventh-graders. They are all more or less the same height and weight as the pupils of the year before, and the year before that. It is easy to delude

9

[3] J. Milton Yinger, "Social Forces Involved in Group Identification or Withdrawal," *Daedalus*, 90 (Spring 1961), 247-262.
[4] *Ibid.*

oneself into thinking that this year's group will be as responsive as last year's to the same lessons and the same motivations. The truth of the matter is that no such assumption is warranted. The social world of the child has changed drastically with each decade. The advent of TV has made incredible differences in the world of our young people. The things that adolescents do and think today as a matter of course were daring, indeed, for their parents when the latter were graduating from college. How many of these changes in the outside world the school can ignore is a question we will have to return to again.

Now let us look at the other side of the coin. If the schools do not change, is this not a good thing? Must conservatism in itself be viewed with suspicion? We can identify motives in resistance to change that we may question; however, are such motives reason enough to support change?

In times such as these there may be a significant social role for a *conserving* institution. That is, when such fantastic things as men orbiting in outer space for days at a time can be accomplished, the ordinary human being is in the same position as the Caribbean natives when they viewed the strange white-winged bird which had brought Columbus to their shores. We are all, more or less, struck dumb with awe, astonishment, and terror.

In the succeeding sections of this chapter, and in many parts of the rest of this book, you will find descriptions of many aspects of education that will suggest the need and urgency of change in the schools. But it is important that we keep this caution in mind: Change in and of itself may be more destructive in terms of social consequences than staying right where we are. Though change may seem past due, we must continually reflect on the total social consequences of what we do with an institution so vital to individual survival as our schools.

PRESSURES TOWARD CHANGE

Despite the conservative nature of the schools over the decades, something new has been added in very recent years: Sputnik. A study of instructional changes that occurred in the New York State schools between 1953 and 1960 revealed that the "rate of instructional innovation . . . *more than doubled within 15 months* after the firing of the Soviet Sputnik I on October 4, 1957." [5]

The recognition of the scientific superiority of our major ideological competitors came as a cruel blow to the American self-image. What better to do than blame the schools! Yet, surely American education could hardly be blamed for what occurred, any more than Soviet education could be given the credit. Logic, however, is not always at the forefront when one's pride is badly hit. The result noted in New York State was seen elsewhere. Changes for which educators had been pleading for years were realized overnight: They were granted more libraries, better science laboratories, higher salaries for teachers, and so forth. International ten-

⁵ Henry Brickell, *Organizing New York State for Educational Change* (Albany, New York: The University of the State of New York, State Education Dept., 1961), p. 18.

sions have thus had a direct impact upon educational practices. The results of this pressure toward change are apparent, but not yet easily assessed. Is it essential that all school students become proficient in a foreign language, *any* foreign language? Should academically able students take considerably more science and mathematics than their less talented colleagues, even if their interests and talents lie in other areas? Should students work harder and longer on school tasks? These questions reflect, in part, some of the consequences of the changes resulting from this particular pressure.

A second pressure for change in the schools comes from the sheer factor of numbers. Not only are more people getting married younger, but more people are having more children. During World War II schools were not built because of scarcity of materials, nor were older buildings replaced or repaired. Then came the war-born baby crop. Beginning with 1946 and for ten years thereafter the school systems of the country were not able to keep up with the need for school construction. In area after area elementary schools were on double session; church basements and even empty houses were used as makeshifts. Then this population increase moved on to the secondary schools. Enrollments jumped 76.6 per cent in the ten years from 1950 to 1960.[6] Not only were there more children going to school, more children were staying in school. With every school generation, more and more youths have stayed longer in school. Places need to be made for them. This pressure, however, also suggests that some internal changes might have to be made in the school structure and offerings. The schools are being pressured to change in this dimension; we shall discuss later the degree to which they have actually been able to respond to such pressure.

A third source of pressure for change has been the exploding nature of the world of knowledge. We are learning almost too much too fast about more and more. Recent discoveries in physics and mathematics have critical meaning for science content in the schools. As one scientist observed, most science courses today are really history; they do not reflect the current state of the discipline. We are learning more, too, about learning itself, with many implications for the educational process.

One aspect of this new knowledge that is really terrifying in its potential is the possible impact of automation. The machines now being built and those on the drawing boards are so fast and so complex that they can manage a good deal more of the world's work than the world can now afford to have done for it. We are probably far less ready for the revolution of automation than for any other that has been mentioned so far. New technologies produce new human expectations and change human interactions. Just consider the problem of leisure: The work week can shrink from 40 hours to 35 hours to 30 hours; how far can a man's working time decline before work becomes leisure? Or how much leisure can our contemporary man handle—unless, of course, educational processes intervene at some point along the way? As change occurs in these fundamental social processes, then the schools are going to adapt—or else!

11

6 National Education Association, *Research Bulletin*, 39, No. 2 (Feb. 1961), 4.

We return, then, to our original question: Whose school is it? The answer is obvious: The school belongs to society. Yet society is not a single, simple entity. The social order is a product of history, of man's adaptations to changing situations, and of the interaction of different civilizations and cultures. Parents, teachers, and children are all products of their period. The school is intimately bound up with the course of national history. Revolutions were never born in the schoolroom, but the schoolroom inevitably reflects revolutions, though often too late and with too little awareness of the forces at work. How well the school of today serves the needs of today, as well as those of tomorrow, is the burden of our examination in the succeeding chapters of this book.

BIBLIOGRAPHY

ALEXANDER, ALBERT, "The Gray Flannel Cover on the American History Textbook," *Social Education*, 24 (Jan. 1960), 11-14. The history that students read in textbooks has only a family resemblance to the real thing.

ARIÈS, PHILLIPPE, *Centuries of Childhood*. New York: Alfred A. Knopf, Inc., 1963. Describes children from medieval to modern times, particularly in France. Delightful and informative.

BAILYN, BERNARD, *Education in the Forming of American Society*. Chapel Hill: University of North Carolina Press, 1960. A re-examination of some of the assumptions regarding educational attitudes of the early colonists.

BOSSARD, JAMES H. S., *The Sociology of Child Development*, rev. ed. New York: Harper & Row, Publishers, 1954. See especially Part VII, "The Changing Status of Childhood," for a vivid and interesting account of children in American history.

BRUNER, JEROME S., *The Process of Education*. Cambridge, Mass.: Harvard University Press, 1961. An examination of some of our assumptions about the learning process and the structure of knowledge that has significant implications for how and what we teach.

FRANK, LAWRENCE K., *Nature and Human Nature*. New Brunswick, N. J.: Rutgers University Press, 1951. How man's new image of himself is shaped by natural and social forces. See especially Chapter IV, "The Cultural Environment."

GORER, GEOFFREY, *The American People*. New York: W. W. Norton & Company, Inc., 1948. A witty British anthropologist takes a critical look at the American scene. See especially his chapter, "The All-American Child."

HEFFERNAN, HELEN, "Pressures on Children and Youth," *California Schools*, 33 (August, 1962), 289-306. Summarizes a survey of educators and parents regarding the problems posed by increased pressures on students.

KELLEY, EARL C., *Education for What Is Real*. New York: Harper & Row, Publishers, 1947. A brief but classic statement, relating early studies in perception with some educational assumptions and practices.

LARRABEE, ERIC, "Childhood in Twentieth-Century America," *The Nation's Children, Vol. III: Problems and Prospects*, ed. Eli Ginzburg. New York: Columbia University Press, 1960. A background paper prepared for the participants in the 1960 White House Conference on Children and Youth.

LEVIN, MARTIN, ed., *Five Boyhoods*. Garden City, N. Y.: Doubleday & Company, Inc., 1962. Fascinating account of the changes in American life as seen in the boyhoods of five perceptive and articulate Americans, who were boys at different times over the last 50 years.

MARCUS, LLOYD, *The Treatment of Minorities in Secondary School Textbooks*. New York: Anti-Defamation League of B'nai B'rith, 1961. A carefully documented study of distortions to be found in textbooks.

PETERSEN, LEN, "Desert Soliloquy," in *Ways of Mankind*, pp. 50-62, ed. Walter Goldschmidt. Boston: Beacon Press, 1954.

———, "Education: The Continuity of Culture," in *Exploring the Ways of Mankind*, ed. Walter Goldschmidt. New York: Holt, Rinehart & Winston, Inc., 1961. This reference and the preceding one are complementary. The first is the script of a radio program originally produced to illustrate the educational process as seen by an anthropologist: A Hopi boy is torn between his Indian culture and the beckoning white culture. The second reference contains selections from five eminent anthropologists discussing culture as educator.

WIGGINS, GLADYS A., *Education and Nationalism: An Historical Interpretation of American Education*. New York: McGraw-Hill Book Company, 1962. A scholarly study showing the central role of education in forming American society.

13

The instant a child is born, his education begins. Why do you think fond parents select blue blankets for baby boys and pink blankets for baby girls? They are intent that the young ones learn their sex identity early, for sure, and forever. The infant or young child learns a great deal in a very short time. Everything we take for granted is brand new to him: color, smell, light, love, taste, and touch. When he first stands on his own two feet, what a triumph of learning, coordination, and sensation—and how different the world looks from this vantage point! Before the child ever comes to school he has learned the most significant lessons of his life. The school can only build on the foundation laid in these early years. If it is a firm foundation, the school can extend the potential; if the foundation is shaky or only partly filled in, then the task of the school is difficult or impossible. And after the child comes to school, the outside world continues as a potent educator.

BEFORE SCHOOL STARTS

The child has learned many things before he even gets inside a formal school classroom. Let us examine some of these briefly.

SOCIETY AS EDUCATOR

3

Does it make a difference whether a child is the eldest, youngest, or middle child? Whether, being oldest, the child is a boy or girl? Studies show that it is quite important to the child's view of himself just what position he has in the family sequence. What he learns, essentially, is the view the other significant people in his immediate small world have of him. The most important thing a person learns—and probably can never unlearn—is this early view of himself, caught from the way his parents react to his presence.

This process of learning about oneself is so complex that we are not sure of all that goes into it. We do know that families differ widely in their responses to the children in their midst. The impact on the child is noticeable by age four or five. The child already knows whether he is a "good" or "bad" child, whether he is loved and valued or unloved and a nuisance. He has some idea of whether he is competent and able or clumsy and stupid. Valuations of his behavior by those around him become part of himself, whether they are objectively true or not.

HE GAINS SKILLS AND KNOWLEDGE

The child in our society is able to acquire a great deal of skill and information long before he enters school. He has learned to speak. His oral vocabulary before entering school may be as many as 30,000 words. He has learned to listen. He can often handle a variety of tools—saw, hammer, screw driver, egg beater. He can play ball, climb a ladder or tree, acquire food by raiding the refrigerator, and he has learned the value of money. Depending on his environment, he has learned various skills basic to all learning.

We tend to think of the "typical" child as living in middle-class suburbia or a small city or town. Such a child does have access to the many skill learnings described. However, a different environment surrounds the child of the slum. He learns many skills too, but they may be different ones. For one thing, the child is less apt to know words and letters. He probably has had little experience in sustained conversation with adults. He has not been reasoned with in order to change his behavior; rather, he has been swiftly slapped or beaten to obtain obedience. But these children are skillful with concrete reality, and also with fantasy. They are more alert to some kinds of behavior cues from adults than are middle-class children.[1]

The child in the isolated rural area likewise has picked up from his environment skills that differ radically from those learned by the middle-class suburban youngster. He may have a smaller oral vocabulary. His skill in playing games with other children may be minimal unless he comes from a very large family. He will be skillful in handling many aspects of his own natural environment, however: dealing with animals, understanding plants, knowing cues to changes in weather, and so forth.

15

[1] Frank Reissman, *The Culturally Deprived Child* (New York: Harper & Row, Publishers, 1962), pp. 26-30.

The child thus comes to school already equipped with many and varied skills. He also comes with a great variety of knowledge and information. A major factor in the information level of the pre-school child today is television. Today's infant probably takes the flickering TV picture as much for granted as he does the sound of his mother's voice. Yet the impact of the two are rather different. The mother is directing her attention to the individual child; the television message is being conveyed to millions. Since the very young child is presumed not to know much about what is on the screen, he is apt to be exposed to the whole range of television offerings—whatever the older persons in the family prefer to see. He may well know more about shooting Indians and boxing than he knows about trees and water and puppies and dirt. Since the young child has no basis upon which to organize these impressions, and since his idea of distance in time or space is rudimentary, what he receives is a jumble of impressions.

Later, as he gains more control over the family, he and perhaps his mother find out that there are special programs for pre-school children. Typically, they have many child participants: a charming young teacher plays games with a few children, they sing songs, she reads a story, and the child viewer is treated as a participant and invited to sing along with the children in the studio. The numerous cartoon programs are also designed to attract this youthful group. Interspersed, of course, are the commercials. And these talk either to the child: "Tell Mother that you want her to get a big box of *Yummies* with the big clown on the package the very next time she goes to the store!" or to the mother who, it is assumed, may be lurking within earshot. *This is a very powerful form of education, and we are not quite sure what it all adds up to.*

It has never been wise to assume that children come to school with nothing inside their heads, but today it would be ridiculous to do so. Not only have these children seen bizarre animals in strange lands, they have been exposed to dramatic social events such as the launching and retrieving of an astronaut, a hurricane sweeping away a town, the inauguration or death of a President. Then add to these the learnings that come from the appeal to the consumer wants of the young. The *Yummies* do look so good on TV. Or the doll house, or the candy bar, or the rocket gun. Everyone else is buying them, you know. All other children like you want these things; don't you want to be like all the others?

Again, we do not know what these experiences really mean in the life of the child, but we can be sure that today's generation has had an exposure different from our own. We can also be sure that most of our schools are not, as of now, planned for this kind of child.[2]

HE LEARNS SOCIAL VALUATIONS OF PERSONS
AND GROUPS

Ours is a society of many groups. These are composed of persons of like interests, like occupations, like neighborhoods. But there are groupings

[2] Educational Policies Commission, *Mass Communication and Education* (Washington, D.C.: National Education Association, 1958).

16

that go deeper than these. The groups that are of major significance in the life of the child, and inevitably in the life of most adults, are those into which he was born—his racial, ethnic, religious, and socio-economic groups.

Americans make much of group identity. Being a country composed of many peoples, we boast, on the one hand, of the cultural richness we have acquired through this kind of diversity; and on the other hand, we punish in many overt and covert ways those who differ from the dominant Anglo-Saxon Protestant majority.

Children, before they come to school, are often able to complete quite accurately the following statements:

People like us ———————. (are best, are not so good, don't belong)
Nice people are those who ——————. (are like us, are clean, are white, live in nice houses)
We don't like ——————. (Jews, Negroes, Catholics, Atheists, Baptists, Armenians, Mexicans)
I can't play with you because you are ——————. (name it)

There were many years when educators and other people preferred to believe that children were innocent of the biases and prejudices and hatreds of their elders. Research has shown this not to be true. Children, sometimes long before they get to school, are aware of significant group differences. The Negro mother has alerted her child to the potential rejection of white playmates. She has educated him in the etiquette of race relations. Similarly, the Jewish child may have learned his religious identity very early for protection or for security. In the ethnic islands that still exist in many of our large cities and in certain locations in rural and small-town America, the children learn at a very young age "who *we* are."

This kind of social learning is particularly significant in America because of one major fact: not all identifiable groups are given the same social valuation. It is *not* equally good to be a Japanese-American or an American Negro. It is, as a matter of social reality, better to have Japanese ancestry. There is an irony here that is not lost upon the lower-rated Negro group: the Japanese are late arrivals on the American scene; the Negro was among the first. The Japanese (as a nation) were our bitter enemy; the Negro has been a compatriot for hundreds of years. American society on the whole provides easier access to social amenities and social power for the Japanese-American than for the Negro. Why do you think this is so? There is no *rational* explanation.

Several generations ago the experience of most children was with a fairly stable, homogeneous neighborhood or community. Most "different" people were too remote in space or status to be clearly within the child's awareness. The social world of the average child of today has changed drastically. Fewer and fewer young people will be raised in the isolation of the ranch or in the psychological comfort of the ethnic island. Inevitably, most youngsters today are going to have contacts across social borders. Populations are moving. Families are moving. Children are moving. This means new kinds of social contacts. And Mother must acquaint the young toddler with who is or who is not "one of ours." A kind of precarious homogeneity is achieved in today's suburbia, but even this is shattered by the sudden directive to Daddy to move to another city, another region, another set of relationships. Perhaps, if he is lucky, he can find an identical suburb for his family to take root in; but he may not always be so lucky. In any event, his young children are taught to sniff out the differences between "us" and "them." Often in identifying the differences, the added ingredient is hate.

White youngsters in communities in which there are no Negroes at all have the same amount and degree of prejudice toward Negroes as those in cities where there is a large Negro population. The stereotypes of who belongs and who does not are part of the common experience of young people no matter where they live in the United States today.

Social class differences are part of the social learning of the pre-school child, though they are usually less obvious than other major learned group differences. Most neighborhoods are fairly homogeneous, and the child's contact with others of markedly inferior or superior socio-economic standing is slight. But the awareness that there are such differences is usually a part of the social equipment of the child even before he encounters them in school.

Another very interesting fact the child has learned before he comes to school is that boys and girls are different. As we noted, the child is taught this difference from the beginning of his life. Every culture provides ways in which boys and girls may learn their social sex roles. In America, this is a continuous process carried on before the child gets to school. The significant thing here is the different social valuations placed on the sex roles, and the different behavioral expectations for each.

The boy is encouraged to be aggressive, to explore, to hide discomfort from physical pain, to want "tough" toys such as guns and ships and soldiers. He is praised when he climbs a high tree and when he comes home, bloodied but unbowed, from a battle with the other five-year-old down the block.

Girls' learning is similar in that they, too, are instructed in what is proper for their sex. Dolls, for instance, are all right. Little girls are given play make-up kits so that they can start early on the road to making themselves sexually attractive. There is considerably more indulgence shown for girls when they cry, but the expectations of neatness and cleanliness are harsher.[3] The lessons of compliance, obedience, carefulness, deference to adults, particularly to older women, have been well learned by most little girls before they reach the first grade.

Confusion regarding sex role valuations is currently a major topic in the discussions of social scientists. We know, for instance, that in the slum family where the father is often absent or even unknown, the mother is the dominant force. Girls in such homes find learning their sex role far easier, or at least they seem to have a model near at hand from whom they can learn. The boys, on the other hand, are confused as to what their social role and social valuation really are. The mother may complain bitterly about irresponsible men and chide her young boy not to grow

18

---

[3] Robert R. Sears, Eleanor E. Maccoby, and Harry Levin, *Patterns of Child Rearing* (New York: Harper & Row, Publishers, 1957), p. 405.

up like his father; yet he does not know what any other kind of man might be like, not having seen many around. He senses that men are not valued because they make trouble, do not provide, are irresponsible, and so forth.

Before he comes to school, then, the young child has learned a truly amazing number of concepts and skills. He knows a great deal about himself (though it may be far from true), he has been able to develop many of the essential tools of social communication, and he has learned how society values persons like himself. Now what happens as he enters school?

AND SO TO SCHOOL

It may take a major effort, but try to think back to your feelings just before you entered first grade. Were you sure? Happy? Eager? Angry? Afraid?

Each child is well educated about school long before he ever gets there. His parents, his older brothers and sisters, the other children on the block who are in school—all have conveyed to him a concept of "school."

For increasing numbers of children, the first-grade experience is preceded by kindergarten or nursery school, but typically these are available primarily to middle-class and upper-class children, and not to all of these. Even for children who have had kindergarten or nursery school experience, first grade, in school, is different. The only group experiences most youngsters have had are the informal mixings and clashings of the street, the neighborhood, and the family. That these street and neighborhood experiences can differ vastly is obvious, yet time and again we observe the first-grade classroom as a setting to which it is assumed that most children come with equal willingness and equal readiness.

In an interesting inquiry regarding the influences of parents on children's entry into school, Stendler and Young interviewed a group of mothers just prior to school opening. The reports from the interviews indicate that the child expects many kinds of learning experiences, and so does the mother. The mother, in fact, views the school as a major socializing agency.

> The child has been told that he must behave himself in school, must mind the teacher, must be quiet, must not interrupt, that the teacher takes the place of his mother and is the boss. In some cases, the teacher has been held over his head as a kind of veiled threat, "You'll have to change your ways when you start first grade." "You won't be able to get away with that stuff in the first grade." "Wait till the teacher sees you acting like that. You won't do it long." Most parents, however, try to present the teacher as a kind of benign socializing agent, "Be nice in school and everyone will be nice to you." "Like the teacher and she'll like you" is the gist of what some children are told.[4]

If parents have succeeded educationally, if school was an experience met with feelings of competence, if education is felt to be one of the

4 Celia B. Stendler and Norman Young, "The Beginning of Formal School Experience," *Child Development*, 21 (1950), 241-55.

marks of the persons "who are like us," then the child will share these attitudes. If the parents have found school experiences distasteful, if they were failures or only partial successes in school, then some of this negative reaction will be passed on to the child. He may be aware of a parental feeling of anxious determination that: "By golly, this child is not going to fail as I did even if I have to wallop him every day." Or he may sense a passive acceptance of expected failure expressed in the idea: "I did not succeed, and since this is my child, the odds are against his succeeding either." And if the experience comes out of minority group rejection, there may be the added implication: "People of our group are not expected to succeed in school; you had better not even try." [5]

Parents often convey, whether they intend to or not, a selective view of which subjects are "easy" and which are not. A mother may indicate to her prospective first-grader that he will find reading easy, but that when it comes to numbers, he will have to pay strict attention; after all, she always had trouble with arithmetic. Or parents may express feelings about boys enjoying school because of the games and science, while girls will like the art, etc. Why do so many girls appear to be conditioned against science? If older siblings or friends have succeeded in school, have found school to be fun and interesting, this is of course what they are going to communicate. But what if it is the reverse?

The first-grade child is no innocent lamb being led to slaughter; he knows—or at least feels he knows—quite a good deal about this new experience. Certainly his feelings are significant educational facts. Nonschool influences have, in this instance, a very direct bearing on one crucial aspect of school success.

OUT-OF-SCHOOL EDUCATION IS A CONTINUING PROCESS

From first grade through twelfth grade the child spends approximately 20 per cent of his waking time in school. The rest of his time is spent at home or in the neighborhood or community. No other institution claims as much of the child's time during these years as the school. Yet out-of-school time is even greater.

During his out-of-school hours, his family, other children in the area, and the mass media are sending millions of messages to the individual about himself, about others, and about society. To the degree that these out-of-school messages reinforce and support the in-school messages, to that degree will the child find his educational road smooth. What he makes of it will depend primarily on his own individual motivations, abilities, and idiosyncrasies.

However, if out-of-school messages, conflict with or depart significantly from in-school messages, the educational process for the individual is indeed a rough one. For instance, the school undoubtedly will emphasize proper speech habits. This is one of the major educational goals of teachers; when students graduate who still use poor grammar and vulgar words, the

---

[5] Robert F. Peck and Cono Galliani, "Intelligence, Ethnicity, and Social Roles in Adolescent Society," *Sociometry*, 25 (March, 1962), 64-72.

school is severely criticized. Yet many children live in families and neighborhoods where all the adults talk in the way the school says no one should. Whose expectations shall the child fulfill? If he fails to do as the teacher says, he will be punished by low grades or nonpromotion; if he departs from neighborhood expectations, he is apt to face family ridicule and peer ostracism.

It has been pointed out by various researchers over a period of years that the American school exemplifies middle-class culture, middle-class virtues, and middle-class values. But many children in the major cities come from very poor homes where the typical experiences of the middle-class child are almost completely absent or unknown:

> In 1950, approximately one child out of every ten in the fourteen largest cities in the United States was "culturally deprived." *By 1960, this figure had risen to one in three.* . . . By 1970, it is estimated there may be one deprived child for every two enrolled in schools in these large cities.[6]

There is abundant evidence that the procedures and goals of the school are not only incompatible with the child's home experiences, but are incomprehensible to him. For instance, the school values good grades on tests and examinations. The child from the middle class is rewarded for a high score when he comes home; when he reports that he is to take a test his parents admonish him to do well and encourage him in his efforts to succeed. In a lower-class home, the test score may be relatively meaningless. Motivations to succeed relate primarily to the basic survival needs: food, shelter, clothing. An experiment in which children were told that if they did well on the tests, they would get a movie ticket, resulted in improved scores from lower-class youngsters.[7] The content of school instruction, likewise, appears very remote from the reality in which the child lives. No school text shows the slum in all its disorders;[8] no lesson concerns itself with telling a girl how to get from the street to her family's apartment without being molested.[9] The child comes to school lacking many of the experiences and motivations that teachers assume he has, and continued attendance at school only serves to widen the gulf. The in-school world appears to be more and more unreal, and the out-of-school world reinforces antischool feelings. The more negative the children become, the more apt the school is to express diapproval and withdrawal; the breach between the two worlds is widened with association rather than closed. The longer some of these young people from culturally deprived areas come to school, the lower are their IQ scores.

Out-of-school influences are in conflict with school purposes for approximately half of our school population: boys. This is somewhat of an exaggeration, but evidence is at hand which shows that throughout their

21

---

[6] Riessman, *The Culturally Deprived Child*, p. 1.

[7] Allison Davis, *Social-Class Influences upon Learning* (Cambridge, Mass.: Harvard University Press, 1948), pp. 86-87.

[8] Otto Klineberg, "Life Is Fun in a Smiling, Fair-Skinned World," *Saturday Review*, XLVI (Feb. 16, 1963), 75-77.

[9] James B. Conant, *Slums and Suburbs* (New York: McGraw-Hill Book Company, 1961), p. 19.

schooling, until college years, boys fare less well than girls. They are failed more often and earlier; they get more failing grades in school subjects; they are more often disciplined; they do not stay in school as long; they end up in reading clinics, counseling centers, and juvenile courts in far greater numbers than girls. Sexton has termed the public school a "female school," and cites statistics to show that on the average: "In Big City three times as many boys as girls are failed. Since failures are found mostly in lower-income groups, this means that lower-income boys are having a worse time in school than any other category of students." [10]

Boys often do more poorly because of the different behavorial expectations of home and school. At home the father (or mother) insists that the boy be aggressive and stand up for his rights; he is taught to fight if need be. In school the teacher is horrified by fighting, stresses cooperation, permits only limited physical expression. Sitting still is a virtue at school; running fast is a virtue at home.

One significant factor in the adolescent out-of-school culture is that it is economically useful. According to advertisers, the teen-age market constitutes the largest amount of uncommitted money available. Most adolescents today do not have to pay bills and provide for their own well-being; they need only spend their money on what they choose to spend it on. They do not, in many instances, contribute any of their earned income to the welfare of their family. If they are not earning money through work, most middle-class adolescents are given an allowance to be freely spent. Their taste, therefore, is a factor in the success of a disc jockey, a movie star, a type of shoe or skirt. The fears and vanities of teen-agers are played upon by the deodorant and cosmetic trade. Magazines pitch their ads to the development of consumer desires in the adolescent. Fads in dress, music, dance, are assiduously promoted through the mass media. And youth responds. [11]

A different and more disturbing aspect of education via the mass media is the contradictory messages they send out. On the one hand, the virtues are upheld; on the other, sensual and self-gratifying activities are displayed in their most tempting forms. Youth is associated with all the things that are "fun": sports cars, liquor, gay parties, alluring clothes and appearance. The eternal verities are challenged by every suggestive advertisement or movie. What is the adolescent to believe?

Unfortunately, the adolescent does not, as of now, turn to the school and his teachers for guidance in the murky field of morals and social values. (Nor does he turn to his church, but that is not our concern here.) The school fails as a source of assurance and guidance because one major component of adolescent culture is an essential rejection of the school. Not that adolescents won't study seriously, and do their tasks as directed (particularly among college-bound, middle-class youngsters), but the things that are important in life, the problems of values and morals,

[10] Patricia C. Sexton, *Education and Income* (New York: The Viking Press, Inc., 1961), p. 277.

[11] Dwight Macdonald, "A Caste, A Culture, A Market," *The New Yorker*, I, II (Nov. 27, Nov. 29, 1958).

are *not* taught in school.[12] If they were, would the students pay them any heed?

The pupil and his parents are also receiving many messages regarding education itself—outside of school. In recent years, for instance, there were several TV series in which a teacher or professor played a leading role: "Our Miss Brooks," "Halls of Ivy," "Mr. Peepers," "Mr. Novak," to name some. What view of teaching, learning, and education was conveyed?

SUMMARY

Though education may be thought of primarily in terms of formal instruction in the schoolroom, probably most of the significant education experienced by an individual takes place before he comes to school and during his out-of-school hours. Though children learn many things before they enter school, their learnings vary with their environment. One cannot assume that all six-year-olds enter school with the same skills, knowledges, and attitudes. There will be tremendous differences between rural, urban, suburban, and slum children. Differences will arise from the individual child's view of himself—learned from his parents and peers—and also from his view of how groups like his own are valued in the larger social world. Boys and girls will bring different learnings and different expectations to school. Inevitably, too, each child will have been educated about education; he will have developed some idea of what schooling and education may mean.

23

BIBLIOGRAPHY

ALLPORT, GORDON W., *The Nature of Prejudice*. Cambridge, Mass.: Addison-Wesley Press, Inc., 1954. The research in the field is summarized and implications drawn by a leading American social psychologist. Probably the standard work in the field.

AMBROSE, EDNA AND ALICE MIEL, *Children's Social Learning*. Washington, D.C.: Association for Supervision and Curriculum Development, NEA, 1958. A review of the research and expert study, with implications for educational programs.

BAILYN, LOTTE, "Mass Media and Children: A Study of Exposure Habits and Cognitive Effects," *Psychological Monographs*, 73, No. 471 (1959), 1-48. Documents the differential response of children to television.

DENNEY, REUEL, "Children of Thoth," *The Astonished Muse*, Chap. 8. Chicago: University of Chicago Press, 1957. A scathing and literate look at the mass media and the child audience.

ELKIN, FREDERICK, *The Child and Society*. New York: Random House (Paperback), 1960. A brief summary of the major social forces that influence and mold the child as he develops.

[12] Thomas Gordon, "Thoughts on Facilitating Two-way Communication about Curriculum and Instruction," *California Journal of Elementary Education*, 30 (May 1962), 237-44.

ERIKSON, ERIK H., *Childhood and Society*. New York: W. W. Norton & Company, Inc., 1950. Combines psychoanalytic insights with anthropological materials to provide insight into the relation between the child and his society.

GINZBURG, ELI, ed., *The Nation's Children, Vol. I: The Family and Social Change*. New York: Columbia University Press, 1960. Background papers published for participants in the 1960 White House Conference on Children and Youth.

GOODMAN, MARY ELLEN, *Race Awareness in Young Children*. Cambridge, Mass.: Addison-Wesley Press, Inc., 1952. The most often cited research on the ways in which young children perceive racial differences.

KARDINER, ABRAM, "When the State Brings up the Child," *Saturday Review*, XLIV (August 26, 1961), 9-11. Psychoanalytic examination of the role of the family in child rearing and of efforts to displace the family, with a firsthand report on the Israeli kibbutzim.

KLEIN, DONALD C. AND ANN ROSS, "Kindergarten Entry: A Study of Role Transition," in *Orthopsychiatry and the School*, pp. 60-69, ed. Morris Kingman. New York: American Orthopsychiatric Association, Inc., 1958. Coming to school makes a great difference to all concerned.

PASSOW, A. HARRY, ed., *Education in Depressed Areas*. New York: Bureau of Publications, Teachers College, Columbia University, 1963. Fifteen reports focus on various aspects of understanding and educating children in slum areas of big cities.

ROWLAND, THOMAS D. AND CALVIN C. NELSON, "Off to School—at What Age?" *Elementary School Journal*, 60 (Oct. 1959), 18-23. Reports variations in school practices, and illustrates responses made by school systems to local pressures.

TRAGER, HELEN AND MARIAN R. YARROW, *They Learn What They Live*. New York: Harper & Row, Publishers, 1952. Describes a research study of the knowledge young children have about intergroup differences and of how different teaching approaches may affect these ideas.

WANN, KENNETH D., MIRIAM S. DORN, AND ELIZABETH ANN LIDDLE, *Fostering Intellectual Development in Young Children*. New York: Bureau of Publications, Teachers College, Columbia University, 1962. Studies of children today demonstrate how much they know and want to know before they enter formal schooling.

WOLFENSTEIN, MARTHA, "Trends in Infant Care," *American Journal of Orthopsychiatry*, 33 (1953), 120-30. How the government booklet, *Infant Care*, has changed with changing social attitudes toward children, since the first edition came out in 1914.

WYLIE, RUTH, *The Self Concept: A Critical Survey of Pertinent Research Literature*. Lincoln: University of Nebraska Press, 1961. Comprehensive review of what is known to date about how a person learns about himself.

If one were to judge by the amount of education available, one would assume that Americans value education and allied intellectual pursuits. The schools loom large as a topic of social conversation, as news in the press, and as subjects for scholarly or popular magazine articles. We can certainly say that Americans are highly interested in their schools and in education; cannot we then conclude that they value knowledge and the fruits of knowledge?

AMERICAN VALUATION OF EDUCATION

The colonists valued education. They founded schools and colleges as soon as their economy became sufficiently stable. The great early leaders of America were remarkably literate and well-educated. But the insistence that all participate in fundamental education in our early colonial history, did not, seemingly, establish a tradition of the school-educated man. Though settlers brought a desire for education for their own children, they also brought a distrust of the man of culture. These settlers, and the millions who came after, were often escaping an aristocratic society in which they were the lower class. The common man's suspicion of the

AMERICAN
VALUES AND
EDUCATION

4

elite was well engrained. In the Old World these laborers and workers could have no dream for a future different from what their parents and grandparents had had before them. The New World, which they built with their own hands, was not the work of persons educated in school. For over 200 years, America's leaders have often boasted of their success, attained without benefit of formal schooling.

In the rather brief history of the United States, persons who have gained the greatest prestige and power and who have amassed gigantic fortunes have been men of action who sought power, and gained it through various means—general ability, business acumen, chicanery, creativity, dishonesty, or bluff. Few questions were asked in early days about how a man came by his money and power, so long as he could command a great deal of both. Most of the persons who gained money and power were not notably intellectual. The "newsboy to president" theme did not arise just from daydreams, but from reality. Many a newsboy did become president of the corporation, and a few even became President of the United States. The legend and the myth emphasize the value and the valor of rising to the top through one's own native wit, innocent of acquaintance with books or culture.

Another theme is also to be noted in our early history. The settlers who flocked into the Northwest Territory were governed under the famous Northwest Ordinance of 1787, which stated: "Religion, morality, and knowledge being necessary to good government and the happiness of mankind, schools and the means of education shall forever be encouraged," and which authorized Congress to set aside one lot in every township for the maintainance of public schools. The long fight for common schools for all, paid for by public funds, was evidence of the recognition that even if one did not value a great amount of education, a certain amount of education was useful. The schools were clearly seen as pathways for upward mobility; they did lead to positions in business and the professions; a father could securely dream of a better future for his child when the schools were there to give him some of the necessary know-how. Organized labor in the 1900's was at the forefront in working for public high schools—*academic* high schools—so that the sons of workers could get the prerequisites necessary for college and university training.

These were practical ambitions. But education might have some drawbacks, too. It might make children look down on parents who were rough and unschooled. Therefore, the school should teach the children just so much and no more. The frills of art, music, foreign languages, and science of the eighteenth century were viewed as distinctly unnecessary and expensive in the early twentieth century.

The development of attitudes toward education has been influenced by two other factors: one, for generations most teachers have been women; and two, education in America is coeducational. How do these factors influence American attitudes toward education? As we have already noted, schools frown upon the out-of-school education boys get regarding what is right and proper boy behavior. The elementary schools, because of the influence of women teachers, tend to have a feminine tone.

This "niceness" is apparent in the secondary school as well, and is possibly a function of the other factor indicated: coeducation. Not only have boys been expected to behave better in school because girls were there, but the girls have done better in school tasks than boys, as pointed out in Chapter 3. Thus, to succeed in school, to identify with school goals, would be to identify with a feminine world and feminine values. This situation may account for some of the suspicion of education that we notice, as well as for the generally low status of the teaching profession. It is the men who dominate the social valuations of the market place, and it is they who have suffered most at the hands of school teachers.

An additional item might be added: the school tasks assigned in many instances have borne no relationship to the practical world. As we have already noted, the out-of-school interests and problems of boys and girls are not part of the school curriculum. Who can take education seriously when it deals with things that are so irrelevant to life? This is the educational experience of millions of young people. When they become parents and citizens, if they then have a less than friendly attitude toward education is it not understandable?

A COMPLEX OF CONTRADICTIONS

During the presidential election campaign of 1952 when Adlai Stevenson first ran against General Eisenhower, "egg-head" was used as a derisive term calculated to lose votes for Mr. Stevenson. Many analyses of the reasons for his loss of the election attributed it to the fact that he was too intellectual. He spoke too well. His jokes were "high-brow." It has been noted, and Stevenson was no exception, that at least since the turn of the century, every Presidential candidate has had himself pictured in a rural setting, whether he knew one end of a cow from the other or not.

Why this semicontempt for the things of the mind? Why this glorification of the rural and provincial? Is the intellectual, the product of education, to be despised? Americans value education, but are suspicious of the educated. Education that is considered "useful," that will get you something—power, money, a good job, a better husband—is all to the good. But education that intrigues one with ideas, suggests new horizons, and challenges old beliefs—this is not practical and might even be dangerous. Perhaps here is one of roots of American conservatism regarding education. Schools that are too different might be inculcating different ideas in children's heads, and these might be upsetting to the standard ways of doing things.

The schools, just because they are one of the most ubiquitous, the most public, and the closest to the individual of all our social institutions, are heirs to many social contradictions.

CONFORMITY VERSUS CREATIVITY

There is a paradox here, the dimensions of which we are just beginning to define. On the one hand, Americans tend to be suspicious of the person of ideas, of the individual who gets involved with what he is learning, who pursues learning for its own sake rather than for practical and self-gratifying ends. Americans also tend to be suspicious of differences, to tolerate but not to reward the eccentric or the strange, and to think that probably most geniuses are slightly cracked, anyway. But on the other hand, we indulge in great waves of self-condemnation, censuring the vulgarity of America's culture, the high level of conformity that is manifest, the lack of initiative and independence and originality in our social world. We feel inferior because we do not think our art, music, literature, or even our movies come up to the creative standards of other nations. What is wrong with us?

Recent inquiries into the nature and nurture of creativity shed light on the situation. We have discovered rather recently that the kind of behavior rewarded by the school tends to reduce the creativity of the child. That is, those who give "different" or "original" answers are apt to be chided by the teacher; those who give answers the teacher expects—the "right" answers—are given approval.

Intelligence tests, for instance, tend to discriminate unfairly in several ways. They discriminate against the child whose language background and motivation are different from the typical middle-class group; they also tend to identify primarily the conforming, rather than the innovating, modes of thinking.

> The one mode tends toward retaining the known, learning the predetermined, and conserving what is. The second mode tends toward revising the known, exploring the undetermined, and constructing what might be. . . . one process represents intellectual acquisitiveness and conformity, the other, intellectual inventiveness and innovation. One focuses on knowing what is already discovered the other focuses on discovering what is yet to be known.[1]

Standard IQ tests only identify one mode of intelligence, with the result that the more conforming kinds of students are given the label of high ability and often, also, the opportunities for higher achievement.

Teachers appear to reflect the public's suspicion of those who do not conform. Those who conform are most likely to succeed in school, and thence out of school. Yet, our culture cannot survive without the inventiveness of creative thinkers; consequently, we must somehow identify and find ways of encouraging them. Will the climate of society permit this kind of educational practice? Will teachers be able to work with the innovator as well as the imitator?

COMPETITION VERSUS COOPERATION

To belong to a group, to be able to work well with others, is held as a high ideal. Parents guide their children in learning how to cooperate with the rest of the family. In school, too, learning how to cooperate in groups with one's classmates and the teacher is continually promoted as a social good. This is a reflection of life in the adult world. The organization man is above all a good joiner, a good member of the team. His cooperative skills must be polished to a high gloss if he is to become the

[1] Jacob W. Getzels and Phillip W. Jackson, *Creativity and Intelligence* (New York: John Wiley & Sons, Inc., 1962), pp. 13-14.

vice-president of the corporation. At the same time they are taught co-operation, children in schools are pitted against one another. This is a competitive world, they are told. The way in which the school awards grades and marks is evidence of its competitive atmosphere: only a certain number of A's can be given; if everyone got an A, there would be no value to it. (Not everyone, remember, can become president of the corporation.) Learn how to sniff out the student who is after your grade, the man who is after your job, and get the better of him. It's a dog-eat-dog sort of world; every man for himself. So let's learn how to meet this world with a good start in school.

THE PRACTICAL VERSUS THE IDEAL

To justify a new school program typically means to show that it will produce a "return." More graduates will get to college, more students will learn to read better earlier, more youngsters will learn job skills. Yet, at the same time, the school must hold up ideal patterns of living, preach morality and duty, and that service to others is better than monetary reward. Cultural activities seem very impractical, but for some reason they seem to be valued. The ambivalence with which many Americans approach works of art ("How much did it cost?") is a symptom of this contradiction.

DEMOCRACY VERSUS AUTHORITY

If schools were (in a naïve sense) truly democratic, then the majority would rule, and determine the procedures to be followed. In practice this would be folly, since immature young people can certainly not be trusted to make decisions about courses of action whose consequences lie beyond their ken. A compromise is often reached via student government, which is apt to be merely a student echo of the decisions of the principal and faculty. Voting is frequently carried on even in primary grades by children who have not the faintest notion of the processes in which they are taking part.

In our society, there is intense suspicion of authority. The expert is questioned. The common man is the best judge of what is good for him, be it taxes, foreign aid, or how to teach reading. At the same time, while suspect, authority is also venerated. The doctor's word can be quoted as though it were natural law to quell a Congressman uneasy about federal aid to medicine. Each discipline attempts to become increasingly esoteric so that only the initiates can understand and thus be accepted as authorities. Education, too, strives towards such Elysian fields. Veneration for the printed word is early inculcated in the young: if it is written *in the book*, it is true!

PURITANISM VERSUS HEDONISM

The immediate gratifaction versus the remote reward is increasingly a battleground for the classroom teacher, as well as for our whole social order. Children expect—or demand—immediate feelings of success and pleasure, or their tasks are slighted or not done well. To look ahead to a distant goal (which may never be reached, since the world may well blow up) becomes increasingly difficult. The value of saving is eroded by the credit manager. Why put off until tomorrow what you can enjoy today with "no money down"? The fruits of this contradiction are increasingly seen in early sexual exploits of the young, earlier marriages, and many more unwanted, illegitimate children. At the same time, the official position of church and school, of preachers and deans of women is that chastity is the only respectable, ethical and moral practice. Compare the advice given young men in *Playboy* magazine with that given young women in *McCall's*.

There is no question but that our schools and our total social order are in existence to convey the idea that it is better to be a citizen of the United States than of any other country. In a world lacking such loyalty and conviction, soldiers defect and societies crumble. Yet Earth, with the advent of rockets, atomic weapons, space satellites, has no boundaries that cannot be breached in little more than the instant it takes to think the deed. What loyalty can then be advocated? How can one understand and behave with concern for those others beyond the seas, and still feel and act with the simple patriotism of *McGuffey's Readers*? Religion, too, falls into this contradiction: how can one accept wholeheartedly one's own belief without somehow demeaning that of others? Can one hold to the true faith and be complacent about the millions who hold to another faith, which to them appears to be quite true? Examining the contradiction between that which is exclusive and yet must somehow also be inclusive leads to perilous territory indeed. The contradiction extends to the clash between the white man's determined assertion of superiority, and his factual numerical inferiority. True, too, is the white man's inability to prove to the satisfaction of all those other millions that he is, in fact, in any significant fashion their superior.

These complex contradictions invade the classroom. They make the teacher's task incredibly difficult. Since each teacher is a creature of his culture, he is torn by each conflict (when he is aware of it), yet has no stable guide leading toward a solution. The situation is certainly no easier for the student, who unfortunately, in too many instances, finds his teacher just as fallible as all the other adults who are confused and distracted by the world in which they live.

ACADEMIC FREEDOM

The freedom to teach and speak as one believes is deeply cherished by scholars. Any infringement of this freedom calls forth anguished cries from the halls of ivy. The tradition of such freedom has been carefully tended for generations. Academic freedom is spoken of with the same reverence one accords such basic documents of human rights as the *Declaration of Independence* or the *Magna Carta*.

Every crisis through which America has passed has produced legislation that would, in effect, limit a teacher's right to instruct as he saw fit. Current efforts to restrict freedom of instruction are focused particularly upon any person who might be a Communist, or who might appear to espouse Communist views. In the minds of some persons there should be restrictions on what a college professor may freely say or teach. But the prevailing opinion in most academic circles is that it is vital to democracy to have a free exchange of ideas.

This position becomes shaky when the argument is related to the public school teacher. These individuals instruct the young who are presumably highly impressionable. Should teachers have the freedom to teach as conscience alone dictates? Tenure laws have been enacted in an effort to provide protection for teachers who might have views that are unpopular in the community. In the majority of school districts, a teacher can attain tenure after two or three years of successful classroom teaching. This means that he cannot be fired without cause, and the cause must be subject to proof in court. In effect, this means that a teacher must demonstrate grave misconduct of some sort before a school system can act to fire him.

Certainly, tenure provides the teacher with economic security. Does it also provide academic freedom? The impression teachers have is that their freedom of expression is restricted even with tenure laws. The evidence would seem to bear them out. The books that teachers utilize in class are subject to censorship by boards of education or individual lay persons who, if their voices are loud enough, can interfere with the teacher's freedom of choice of subject matter. Teachers have been shifted from one subject to another because what they taught was considered unacceptable. Failure to accede to pressures, from whatever source, can result in punitive retaliation by administrators who assign the worst rooms, the worst sections, and outworn books to resistant teachers. Life can be made unpleasant for such teachers if there is a wish to do so; while proof of invasion of academic freedom may be hard to obtain, the typical public school teacher feels far less free than his colleagues in the college and university.

There is irony in observing that the typical public school teacher is unaware of his lack of academic freedom. Most teachers deviate not at all from the expected. And, if they note other teachers who do, they may be among the first to cast stones.

31

SPECIFIC TARGETS OF SCHOOL CRITICS

Earlier generations were critical of the schools because they were godless. Horace Mann, the early educational crusader, was viciously attacked for his forthright position on secular schools. We have already mentioned the suspicion of the public regarding educational frills, such as art and music.

Today the schools have been a source of public uneasiness because of purported subversive teaching. One of the first symptoms of suspicion of teachers was the rash of teacher's loyalty oaths. Although these oaths had been required in a few places prior to 1940, it was in the years during and after World War II that these oaths became widespread. In some instances the oaths were required of all public employees, but in many other instances only teachers were required to assert their loyalty. In one state, at least, authors of textbooks that may be purchased by the public schools must swear that they are not and never have been "disloyal."

Loyalty to one's country is unquestionably a desirable state of mind, but what is of interest to us is that educators have been singled out for particular attention. Are teachers more prone to be subversive than other people? The facts seem to indicate that very few teachers could be considered subversive in any definition of the term. Research shows that teachers are apt to be more conservative than the average person in their income bracket, are not very active politically nor politically interested. Why, then, are they the objects of such special anxiety as seems indicated by the requirement for teacher loyalty oaths?

I would suggest that teachers are a nearby and vulnerable target, a scapegoat for the fears of ideological attack from the Communist world. There may be other reasons, too, why the public wants to immunize, so to speak, the teacher group. After all, the teacher is "educated." He presumably is one who is conversant with the new, the recent, the avant-garde in the world of knowledge. Ideas, as is well known by dictators, are dangerous unless carefully controlled. When the average American is anxious about his future, he too becomes the victim of the fear of ideas.

Not all ideas are equally dangerous. Ideas certainly can and do challenge the known view of the universe; take modern physics for a very potent example. Yet we do not consider the physicist disloyal because he suggests that what our senses tell us about our world is probably not correct. We do find this somewhat disturbing. We may feel uneasy about the potentials of science to push out into the unknowns of the universe, as well as to destroy all that is close and dear. But we cannot attack the physicist; he, after all, is only seeking the laws of nature. There are easier and handier targets.

Teachers of the social sciences have been particularly selected as targets of the displaced attack. The content of the social studies in schools has been exhaustively scrutinized. A few years ago, any book on Communism or Russia was suspect; today the pendulum has swung so that courses or units on the errors of Communism are to be taught in the schools. In some areas of the country any discussion of the United Nations is considered taboo. UNESCO is the agency of the UN that has particularly concerned some critics of education who do not feel children should be permitted to study this aspect of our foreign relations.

The social studies are particularly available for public attack because the realities of the social world are harsh and often unpleasant. There are innumerable unsolved problems with which democracy must grapple. To what extent should young people be exposed to social reality? To what extent should our political and social leaders be considered as fallible human beings?

Literature, too, may be a cause of public concern, since the modern writer has few of the reticences of his Victorian predecessors. Teachers and librarians have, for instance, been severely reprimanded for permitting students to read J. D. Salinger's modern classic about adolescence, *The Catcher in the Rye*. Books by authors whose own views have been subject to public questioning are removed from school and library shelves.

Some school critics can certainly be put in the category of professional attackers, who gain notoriety and financial gain through channeling public fears towards a convenient target. That this target is often the school is to be deplored. But we cannot as easily dismiss the average citizen who responds to these attacks, or who is himself made uneasy by teaching which he feels leads young people into dangerous realms.

SUMMARY

American attitudes toward education are highly ambivalent. On the one hand, education is prized and valued as a significant asset in the individual's personal striving; on the other hand, education as intellectual consideration of significant ideas, as an end in itself, is suspect.

The schools have been the object of particular attack and criticism, much of which comes from a climate of opinion that makes the scapegoat phenomenon operative. While the schools can certainly be legitimately criticized on many grounds, much criticism appears to be displaced and unwarranted. The fear of teachers and of the educated person as potentially subversive appears in the general use of loyalty oaths, although teacher disloyalty has never been shown to be a major social problem.

In this climate of opinion, American education is forced to undergo continual self-evaluation and self-criticism. That the schools are lively and changing, that reforms are being made, is as much a cause as a result of the penchant of Americans for looking at the schools when things are not going right in the larger social context.

33

BIBLIOGRAPHY

BARZUN, JACQUES, *The House of Intellect*. New York: Harper & Row, Publishers, 1959. Penetrating essays that show one view of the anti-intellectual situation in America today.

BENNE, KENNETH, *A Conception of Authority*. New York: Teachers College, Columbia University, 1943. An adroit analysis of the role of authority in social relationships with particular reference to education.

BOORSTIN, DANIEL J., *The Image: or What Happened to the American Dream*. New York: Atheneum Publishers, 1962. An examination of some of the incongruities in the American social fabric.

BROUDY, HARRY S., "An Analysis of Anti-Intellectualism," *Education Theory*, IV (July 1954), 187-99. A philosophical position.

FRANK, LAWRENCE K., *Society as the Patient*. New Brunswick, N. J.: Rutgers University Press, 1948. A collection of essays by an educator and psychologist, with particular attention given to the role of education in constructing the good society.

Freedom-to-Read Bulletin. New York: American Book Publishers Council, Inc. An occasional publication that provides a state-by-state account of the activities of those who would censor the readings of others, either legally or by various kinds of pressure tactics. A dismal record.

HENRY, JULES, *Culture Against Man*. New York: Random House, 1963. An anthropologist turns his inquiring eye upon crucial factors in American life.

HOFSTADTER, RICHARD, *Anti-intellectualism in American Life.* New York: Alfred A. Knopf, Inc., 1962. A scholarly recital of the trials and tribulations of the intellectual through the course of American history.

HOLMES, BRIAN, *American Criticism of American Education.* Columbus, Ohio: The College of Education, The Ohio State University, 1956. A British educator brilliantly discusses American views of American education and contrasts the reality of European education, particularly British.

HULLFISH, H. GORDON, *Educational Freedom in an Age of Anxiety,* Twelfth Yearbook of the John Dewey Society. New York: Harper & Row, Publishers, 1953. A distinguished group of scholars examine the forces that affect freedom of inquiry.

IVERSEN, ROBERT W., *The Communists and the Schools.* New York: Harcourt, Brace & World, Inc., 1959. A carefully documented study of the Communist party and its relationship to education at all levels.

LERNER, MAX, *America as a Civilization.* New York: Simon and Schuster, Inc., 1960. For a well-written survey of the state of American culture, this volume is outstanding.

MEAD, MARGARET, *The School in American Culture.* Cambridge, Mass.: Harvard University Press, 1955. An anthropologist presents a different view of the function of education in the past, present, and future.

MYRDAL, GUNNAR, *An American Dilemma.* New York: Harper & Row, Publishers, 1944. The classic statement on the contradiction between American beliefs and behavior, with particular reference to the role of the Negro in America.

NELSON, JACK, AND GENE ROBERTS, *The Censors and the Schools.* Boston: Little, Brown & Co., 1963. Two journalists report on various attempts by individuals and groups to impose their own varieties of the truth on American schools and to determine the books children can read.

RAYWID, MARY ANNE, *The Ax-Grinders.* New York: The Macmillan Company, 1962. Recent attacks on the schools, with analysis of two typical situations; hypotheses are suggested regarding why such attacks occur.

ROOT, E. MERRILL, *Brain-Washing in the High School.* New York: Devin-Adair, 1959. A particularly virulent example of the selective perception of school critics. This author "proves" that current history textbooks are generally subversive.

STEWART, GEORGE R., *The Year of the Oath.* Garden City, N. Y.: Doubleday & Company, Inc., 1950. The fight for academic freedom at the University of California. A case study of what happened when the fear of academic subversives took over a campus.

WILLIAMS, ROBIN, *American Society.* New York: Alfred A. Knopf, Inc., 1960. A sociological report on the state of American civilization.

34

A subtitle for this chapter might well be "How the people get the schools they deserve."

The American system of governing the educational process is unique. Other democratic nations do not follow our practices. Therefore, we cannot claim that our particular methods of control are the only democratic possibilities. We can certainly boast, if that is the proper term, that the schools we have are what we, the people, want. To what extent our wishes are or should be molded or guided by professional educators is an area for us to consider. This chapter describes in general, how policies and decisions are made for the schools of the United States.

THE CITIZENS HAVE THEIR SAY

POLICY INFLUENCE—DIRECT: I

The most direct method whereby the citizen exercises his control of education is through election. Why school boards ever became elective in the first place is an interesting historical tale. We cannot trace all of that history here, but suffice it to say that the frugal colonist and fervent church member made quite sure that

DEMOCRACY'S
SCHOOLS

5

he knew where his school money went. The concept of lay control of the public schools was strongly espoused by Thomas Jefferson, who wanted school supervisors or inspectors to be elected. The sectarian and ethnic differences that divided many communities in the middle states worked against any strong state control, since fear of the propagation of any minority religious view prevented the widespread acceptance of selection of school trustees by a higher authority. Another factor that led to the election of school trustees, judges, and other critical governmental functionaries was fear of the development of an elite, hereditary society like those from which the early settlers had fled.

That professional educators had no say in what they were to be paid, in their working conditions, or in what they were to teach in colonial times is a reflection partly on the low state of the profession at that time, and partly on the social conditions that then existed. Most early school teachers were itinerants, often barely literate themselves, who taught out of laziness or lack of any other skill. It was obvious that such persons were not qualified to decide so crucial a question as what to do with public funds. The view of the educator as probably not a very practical person when it comes to something significant like money is still with us today. Parenthetically, one might point out that teachers and professors are considered very good credit risks, and it is reported (though not proven) that the Internal Revenue Service tends to view professors' and teachers' returns as somewhat more reliable than most because they "are too dumb or too smart to cheat."

In the United States today, 95 per cent of the school districts are run by local school boards elected by popular vote. These boards, usually composed of five to seven members, are usually nominated by petition of qualified voters. Most school-board members are elected on a nonpartisan basis, and usually at an election held apart from other elections. In most instances any eligible voter is eligible to serve on a school board, and he can succeed himself an indefinite number of times. He is rarely paid for his services.

Studies of school-board membership show that members represent business and professional interests, with incomes higher than the average, and with higher than average education. This is true despite the fact that the law in no state indicates income as a requirement for school-board membership, or spells out in more than vague terms what might constitute adequate education for the position.

It is tempting to conclude that the upperclass bias in school-board representation will of necessity promote a conservative approach to school problems. In certain instances, this may well be so. It is sometimes argued, however, that because school-board members come from the upper end of the socio-economic continuum they will tend to support more liberal views of education.[1] It is possible that better educated persons will be less apt to be frightened by new ideas, since they have had wider experience. The number of school boards that have demanded withdrawal of "controversial" books, fired a teacher accused of deviant ideas, or

[1] W. W. Charters, "Social Class Analysis and the Control of Public Education," *Harvard Educational Review*, XXIII (Fall, 1953), 268-83.

insisted on a strictly chauvinistic approach to civics and history is not known; nor is the number known of those that have resisted the pressure to do these things. However, the former instances are the ones that tend to be publicized. School boards have earned a reputation for conservatism.

To what extent school decisions are class biased because of the board's composition is unclear, but research bears out the impression that better schools and better teachers are found in better parts of cities. Presumably the board sets policies for a total community, but discrepancies in facilities and other measures of educational resources are so great between high-income and low-income neighborhoods in many areas that it is hard to escape the conclusion that, if the school boards are not responsible, then at the least, they are remiss.

Sexton, in a careful and recent study of such discrimination by socio-economic level, makes it clear that the class bias of the total school structure starts at the top. In the area of her study, school-board elections drew a small percentage of the electorate; and, according to Sexton, a much higher percentage of conservatives than nonconservatives were elected.

> Lower-income individuals and organizations have not shown much interest in school-board elections, regarding them often as of rather minor importance compared with "political" elections. This is probably directly attributable to the generally unsatisfactory experiences lower-income groups have had in school, and to the sense of alienation that has resulted from these experiences.[2]

37

School-board members do not necessarily agree with professional educators on the crucial issues facing education. Regarding federal aid to education, for instance, school-board members are generally opposed, while the NEA, representing the largest group of educators in the country, has been working diligently for federal aid for over twenty years.

The policies of school boards in the United States generally reflect the thinking of the upper socio-economic levels of the community not only because those who serve are from these levels, but because of the informal channels whereby their decisions are influenced. In the usual course of his day, it is unlikely that the average school-board member would come in contact with the minority or lower-class groups in his own community. His very life pattern insulates him from contacts with these kinds of people. He cannot, except by surmise, know what they need or want in terms of education.[3]

Then too, minority group members are hesitant about calling upon school personnel to make their wants known. They feel conspicuously uneducated, poorly dressed, perhaps have a heavy foreign accent, and share a general lower-class antipathy toward authority in all of its forms. The social order tends to operate against the lower-class or minority-group person's being able to help himself with the kind of effective personal and

[2] Patricia C. Sexton, *Education and Income* (New York: The Viking Press, Inc., 1961), p. 237.

[3] W. Lloyd Warner, *Democracy in Jonesville: A Study in Quality and Inequality* (New York: Harper & Row, Publishers, 1949), p. 195.

social pressure available to others. As Sexton suggests, a school board would have to *want* voluntarily to work to help the underprivileged.

The people elect their representatives to the school board, and then what happens? Are these persons really powerful in the direction of school affairs, or are they puppets who just do what the superintendent tells them to do? Legally, almost all school boards have the power to enter into contracts, levy taxes, disperse school funds, acquire property, enter into bonded indebtedness, enact changes in the school curriculum, and establish procedures for hiring and firing school personnel.

The most important task of the school board is to select the chief school officer for its district. If the system is quite small, boards may enter actively into the hiring of other staff members, but typically they permit the school official to act on his own, reporting to them his recommendations for such appointments, which they then formally approve.

Assuming that the average school board represents the more conservative view of the community, it would seem that most boards would select educational leaders who appear to support such a view. Certainly, the superintendent's tenure is dependent upon his ability to anticipate what his board will or will not support, and to identify the ways in which board members' opinions may or may not be influenced.

Through their votes, the people choose the legal policy-makers for the schools, but they are, in effect, choosing persons whose significant community includes only a part of the population. Lay control of education in America, then, in one formal sense, exists only as an ideal possibility.

POLICY INFLUENCE—DIRECT: II

The second legal and formal way in which the American lay public gets into the educational act is through the opportunities provided to vote on school bonds or increases in school taxes.

In order to understand how citizens control school finance it is important to know something about the underlying structure. Most school districts are financed from local tax sources. The amount of the tax and the extent to which a school district may go into debt (through issuing bonds) are subject to voter approval in most school districts. The law usually stipulates that of those voting, a majority of 60 per cent or more will be required to approve the measure. Eligibility to vote in school finance elections is generally based on the same requirements as those for voting in any election, with some interesting exceptions. In three states, no registration is needed to vote in such elections. In Arkansas and Texas a poll tax receipt is necessary. Four states, Arizona, Michigan, New Mexico, and Utah, allow only voters who own real property to vote. Six states permit a simple oath to establish eligibility to vote. In several states the voters do not have the opportunity to express directly their wishes on school finance matters.

The other interesting aspect of school finance is that most school districts are financially independent of any other governmental body. They can raise their own taxes and float their own bond issues without approval of a city, county, or other agency. The limitations upon their authority come from state legislation, setting a limit on the tax level, establishing the times and procedures for school elections, the conduct of the sale of bonds, and so forth. As in many other areas of education, the states will vary, and sometimes districts within a state will vary. Of interest to us, however, is that the people are directly consulted about the level of financial support they deem adequate in most school districts in the country. If the local citizenry wishes to pay a great deal for schools, they can do so. If they do not want to increase their tax bill for schools, they can also indicate this opinion.

As has been noted, school-board elections typically call forth a rather low level of voter interest. In school financial elections, turnouts are also low. A recent research inquiry into school financial elections and voter turnout reveals interesting, if somewhat disturbing findings. The most notable finding is that the larger the vote, the more apt is the school tax or bond issue to be defeated. Most of those who will vote for increases, the "yes" voters, are interested enough to go to the polls. Efforts to get more people to vote means turning up more "no" votes. Voting statistics do not show any significant increase in the amount of voter interest shown over the past ten years despite the furor in the press regarding the plight of education today. The really grave problem facing a school board or school administrator is the fact that having a larger voter interest seems to work against increased school support by the public![4]

Much of the public shows low involvement in school problems. Involvement in local school affairs is high with young parents, declines as the children grow older, and tends to disappear when the children are gone.

Complaints from all sides have been heard regarding the low pay for teachers, which is seen as a factor in the recruitment of mediocre personnel into teaching. Since raising salaries costs money, it is obvious that either the public really does not care enough about education to pay for it, or the "scapegoat" phenomenon is operating. Since the average man cannot get at the taxing powers of other governmental units but can have his say on school issues, he is apt to say "no" if you rouse him enough to vote at all. Perhaps this confirms our previous hypothesis regarding the ambivalence of the average American toward education. It is a good thing in the abstract, he says, but when it comes to paying for it, he has not been convinced sufficiently to overcome his innate distaste for raising his own tax bill no matter who the beneficiary might be.

Voting for school funds is only part of the story, of course, and is not the only way in which control of education is exercised through finances. The superintendent typically submits a budget to his school board. They study it. They may hold public hearings on the budget at which time interested groups may present their ideas regarding the amount of the budget and/or the way in which it is distributed.

The superintendent, in making up his budget, has to know what his school board is willing to pay for. A superintendent may deliberately inflate his requests so that when asked to scale them down, he can cut

[4] Richard F. Carter and William C. Savard, *Influence of Voter Turnout on School Bond and Tax Elections*, Cooperative Research Monograph No. 5, U.S. Department of Health, Education and Welfare (Washington, D.C.: U. S. Government Printing Office, 1961).

items that were not essential anyway and can thus get the budget he really wanted. Shall the available money be allocated to teacher salary increases one year, and the next year to improving playground facilities? Shall a new gym or a new library be built, if there is not enough money for both? How long shall textbooks be kept before being replaced? How often shall schools be repainted? These are all money questions. But they are all policy questions, some dealing directly with significant educational issues. In terms of the program of a school and the education of children, it does make a difference whether a new library or a new gym is built.

Since schools purchase all kinds of supplies, the issue often arises of whether the school board, since it is using public money, should not get the supplies from the lowest bidder and thus save as much as possible. A contrary view, however, is that since local money will be used, it should be spent locally, even if local suppliers cannot sell at competitive prices. The smaller the district and the larger the school budget looms in terms of local industry, the more acute will this problem be.[5] The American is again caught on the horns of a dilemma. The ideal school, good but cheap, is a delusion dearly held, but a delusion nonetheless.

CONTROL OF THE SCHOOLS

INDIRECT

The public has its say about the schools in a direct fashion when it elects a school board and votes on school finance questions. The public also makes its wishes known through indirect means. Some of these are obvious and some are subtle.

The most obvious kind of pressure is that of special interest groups. The schools are a ready-made target for all kinds of messages, if the message can only get through. Many groups with many special programs inundate the schools with free or inexpensive materials. Films and filmstrips used by many schools have been produced primarily to put a given corporation's name or product before the children, and secondarily to do a teaching task. Such materials are often well constructed, professionally produced, and a genuine aid to the teacher. The question that must be answered, however, is whether it is proper to use such materials, no matter how well developed, since the school is thus letting itself be used for noneducational ends. Spokesmen for producers of such material contend, of course, that this is the American way, and that they should have just as ready access to children in school as anyone out of school as long as they observe the proper etiquette.

The question would be academic except for the fact that millions of dollars are spent to produce and distribute such material. Teachers and other school personnel are continually being sent or given copies of material to be used with students. As many teachers have testified, you can quickly become submerged by a flood of materials if you once indicate an interest.

[5] Arthur J. Vidich and Joseph Bensman, *Small Town in Mass Society* (Princeton, New Jersey: Princeton University Press, 1958), pp. 171-97.

There are numerous groups, in addition to industries and businesses, that wish to promote a particular viewpoint. The United States Chamber of Commerce, for instance, has publications for both teachers and students that present its particular view of the American economy. Other groups, such as the Anti-Defamation League of the B'nai B'rith, have materials, again for both teachers and students, that present their viewpoints regarding intergroup relations. There is hardly a field in which some group has not made an effort to put into the hands of students and teachers material that will influence their attitudes.

We have already mentioned the scapegoat phenomenon in relation to the schools. That this may lie behind some public criticism is undoubtedly true. But critics of school programs may have other motivations. Whatever the source of the criticism, however, schools are particularly vulnerable to pressure by citizens, acting either individually or as spokesmen for groups. The very localism of the public school in the United States may be a disadvantage when such pressures occur:

> . . . at the national level, no one group has the kind of power to interfere with the educational program that one sees every day under a system of local control. The rabble rousers who can successfully frighten a large city school system like that of Los Angeles into dropping an essay contest on the United Nations would not have a chance in a federal school system.
> . . . It is local control of education which provides a greater opportunity for national pressure groups to dominate the educational programs of the public schools on a *national* basis. The reason is that local school boards are unable to withstand the pressures which can be generated by powerful national organizations which know what they want from the school.[6]

41

This argument by Lieberman makes the case against local control rather persuasive. Certainly we can see here, and in the numerous case studies of schools that have been the objects of attacks by extremist individuals and groups, that our decentralized system provides a ready means of control for those adept at pressure techniques.

Another kind of pressure that the public exercises is perhaps more subtle. This has to do with individual parent or patron contact with the school. Although it is the avowed policy of the schools to encourage and promote parental interest, there is considerable feeling that a good thing can be overdone. In identifying reasons for wanting to move or to remain in certain schools, for instance, some teachers indicated that they preferred schools in lower-class neighborhoods because the parents did not try to "run the schools." [7] Although teachers may prefer situations in which parents keep their distance, the facts indicate that the more aggressive approach of middle-class and upper-class parents to school affairs results in theirs being the attitudes and wishes that command the attention of school personnel. Sexton points out that higher-income parents were far more apt to belong to parent-teacher associations than lower-income groups.

[6] Myron Lieberman, *The Future of Public Education* (Chicago: University of Chicago Press, 1960), p. 55.

[7] Howard S. Becker, "The Career of the Chicago Public Schoolteacher," *American Journal of Sociology* (March 1952), pp. 470-77.

Furthermore, upper-income parents frequently consult with teachers, counselors, the school principal, the superintendent, and even school-board members about their children and school affairs. Lower-income parents seldom talk with any of these people. When an upper-income parent has a grievance, he talks to the appropriate person at school about it; he talks this person's language and he regards himself as at least an equal; he is usually educated, articulate, and impressive, a person to be respected and reckoned with. Whatever the complaint is about . . . chances are it will be given serious attention.[8]

But the lower-income person has no such assurance of being heard. His ability to articulate his feelings is less adequate; he may not even be sure just why he is critical of the schools. It would not be conceivable to such persons to call the superintendent, and rarely do they ask even to speak to a principal or teacher. They do not come to school open-house events. At the secondary school level, many an adolescent is visibly embarrassed if his parents turn up and appear uncouth or poorly dressed. Thus, the parental pressures on the school will come from the upper-income groups and will reinforce the class bias already present in the school board.

Interestingly enough, when a large sample of school principals were asked to identify the forces that had most influence on changing the instructional pattern, local lay groups and P.T.A.'s were ranked far below professional activities and studies. When asked regarding pressure for students to do more work in and out of schools, principals listed higher admission standards to college as most significant, but nearly half the school systems reporting indicated that general public demand was a major source of pressure. Urging by a few influential citizens was considered important in only about 10 per cent of the schools.[9]

While the principals who responded were undoubtedly expressing what they truly believed to be the facts, we can suggest that these data are only part of the story. A principal may hardly be aware of all the pressures exerted on him, particularly if he tends to agree with the dominant attitude of the middle-class group in his community. He may not know they are influencing him because in all actuality they are merely substantiating his own feelings and beliefs regarding what is right and proper and to be valued.

What we have been looking at so far is the extent of public control over what goes on in the schools. We have seen that the public has two direct ways of influencing school practices: through their election of school-board members and through their votes at school finance elections. In addition, sectors of the public can influence schools by use of pressure devices for commercial purposes or to insist on a given ideological position. Less obvious influence is that exerted by individual parents or groups of parents who create a climate of acceptance or rejection, or who actively work for or against a specific program. What control, then, does the professional educator have over what goes on in the schools?

[8] Sexton, *Education and Income*, p. 228.
[9] *Principals Look at the Schools* (Washington, D.C.: National Education Association, 1962), pp. 29-31.

Disputes about education and the schools are difficult to resolve for one very good reason: ultimate responsibility for what happens in the school is not clearly assigned. Since the public exercises so much control, both directly and indirectly, is it responsible for school programs? Or are the educators, who do the day-to-day job of keeping school, responsible for what happens in the schools?

The line that separates the public and the profession is not clear. One of the major problems a superintendent faces is helping a school board identify those areas in which it is most appropriate for it to function. But a school board or an individual member may not agree with the definition provided by the superintendent. Thus we find a continual process of accommodation and adjustment between the public and the professional, a kind of uneasy truce, with potential battle lines forming and reforming depending on the current climate of society and school relations.

The schools are continually faced with actual or potential conflict with the public. Several factors contribute to this. One, as we have described, is the tradition and exercise of local public control over major aspects of school operation.

A second significant factor is the recency with which education has become a profession. As an example, most education associations are open to membership to anyone who pays dues. Only in the last few years have any efforts been made by any educational organization to establish *professional* requirements for membership; that is, appropriate training and certification. (This will be discussed in greater detail in Chapter 12.)

43

A third significant factor that makes school-public conflict almost inevitable at one time or another is the variety of perceptions of the task of the school, coupled with the relative lack of adequate power over the educational process held by either the school or lay public. The public, for instance, tends to hold nonintellectual goals for education as being more important than educators, who rank intellectual goals as more significant.[10] Because differences of opinion concerning the proper function of the schools are the sources of a debate in which neither side has enough power effectively to impose its view on the other, the school controversies we repeatedly read and hear about cannot be expected to cease.

SUMMARY

In this chapter, we have examined the sources of power available to the public to get the schools some of the people want. The public not only has a great deal of power over the schools legally; it also has considerable informal and covert power, which to date has served to make the schools effective for serving middle-class values and vulnerable to local pressure at many points.

[10] Lawrence W. Downey, *The Task of Public Education: the Perceptions of People* (Chicago: Midwest Administration Center, University of Chicago, 1960), p. 48.

Conflict in the school situation is almost unavoidable since the roles of the public and the professional are not clearly defined and neither group has sufficient power to make its view of education prevail.

There is a basic question with which we must end this chapter: Should the public get the schools it *wants* or the schools it *ought* to have? Because there is a multiplicity of publics, as well as many differences in the theories and convictions held by educators, the question can probably never be answered definitively for the nation as a whole. In addition, as we shall see in the next two chapters, regional differences, differences in type of community, and differences in kinds of school systems all contribute to a lack of uniformity concerning what is desirable and what is desired.

BIBLIOGRAPHY

AMERICAN ASSOCIATION OF SCHOOL ADMINISTRATORS, *Choosing Free Materials*. Washington, D.C.: AASA, 1955. An example of one set of criteria, established by an educational group, to guide selection among the masses of free materials for school use.

DARLING, EDWARD, *How We Fought for Our Schools*. New York: W. W. Norton & Company, Inc., 1954. How a school system became embroiled in public attack and defense. Not a book for scholars.

GOLDWIN, ROBERT A. AND DON SHOEMAKER, *The Case of the Lively Ghost*, Case Stories in American Politics, No. 1. Chicago: American Foundation for Political Education, 1957. Dramatic personalization of the decision facing a school board on the issue of school desegregation.

GROSS, NEAL, *Who Runs Our Schools?* New York: John Wiley & Sons, Inc., 1957. Research report on school board membership and school policies.

————, WARD S. MASON, AND ALEXANDER W. MC EACHERN, *Explorations in Role Analysis: Studies of the School Superintendency Role*. New York: John Wiley & Sons, Inc., 1958. Detailed research report, with illuminating material on the sources of school-board and superintendent conflict and accomodation.

HALL, MORRILL M., *Provisions Governing Membership on Local Boards of Education*. United States Office of Education Bulletin No. 13. Washington, D.C.: Government Printing Office, 1957. Basic statistics regarding school boards throughout the country.

LADD, EDWARD T., AND WILLIAM C. SAYRES, eds., *Social Aspects Of Education: A Casebook*. Englewood Cliffs, N. J.: Prentice-Hall, Inc., 1962. Authentic cases of school systems in action, many illustrating the involvement of local community concerns with the government of the schools.

MALONEY, JOSEPH F., *"The Lonesome Train" in Levittown*, The Inter-University Case Program, No. 39. University: The University of Alabama Press, 1958. Demonstrates, via an authentic case, the interrelationships of public, school-board, and school leadership. Two other cases in this series, No. 15 and No. 51, are also of interest to the student of administrative policy and public education.

MARTIN, ROSCOE C., *Government and the Suburban School*. Syracuse: Syracuse University Press, 1962. Focusing on suburbia, this author presents a valuable discussion of the relationship between the public schools and the ways the public makes decisions about the schools.

NATIONAL COMMISSION FOR THE DEFENSE OF DEMOCRACY THROUGH EDUCATION, *Reports*. Washington, D.C.: The National Education Association, published periodically. The reports of the Commission's findings make fascinating reading as they show the many difficulties of providing adequate education within the democratic structure of American educational government.

OSTROM, VINCENT, "Education and Politics," in *Social Forces Influencing American Education*, 60th Yearbook, National Society for the Study of Education, Part II, pp. 8-45. Chicago: University of Chicago Press, 1961. The complexity of school "government" is analysed by a political scientist, with vivid examples of local pressure groups.

WALLER, WILLARD, *The Sociology of Teaching*, Chap. III. New York: John Wiley & Sons, Inc., 1932. A master of sociological analysis identifies the superintendent and school-board relationship.

WARNER, W. LLOYD, R. J. HAVIGHURST, AND M. B. LOWEB, *Who Shall Be Educated? The Challenge of Unequal Opportunities*. New York: Harper & Row, Publishers, 1944. Substantiates the later findings of Sexton regarding the differential allotment of public resources according to the socio-economic status of the community and neighborhood.

45

America's schools are remarkable for their differences. Our decentralized educational program makes for interesting variations in school practice. If everybody stayed in one location, these differences would be of only academic interest. But Americans are on the move. What happens educationally in one part of the country can have repercussions elsewhere. Despite this mobility, however, local characteristics tend to persist and influence school practices. It is the differences that emerge that we wish to examine here.

THE RURAL SCHOOL

In the American past stands the cherished image of the little red schoolhouse. Here children of all ages were housed in one room, taught by one teacher. If it was a man teacher, the big boys had to be beaten physically before he could try to teach them anything. If it was a woman teacher, there were other ways of testing her to see if she could control the group. The reading matter was often the famous *McGuffey Readers*, where morality was preached, along with phonics and spelling.

THE SCHOOL
IN THE
COMMUNITY
SETTING

6

This vision of the American schoolhouse was enshrined in the literature of the day. How many of us were passionate participants in the drama of the rural elementary school conveyed in the sun-dappled and tear-stained pages of *Rebecca of Sunnybrook Farm*? This view of the innocent rural life is a cherished one. The realities of farm life eighty years ago were harsh and often desperate, but what memory conserves is a sense of pastoral peace, of a place where values were secure, seasons were dependable, and virtue was rewarded.

An objective view of the education provided in the one-room school at the turn of the century indicates that it barely served the requirements of literacy. The teachers were often only a year or so older than their oldest student, had perhaps one or two years of high school or "normal school," and could call upon very few resources for instruction.

What is significant to us, however, is the nostalgia of many for what they imagine to be the virtues of this kind of school and schooling.

Rural schools today are apt to be quite different from the remembered model. Hardsurfaced all-weather highways have served to accelerate the process of school consolidation. The one-room one-teacher schoolhouse is becoming more and more rare. The consolidated schools now provide the grade-by-grade education typical of the town and city school.

Do we have a setting for education in rural areas of America that is distinctly different? Are not small towns and outlying farms as accessible as other areas to mass media, television, magazines, newspapers? Is not the whole country becoming just one demonstration of the Madison Avenue and Hollywood versions of what life is like? Rural America is undoubtedly facing some major adjustments. The depression foreclosures and the dust storms forced thousands to leave agricultural pursuits during the 1930's. Today, economists state that the only way to achieve a stable agricultural level without vast expenditures for price support and surplus storage is for a goodly percentage of farmers to leave farming. Only about 9 per cent of the population is needed to produce all the food and agricultural products needed. Although the single-family farm is still the pattern, the percentage of acreage held in large farms is increasing steadily. For efficient and profitable farming today vast expenditures are needed for fertilizer, expensive machinery, irrigation, pest control, and so forth. Farming is a scientific enterprise requiring training and intelligence.

Rural areas are being pressed by these forces. Yet, rural America still retains distinctive patterns. The values held there are more conservative. For example, a subscription to *Life* magazine for school use in a small rural town was not renewed when parents protested the liquor ads and the "naked women." [1] A study of the values held by the rural adolescent show him to be far more conservative than his urban counterpart. He is more likely to have become part of the productive family unit and to share his family's views. Although he, like his city peer, differs with his parents on points of etiquette and behavior, he is no rebel when it comes to basic values. Even though rural values have shifted, indicating less sus-

47

[1] Art Gallaher, Jr., *Plainville: Fifteen Years Later* (New York: Columbia University Press, 1961), p. 30.

picion of innovation and change, the values of nonrural adolescents have shifted far more.[2]

To grow up in rural America still means to experience a way of life distinctly different from that known by the majority of America's children. The rural child, for instance, must travel for at least ten miles to have as many social contacts as a city child has within one block. But farm families are apt to know more about even distant neighbors than apartment house dwellers know about those who live on the same floor. Main Street is still a place where anonymity is impossible. If Johnny heaves a rock through the grocer's window, almost any adult seeing the act can tell you whose child he is. In the city, on the other hand, he can blend into the background, among hundreds of other children, and disappear. Social pressure in the rural area is greater since everyone is much better known and there are relatively few persons on whom to concentrate one's attention. The city-bred person who tries teaching in a rural area will find himself suddenly far more conspicuous than he might wish. The rural teacher must be ready to adhere to rural patterns of living. Teachers who persist in rural schools are apt to have grown up in this style of life, and to have no great urgings to be "different" or intellectual or sophisticated. The town schools, which both town and farm children attend, are apt to have school boards dominated by farmers. The results may be like those found in Springdale, where, although most of the graduates of the high school would proceed to college or find employment in business or industry, the school curriculum was of little help: "Agricultural training is overemphasized and perpetuates a tradition of what has largely become useless training." [3]

In rural and small town culture, class differences are much less significant than they are in the city and suburbia. Although status is important and can be recognized, the differences are less in absolute terms and more in such things as "style of life." The vastly different social class learnings that separate a slum child of a big city from the middle-class apartment-house dweller in that same city exist less drastically in the rural areas and small towns of America. There is a homogeneity of core values and core experiences that reduces class differences to relative amounts of available money, to dress, and to possession of items of conspicuous consumption like new refrigerators.[4]

A recent summary of the education provided rural youth indicated that although there are good programs in many places, on the whole, rural schools lack specialized programs for the talented, have inadequate vocational programs, rarely have fully staffed guidance programs, and do not have the breadth of curricular offerings, particularly in the arts, that are available in other school areas. Children with various learning defects

48

[2] Robert S. Bealer and Fern K. Willits, "Rural Youth: A Case Study in the Rebelliousness of Adolescents," *Annals of the American Academy of Political and Social Science*, 338 (November 1961), 63-69.

[3] Arthur J. Vidich and Joseph Bensman, *Small Town in Mass Society: Class, Power and Religion in a Rural Community* (Princeton, N. J.: Princeton University Press, 1958), p. 179.

[4] Gallaher, *Plainville*, Chap. vi. See also Roger Barker and Herbert F. Wright, *Midwest and Its Children: the Pyschological Ecology of an American Town* (New York: Harper & Row, Publishers, 1954).

are usually not cared for by special programs. Instructional materials are insufficient in quantity and variety.

> It almost seems that the importance of materials to teaching and learning is yet to take root in the thinking of those responsible for our rural schools. . . . Many teachers meet their classes day after day armed with little more than a set of textbooks, a dictionary, a blackboard, an outdated set of encyclopedias, and the State-provided course of study.[5]

It is clear that education in rural America is faced with some difficult problems. Given the conservative nature of the community and the more limited funds available, the school can provide only a few windows on the outside world. Yet, it is into this outside world that many rural youths must migrate.

EDUCATION IN SUBURBIA

When there is a lag in social conversation, a good gambit is to deplore or extol suburban living. This is bound to keep everyone excited and involved for at least a half hour. There is no doubt that suburban living is a highly controversial subject. Is suburbia good or bad? Are these communities going to make for better family living or will they undermine it?

The facts about suburbia are challenging. Urban living has been a significant part of American life from colonial times, despite our feelings about rural living and the wide open spaces. The phenomenon we are living with today is really urban deconcentration. Persons acculturated in the cities are moving out to the greener grass of the surrounding suburbs. When the rural person migrates to town, he typically finds location in the central city. He usually enters the city at or near the bottom of the economic ladder. Only when he or his children have moved up in the socio-economic scale can they afford to think about a ranch house (*sic*) outside the city. Thus, the suburban dweller is really a city man transplanted.

The suburb is not a particularly new phenomenon. Street-car lines and commuter trains fanned far out into the countryside long before the mass rush to suburbia began. These earlier suburbs were often associated with the wealthy (e.g., Philadelphia's Main Line). Large, gracious homes, with ample space for stable and horses, were the mode in many early suburbs.

The difference in the picture of suburbia today is most impressive. Suburbia is now not populated primarily by the wealthy. In fact, many of the developments are rather dreary tracts of cheap small houses on little pockets of lawn. The term "development" is a key to the social patterns that we note in surburbia. Typcially, a contractor will have 150 homes in one price range in one development and in a nearby development, another 150 homes in a vastly different price range.

This results in a new kind of segregation: segregation by income. Although each child in such a development may have many others to play

---
[5] Robert M. Isenberg, "Are Rural Youth Getting an Equal Break Academically?" *Extension Service Review*, 34 (August 1963), 146-47.

with, the value systems and life patterns of all tend to be similar. Or at least most of the families strive toward some common picture of what life should be like for them, derived from faithful reading of women's magazines, where careful instruction is given regarding what is good taste and what is not. And good taste, the reader is informed, does not really require much money; only ingenuity and a sense of what is "fun" or, to put it in terms of reality, what will impress visitors.

The pattern of living in suburbia is regulated by the ebb and flow of the commuting fathers. Although the work day has been shortened, and suburbia has flourished because of the two-day week end, the hours taken to get to work and back actually mean that the breadwinner is away from home as many hours as twenty years ago if not more. The effective management of the house is left to the mother.

Suburban living is not necessarily easy. There is considerable documentation that the isolation of the women and children tends to increase feelings of entrapment and thus tension among family members. The higher the education of the wife—and suburbia tends to attract an increasing number of families with ever more education—the more she will feel cut off from significant activities. The husband and father is apt to feel alienated from his children since he sees so little of them. During his few free hours at home, he is apt to be caught with the do-it-yourself demands of home maintenance.

These problems of adjustment appear acute at the present moment in some areas. Yet, we are beginning to see, entering the ranks of the young married, persons whose whole life has been lived in suburbia. What was a trap or an illusion to their parents is familiar territory to them. Perhaps suburbanitis, as a neurotic pattern, will decline within another generation, given some educational help.

The suburban offspring are as effectively insulated from the larger society as are the rural youths of Plainville. The homogeneity of the families, which may be actual or only hoped for, tends to focus attention on personal idiosyncracies rather than on social or economic differences. This focusing on individual deviations has, it seems, promoted intense striving to be as much like other people as possible. To be too different from what is expected of people in *this* "development" at *this* income level is to be uncomfortably conspicuous.

Parents, particularly young ones who are on the upward mobile belt, find that the husband's job success appears to depend on being a good organization man. These parents hope their offspring will have a successful, smooth life, and so they work hard at making them organization children.

For suburban youth, the car and the telephone are life's essentials. Lacking adequate public transportation, the only way adolescents can get together is either by car or by phone, and they use both abundantly. The school draws them together from a wide area and promotes their social mixing and social development; the family must supply the wherewithal to meet the needs thus fostered. More and more homes in suburbia must have an extra car for junior and an extra telephone line for junior miss.

Being constantly on the move, either driving or talking, the teen-ager has found television too static and attention-demanding. Instead, he has rediscovered radio. The development of the small transistor radio has meant that he can take his entertainment with him—a kind of background noise that can be tuned in or out at will. During the high-school years, there is a noticeable slackening of interest in television, particularly in suburbia. The radio disc jockey and the current song hits or singers are what the adolescent has to know to be "in."

The greatest growth of suburbia has occurred in the postwar years. Not only are the developments new, the schools are also new. Thus, suburbia's schools can incorporate the latest devices and most modern furniture and equipment. As growth continues at a steady pace, the major problem faced by many suburban school districts is just keeping up with the numbers of children. New school building construction becomes a big business.

The suburban schools are modern in appearance and their programs indicate what the upwardly mobile middle class currently wants in terms of education. Parent pressure has forced many suburban schools to start foreign language programs in the elementary grades. Special classes for handicapped and gifted children proliferate in suburbia. Outstanding as a characteristic of suburban schools are the club programs. Some secondary schools have over a hundred such voluntary activities, all vying for the students' time and attention.

These activities also serve the further purpose of preparing college-bound youths for their role in the club and activity life of the college or university. Students become well versed in the arts of group management and become politically astute in their maneuvers for power and status, where it counts, among their peers. For decades, schools have struggled with the problem of exclusive, often secret, fraternities and sororities. In some suburban areas, these groups are vital and virulent, even though illegal. Often they become a means for achieving status and social mobility. If the child gets into the right group in high school, he has a better chance to be bid for a high-status fraternity at State University. In a few communities, it has been reported that active recruiting for sororities and fraternities takes place at the junior high level several years before the children have even moved up to senior high. Many of the efforts of school administrators to eradicate such groups are nullified by the active support of adults in the community. If the groups are disbanded, they reappear in another guise.

The schools of suburbia are paradoxically situated; they both benefit and suffer from the lively public interest in them. Some of the schools with the highest salaries and highest costs per pupil are in suburban areas. Students from these schools get into the best colleges and win many awards and scholarships. Educationally, these are very rich areas. Parents select homes in certain suburbs because of the reputation of the schools. School programs are keenly supported; P.T.A. groups at the elementary level are active, with many men participating. Yet, some of the most strenuous attacks upon the schools have come from suburbia. The educated parent is most likely to note and to do something about some real or imagined school lack. Pasadena, California; Arlington, Virginia; Montgomery County, Maryland; Tenafly, New Jersey are wealthy suburban school districts in which the public schools have suffered vicious attacks.

Some of these attacks have been spearheaded by the archconservative groups, who see a Communist behind every textbook.[6] Other parental pressure groups appear to be a response to acute anxiety regarding the admission of students to status universities and colleges. Complaints are heard that schools are not "pushing" children hard enough. Parents demand homework in first grade. Thus, while the schools are well supported, they are often exposed to excessive public interference.

Lacking a social milieu that effectively exposes them to differences on an interpersonal level, suburban youths grow up fairly well convinced of the value of being like everyone else. The rebellious youth is more apt to be spoiled than angry. Suburbia provides abundantly for its young, so much so that they respond with ever increasing material demands. The casual, though often nasty, delinquencies of the suburban area appear to arise almost as much from boredom as from anything else.

The goals sought by these young people are, in most instances, obviously attainable by them: college, white-collar jobs, adequate incomes to support future homes and families of their own. There is only a minority of young people who seem aroused by or interested in the moral and social problems of the day. The rest, though dutifully reporting on housing, crime, or international affairs for school themes, are not touched to the soul. When their insularity is challenged, they bristle and counterattack.

Suburban life, on these counts, then, has been seen as a force toward a kind of social passivity, toward a loss of the *élan vital* that propelled the United States so rapidly forward in previous decades.

The school in suburbia, like its counterpart in rural areas, has the task of countering social isolation. Social reality is, in one sense, as remote from Levittown as from Plainville. The acute, real problems that must be solved, however, will most likely be the task of the children who are produced from suburbia, rather than of the children from city and rural America. It is possible that suburban isolation may grossly interfere with suburban-raised generations' perception of and, therefore, ability to solve the problems of the future.

BIG CITY

Man has lived in cities for centuries. Being a gregarious animal, he did not find great concentrations of his fellow man distasteful. Americans have built some of the great cities of the world in a relatively short time.

The city was the first home for most immigrants. Even those whose goal was homestead land on the frontier passed through the cities. Most immigrants stayed in the city for at least one generation. Ethnic concentrations in the slums of American cities have been a familiar part of our social landscape for several hundred years.

[6] Mary Ann Raywid, *The Ax-Grinders: Critics of Our Public Schools* (New York: The Macmillan Company, 1962).

For the immigrant parent, the city school was the important Americanizing agency. Here was where the children came into their first contact with Americans. The youngsters were soon able either to guide their parents into American ways or to leave home. The school was the quickest way out of the tenement.

As one immigrant group became Americanized and moved out, another moved in to take its place. Studies of New York neighborhoods show the changing ethnic pattern over several generations as group succeeded group.

The city was also an attractive place for middle-class and upper-class Americans. Here they could enjoy theaters, restaurants, and the society of their peers. For some, the city was the place for work and business, for advancement and the achievement of power. For others, it meant escape from the narrowness of rural and small town life; in the city a person could dare to be different and could find others who shared a different view of life.

Today's American city appears to be entering a new phase, with some highly significant implications for education. Cities have been big; they are getting bigger. While much of the city is spilling into suburbia, the suburban fringe is moving even farther out. The highly concentrated living associated with city dwelling now encompasses more acreage and, thus, more people than ever before. But as suburbia spreads farther and farther from the center of the city, suburban dwellers resist coming in for shopping or fun. Stores are finding it profitable to have branches in large shopping centers that cater to suburbia. Some business firms have found that employees are just as happy if the firm is also located in suburbia. For example, electronics firms are favorites of suburban developers, as they bring in skilled researchers but few or no blue-collar personnel who might form unions and that sort of thing.

Thus, the centers of many of today's big cities are decaying. Businesses are no longer prospering. Even though thousands of workers come into the city for clerical and white-collar activities, they find it easier to carry on their personal consumer activities near home—in suburbia, that is.

But housing is still a problem in the big cities. With thousands moving out to the suburbs, thousands are moving in. This is, in a sense, the old movement of population groups, but with a difference. The older ethnic migrations found the city only a temporary stopping point. Today's city migrant is caught; he cannot see a way out of the city no matter how hard he may try. The new migrant to the city is most apt to be a Negro. In 1900, 90 per cent of the nation's Negroes lived in the rural South; today only about 50 per cent live there. The remaining 50 per cent are now concentrated mostly in large cities, and of these cities, only four are in the South. Four northern cities outrank even Washington, D.C. in the number of Negroes. New York State now has more Negroes in its population than any other state. Other large groups of new migrants to the cities are the Puerto Ricans and Mexican-Americans.

Today's city slum is a trap rather than a way station. The dwellers there can hardly hope for, much less see, a way out. The suburb is a white collar choking them in. If and when they do manage to find stable jobs, housing is tightly restricted. What has been noted is that the old segregation of schools in the South is being duplicated by the newer segregation of schools in the North, the result of segregation in housing. For as the cities become the major housing areas for nonwhites and Spanish-speaking migrants, so the suburbs become the communities for the whites of whatever ethnic or religious strain.

A new force may, in time, change the desolate picture of the central city. The Negro protest movement, with sit-ins, picketings, mass marches, has swept across the country from one major city to another. The object of these activities is to open new job opportunities, break housing restrictions, desegregate city schools, and open up other services and accommodations to all. The country as a whole has been taken by surprise by the swiftness with which this protest movement has grown. The apathetic Negro, defeated and passive, is on the way out. A new militant leadership is rousing the Negro in community after community. How long it will take before complete integration of the Negro in American society is accomplished we cannot say, but it will undoubtedly be generations before the blight of the slum is completely gone.[7]

We will return to the impact of slum life on these particularly disadvantaged groups, but we must consider as well the effects of city life on children not trapped by race in a ghetto. The city child typically lives in a multifamily unit. He is surrounded by thousands of other people all day and all night. He has little place to play, and the place in which he can play may often be unsafe or crowded or dirty. To find recreation, he must either be part of an organized group in a settlement house or club or he must seek recreation within his own family apartment—in front of the TV, with a book, or with one or two friends. He cannot roam widely unless his family permits it, but the temptation to roam is not very great; all he will see is more blocks of apartment houses, small stores, big buildings. The things that make a city attractive to many adults—the museums, theaters, restaurants, lectures, concerts—are not attractions for young people. The city child, to find what might be especially designed for him, must have alert, interested, and available parents who escort him to his special activity.

The slum child lives an even more restricted life. He often lacks a parent who could take him to special children's activities, if the parent knew such existed—and most of them do not. As the child grows older, he may find himself physically restricted by the territorial claims of rival youth gangs, so he dare not leave his own block.

Big American cities, for persons of either wealth or poverty, are not exactly delightful places for living. As has been noted, public services in the cities tend to be neglected: parks are few and often ill-kept, schools are under-supported and old, standards are low for police protection and for public sanitation. The air is increasingly polluted by industrial waste and automobile exhausts. Urban renewal has promised to solve all of these problems, but so far the promise has not been met. In fact, critics of current urban renewal policies suggest that they have created new problems on top of old ones. Disorganized as slum living may appear, it still provides

[7] "The Negro Revolution," four articles in *Dissent*, X, No. 3 (Summer 1963), 205-33.

a neighborhood and some sense of community; the huge complexes of apartments that make up the typical urban renewal development destroy these established relationships, and do not provide a setting where new community feeling can grow. The deprived are now also the dispossessed.

The problem of schools in urban areas have been intensified in recent years because of these multiple social problems. The city school derives its model from a suburban or at least small-city view of life. The curriculum, the materials of instruction, the motivational practices are middle class. The typical picture of family life in the primary-grade reader shows a suburban ranch house with a jolly family and its jolly pets. The people in the texts are all white, too, unless they are obviously foreign.

The city child cannot see himself in the school's terms. He knows he does not live this kind of life. If he is nonwhite, he cannot see himself in the picture at all. The apartment dweller, if middle class, will find the school's goals and the learning goads utilized not too alien. But the slum child is almost completely out of touch with the orientation of the school. He knows that ambition will get him nowhere. He has no reason to value more education. He has no place to do homework, and rarely anyone at home who cares if he does it or not.

Schools that serve the slum areas of big cities are often tense and uneasy institutions. Reports of student violence and disorder make the press regularly. Research indicates that maintaining classroom dicipline is the hardest task for the teacher at almost every grade level and, in fact, takes more time in some elementary classrooms than instruction. The demoralization of teachers and other school personnel in these schools has been documented. While there are many fine persons who have found a way to live with such social disorganization, the typical teacher, unfortunately, is not comfortable. The middle-class teacher, either Negro or white, cannot or will not realize that the slum child starts, educationally, from a different place than the middle-class child. It is very hard, says a big city administrator, to get experienced teachers to remain in central city schools; new teachers request positions in outlying "good" districts, or refuse jobs. The big city is in a poor bargaining position in the current competition for qualified teachers. As a result, schools that require extremely able teachers get and keep those whom no one else wants.[8]

As we have seen, city school boards are dominated by professional and business persons who view education and the needs of their communities from a particular vantage point. That their view is out of touch with reality is now becoming clear; big city school systems are in trouble. Although rural areas and suburban areas have been able to establish the kinds of schools they want, city dwellers have not been so fortunate. Current population shifts and the obvious failure of the schools to educate effectively a large proportion of the city's youngsters has prompted a serious new look at big city educational programs.

55

[8] *Fourth Annual Educational Conference on Problems of Segregation and Desegregation of Public Schools* (Washington, D.C.: U.S. Commission on Civil Rights, May 3-4, 1962). Testimony of Dr. Houston R. Jackson, Baltimore, Maryland.

A school's setting determines many aspects of its program. There are observable differences in approach between the rural school, the suburban school, and the big city school. Each locale, in turn, provides a different out-of-school setting for children and youth so that here, too, differential learning takes place.

The ideal model of the school that we have inherited does not coincide with the reality of social life in many places. It is this lack of congruence that is certainly one of the most deeply challenging aspects of modern education. How can the rural school change (be permitted to change) to equip the surplus rural population to cope with an electronic, urban society? How can the suburban school unwrap its swaddled youth and bring compassion, understanding, and a sense of mission to the future leaders emerging from these environs? Can the big city school system dare utilize the findings of anthropology, sociology, and psychology, and adapt its program in order to stop the tragic waste of human talent resulting from current programs?

These are intensely difficult questions. Some educators may not know these questions exist. Others may ignore them. Yet, many others are striving valiantly to find feasible solutions. However, no educational solution can take place in a vacuum. The public, too, must hear the questions and be willing to work toward answers.

56

BIBLIOGRAPHY

AGEE, JAMES AND WALKER EVANS, *Let Us Now Praise Famous Men*. Boston: Houghton Mifflin Company, 1960 (originally published 1941). A poetic and disturbing report, in words and pictures, of three tenant families in the rural South during the depression years.

ALLEN, GEORGE N., *Undercover Teacher*. Garden City, N. Y.: Doubleday & Company, Inc., 1960. A newspaper reporter becomes a junior high teacher in a New York City slum school. His report is illuminating, frightening, and sympathetic.

BARCLAY, DOROTHY, *Understanding the City Child: A Book for Parents*. New York: Franklin Watts, Inc., 1959. A useful look at city life with particular emphasis on the child at home. An introduction contrasts city life of the 1920's with that of today.

BERGER, BENNET M., *Working Class Suburb: A Study of Auto Workers in Suburbia*. Berkeley: University of California Press, 1960. Is a working-class suburb different from a middle-class one?

BRAITHWAITE, E. R., *To Sir, with Love*. Englewood Cliffs, N. J.: Prentice-Hall, Inc., 1959. What it is like to teach in a British slum secondary school, particularly if you are a Negro teacher.

CHANDLER, B. J., LINDLEY J. STILES, AND JOHN I. KITSUSE, eds., *Education in Urban Society*. New York: Dodd, Mead & Co., 1962. A distinguished collection of articles on the special problems of city schools.

CONANT, JAMES B., *Slums and Suburbs*. New York: McGraw-Hill Book Company, 1961. This report by Dr. Conant drew national attention to the social dynamite existing in the slums.

GORDON, RICHARD E., KATHERINE K. GORDON, AND MAX GUNTHER, *The Split-Level Trap*. New York: Bernard Geis Associates, distributed by Random House, 1960. Case histories of individuals and families who live in suburbia, with particular attention to the influence of suburban life on mental health.

HALSEY, MARGARET, *This Demi-Paradise*. New York: Avon Books, 1960. (Paperback.) A perceptive and witty diary of life in a suburb.

HUNTER, EVANS, *The Blackboard Jungle*. New York: Simon and Schuster, Inc., 1954. A bitter and chilling novel about life in a vocational high school. Overdone, but uncomfortably close to school reality.

JACOBS, JANE, *The Death and Life of Great American Cities*. New York: Random House, 1961. A critical evaluation of urban renewal projects and their impact on people.

KOLB, JOHN H., "Rural Youth," *The Nation's Children, Problems and Prospects*, Vol. III, ed. Eli Ginzburg. New York: Columbia University Press, 1960. Background paper for the 1960 White House Conference on Children and Youth.

KRAMER, JUDITH R. AND SEYMOUR LEVENTMAN, *Children of the Gilded Ghetto*. New Haven: Yale University Press, 1961. A sociological study of three generations of Jews in the suburb of a midwestern city.

MEAD, MARGARET, *The School in American Culture*. Cambridge: Harvard University Press, 1950. See especially the description of the idealized image of the little red schoolhouse.

MUMFORD, LEWIS, *The City in History*. New York: Harcourt Brace & World, Inc., 1961. A marvelous, if lengthy, story of cities, with a particularly caustic account of the excesses in urban development today.

PATTERSON, FRANKLIN, *Public Affairs and the High School*. Medford, Mass.: Tufts University, 1962. A summer pilot program to enlist youth's active interest in public concerns and public service.

PATTON, FRANCES GRAY, *Good Morning, Miss Dove*. New York: Dodd, Mead & Co., 1954. Fictional account of life of a small-town schoolteacher. Vividly illustrates the sentimental view of the idealized school in the American tradition.

SMITH, ROBERT PAUL, *"Where Did You Go?" "Out." "What Did You Do?" "Nothing."* New York: W. W. Norton & Company, Inc., 1956. A nostalgic recall of the delights of childhood in an earlier age.

SPECTORSKY, A. C., *The Exurbanites*. New York: Berkley Publishing Corp., 1955. (Paperback.) A needling report on the way-out suburbs.

STONG, PHIL, *If School Keeps*. New York: Fred A. Stokes Co., 1961. A biting reminiscence of rural schooling.

The Exploding Metropolis. By the editors of *Fortune*. Garden City, N. Y.. A Doubleday Anchor Book, 1958. (Paperbound.) A series of essays on the situation of the city today.

WHYTE, WM. H., *The Organization Man*. Garden City, N. Y.: A Doubleday Anchor Book, 1957. (Paperbound.) See especially Part VII, "The New Suburbia: Organization Man at Home."

57

Schools differ because of the kinds of communities in which they are set. They also differ according to the region in which they are located. Such differences arise in large measure from the history of the region, but more significantly, because the schools are a local product. Whether localism is or is not desirable is a continuing American debate. Furthermore, there are vigorous nonpublic schools that enroll a significant segment of the children and affect public schooling in some localities. What about them? Are they very different, and if so, what public controls for them are right, proper, and legal? Finally, are differences becoming accentuated, or is a national system evolving? It is to these questions that we turn our attention in this chapter.

REGIONAL DIFFERENCES

The patterns of rural, urban, and suburban living are sufficiently dissimilar to create some different educational practices and pose different educational problems. Regional differences slice the pie in another fashion. Although on the surface Westchester County,

VARIATIONS ON THE THEME

7

New York, might appear similar to Atherton, California, these expensive suburbs have a regional flavor that has some significance for the school. One study showed that school programs in the Far West tended to emphasize the socializing function of the school; in the South, the concern appeared to be more with personal development, particularly physical; the eastern states preferred an emphasis on moral behavior, the world, and citizenship; while the Midwest seemed to be in the middle of the road.[1]

Outstanding in terms of a regional problem is the desegregation of the schools of the South. All of the 17 states and the District of Columbia, where school segregation was enforced by law prior to 1954, have some kind of integration. The path toward such integration has been a thorny one, fought on every level of the community, the state, and the nation.

The story of education for both Negroes and whites in the South is not particularly encouraging. Southern states in general have been at the bottom of the list in terms of the amount of money per pupil spent on education ever since statistics of such things were first compiled. The education provided for Negroes lagged behind the education for whites. Until the 1950's, in most southern states, Negro schools were less well equipped and tended to be older, with larger classes, a shorter school year, fewer special services or facilities, and lower salaries for teachers.

The defense of segregation has rested on the doctrine that such separation was acceptable as long as the facilities provided were equal. That this equality did not exist in fact bothered very few persons in power until the shift in the general climate of opinion indicated that even separate *and* equal facilities would have to go. In a drive to create separate equality during the 1950's, many southern states spent unprecedented amounts on Negro schooling. Salaries were equalized. Facilities were improved and more services provided. However, the concept of separation of the races had lost its legal support, and these efforts only served to reduce Negro pressure in some areas, but did not eliminate the drive toward integration.

The overwhelming pressures of the racial controversy have influenced much of the instruction and content in southern schools. Books and magazines are screened for positions offensive to the white power group in the community. The birthday of Robert E. Lee is a school holiday in many southern states. A Confederate flag in and around school property is not even noticed. The Civil War is renamed The War Between the States, and is refought with every generation of students.

Schools in states on the eastern seaboard reflect another kind of crucial social problem. Here too, in the urban centers, segregation by housing has become an explosive issue. The eastern states are among the few where competition from parochial and private schools is a concern for public educators. In some cities in the East, for instance, parochial school enrollments almost equal and in one or two instances exceed that in public schools. When Catholics serve on school boards, research shows

---

[1] L. W. Downey, *The Task of Public Education: the Perceptions of People* (Chicago: University of Chicago Press, Midwest Administration Center, 1960), pp. 37-44.

that they tend to be motivated much more to represent a special interest than are non-Catholics.[2]

The East also supports non-Catholic private schools, many of which are very expensive and attract an elite student body. In a city like New York, many middle-class and upper-class parents face the decision, so they say, of either enrolling their children in a private school, or moving to the suburbs where public education is "safe."

The heavy industrial and commercial development of the East has long supported vocational programs to fit young people for jobs in business and industry. By contrast, the South has few vocational programs, and traditionally hardly any for Negroes. Thus, the South has been poor in technologically trained manpower for generations. The movement of some industry to the cheaper, nonunion labor area of the South has promoted more interest in vocational programs in recent years.

The Far West has developed a different style of education. California is the dominant state in terms of sheer numbers of people, amount of money, and centers of influence. Relatively few children go to private or parochial schools. Most college-bound students will attend public junior colleges, state colleges, or the State University.

The adult population, in most instances, has been born and reared in another part of the contry. There is high mobility among the communities in California itself, with persons moving from suburb to suburb with job changes or income increases. The climate encourages year-round outdoor activities, which are reflected in the school programs. The emphasis on "getting along," on being a good member of the group, on being active in many kinds of clubs and organized activities, on having a good time, can be noted in school planning and practices.

Although there appears to be a more modern tone to the curriculum and a greater air of experimentation and trying out of new approaches, there does not seem to be much evidence that the schools of the West actually are any more "progressive" than schools in the East. The multiplicity of materials and services and the newness of so many schools would tend to convey such an impression, but it is not verified by reports of practice.

The schools of the Midwest, outside the big cities, tend to be oriented toward rural and conservative values. Some of the states have a very high percentage of small high schools where only a minimal program is possible, because of local resistance to the consolidation of school districts. Athletics are important, and experimentation is relatively rare.

These generalizations about regional differences are too brief to be completely accurate. In each region there are schools that do not fit the pattern described. Regional differences may underly some school problems, but, except for the South, there are apt to be more differences between urban, and rural, and suburban schools than between schools of different regions.

[2] Neal Gross, Ward S. Mason, Alexander W. McEachern, *Explorations in Role Analysis* (New York: John Wiley & Sons, Inc., 1958), p. 199.

Most children attend public schools. Yet, an increasing number are enrolling in private and church-related schools. How different are these schools? What is the relationship of these schools to public schools and to society at large?

The numbers of children attending nonpublic schools, as well as the proportion of such children in the total population, have been increasing. In 1900 about 8 per cent of school children were enrolled in such schools; in 1960 the percentage of children had almost doubled, amounting to approximately 6.5 million students. Of this number, it is estimated that 80 to 85 per cent are in the parochial schools of the Roman Catholic church.[3]

The private schools can be divided into two groups: the schools operating primarily for the profit of the owner, and the nonprofit schools functioning with a board of directors and endowment funds. Schools of the first group typically are mediocre in staff and performance. If they are boarding schools, they are apt to be caretakers for children that parents are unwilling to have around or are unable to control. The facilities and equipment are usually below those of the public schools, and since salaries are low, the teachers are often not certificated for regular school employment.

The second group includes the exclusive preparatory schools and the exclusive private day and boarding schools. Typically, these schools attract and enroll a student body from the upper-middle-class and upper-class community. The goal of most of them is to prepare students for college and university or, in the case of some of the girls' schools—the modern versions of the old-fashioned "finishing" school—to provide them also with the skills and etiquette of the upper-class lady.

These schools have several characteristics that make them different from the public schools. The policy direction of the school usually comes from a self-perpetuating board, often made up of alumni or large donors. The board is answerable to no one so long as the school remains within the legal definition of a non-profit organization. This frees the school from the kinds of local pressures and restrictions that limit the kinds of things public schools can do. As a result, we find some private schools, including some of the most exclusive, experimenting with different kinds of instructional procedures and programs.[4]

However, the independent private school is vulnerable to pressures, too. If the board is dominated by donors, or persons are put on the board with the hope that they will become donors, then the director of the school and his staff may be subject to considerable overt or covert board pressure. Also, since the school must obtain much of its financing from tuition,

61

[3] Burton Clark, *Educating the Expert Society* (San Francisco: Chandler Publishing Co., 1962), p. 133.

[4] David Mallery, *New Approaches in Education* (Boston: National Council of Independent Schools, 1961).

parents must not be too distressed by what the school is doing lest they withdraw a child. Since attendance is voluntary, the school can be effectively threatened by significant numbers of parental withdrawals, a course of action not open to public school parents.

The private school, in order to maintain freedom and support, must be extremely conscious of its public image. The more impressive this image, the more it is associated with the elite, with wealth, power, and "old families," the more free the school can feel to develop a good program and also be assured of needed support.

The exclusive private schools attract two kinds of students: those who consider attending such schools a birthright, the thing that everyone does as a matter of course, and those whose parents wish they could feel this way. The preparatory school is seen as one of the rungs in the ladder of upward social mobility. Not just any private school, however, but the *right* private school. A girl cannot hope to aspire to a real debut to society in any of the major cities if she has not attended an acceptable private school. The boy who is accepted into the exclusive circle has started his journey to prestige and status, which will send him, as the next step, to an Ivy League college. Here he meets the future business, legal, and political leaders of the country and can hope to be one of them; if not a president, at least a vice-president.[5]

A careful examination of the life and educational careers of business aristocracy makes it quite clear that going to the "proper" prep school is essential to upper-class status.[6] However, the notion that private preparatory schools produce better intellectual material for the high status universities has been effectively disproved in recent years. A number of Ivy League colleges report students educated in public schools work harder and tend to do better than the preparatory school graduate, and certainly no worse. Private school students are no longer the majority group on campus. Thus, the major reason remaining to utilize the private school as one gateway to college is the prestige attendant upon rubbing shoulders with the *really* rich. This motivation serves to enroll significant numbers of students in private schools. The educational differential may unfortunately be the last factor weighed.

The church-related or parochial school presents a different educational environment from either public or independent private schools. Perhaps the most striking thing about parochial education in the United States is the uneasy feeling on the part of the public toward such schools. Although some of the Protestant denominations support parochial schools below the college level, the overwhelming majority of parochial schools are Roman Catholic. The attitude of the public toward such schools reflects attitudes toward the Catholic church, its manner of functioning, and its dogma.

Parochial school history in America is peculiarly American. The church

---

[5] Vance Packard, *The Status Seekers* (New York: David McKay Co., Inc., 1959), pp. 204-13.
[6] E. Digby Baltzell, *Philadelphia Gentlemen: The Making of a National Upper Class* (New York: Free Press of Glencoe, Inc., 1958), pp. 292-319.

schools have had an ethnic base as much as they have had a religious base. Irish Catholics, immigrating in large numbers in the latter half of the nineteenth century, supported the urgings of the church to establish separate schools. Such schools also provided support from fellow countrymen in a new land. Separate ethnic churches were established by different immigrant groups, which still exist in some areas today. Most Catholics, however, like their fellow Americans, are no longer closely identified with their ethnic origins. The parish churches, particularly in suburbia, draw congregations that appear to differ very little from Protestant church populations.

The parochial elementary school is typically administered by a teaching-principal, a nun, who is in turn supervised by the local parish priest. The over-all direction for the parochial schools in a given area is usually in the hands of the archdiocese.

Of significance is the fact that great variations can occur in the kinds of educational programs pursued from one diocese to another. Also, according to Fichter, the individual parish church school has considerable freedom of decision.[7] Most of the curriculum and course content appears to be very similar to that of the public schools.

A recent analysis of textbooks published for parochial schools in the areas of science and mathematics, revealed, however, some striking differences. At numerous points, sectarian dogma was included along with standard information. The question that this study raises impinges on national policy. National Defense Education Act funds are provided to nonpublic schools for the teaching of secular subjects as defined by the Act: science, mathematics and foreign language. The results of this study show that in many instances there may be no such thing as a secular subject in a sectarian school. This issue may seriously challenge the utilization of NDEA funds wherever sectarian purposes are so intricately imbedded in the subject matter taught.[8]

Because the teaching staff in most Catholic parochial schools is made up of members of religious orders, their participation in community activities is nil compared to that of their public school colleagues. The Catholic schools work to produce active parent involvement in the schools through their own parent organizations. But the teacher in the Catholic school does not have the community visibility that the public school teacher has.

The relations between government and the church schools are very uneasy. The historic separation of church from state is strongly written into the Constitution and has been a sore point for decades. The issue is still unclear. Since education is the concern of the state and not the federal government, we find interesting differences in the control the states see fit to exercise over church-related schools. When Oregon once attempted to legislate all private and parochial schools out of existence, the Supreme Court declared that although the state rightly had an interest

63

[7] Joseph H. Fichter, S.J., *Parochial School: A Sociological Study* (Notre Dame, Indiana: The University of Notre Dame Press, 1958).

[8] George R. LaNoue, "The National Defense Education Act and 'Secular' Subjects," *Phi Delta Kappan*, 43 (June 1962), 380-88.

in the education of all future citizens, parents had an equal right to select the educational pathway that suited them best. State governments have been struggling for a long time to determine just what is proper in terms of their responsibility. Each state defines it differently. For instance, three-fourths of the states provide by law that private school education shall be "equivalent" to public school education. In some states, in order to meet this requirement, the private school personnel must register with a local, county, or state board; in other states these schools must meet the approval of one or another of these boards. In some states the standards for employment of teachers are spelled out by legislation. In a few states administrators must make reports, sometimes in great detail, regarding the operation of their schools. Some states specify what is to be taught in all aspects of the curriculum except religion. Lessons on the Constitution and other aspects of citizenship are required by some states in private as well as public schools. Under their police powers, the various states have sought ways of regulating or approving private and parochial schools.

It is clear that Americans face a dilemma in their attitudes toward church schools. The Roman Catholic church, on the one hand, feels that it is the duty and obligation of every Catholic parent to send his children to a church school and to support this school. The Presbyterians, on the other hand, take an equally strong position in opposing church-supported schools of any denomination, on grounds that they have a weakening effect upon the public schools.[9]

Americans are reported to be the most heavily church-affiliated of any Western nation. Yet, the tradition of public nonsectarian schools has been the inevitable result of the many different religious groups that flourish. The fact that one church, however, has successfully established and seems bound to increase its own school system makes for public unease in some quarters.

> We are convinced that in the event the parochial schools become dominant, the free public schools will not only be made less effective, but the health of the body politic will be weakened and freedom in the community diminished.[10]

What effect does parochial school education have? Catholics who attended parochial schools, when compared with those who attended public schools tend to be differentiated primarily in areas related to recurrent religious concerns: performance of religious duties and financial support for religious education. That secondary education efforts of the church are directed more toward girls than boys suggests an interest in the influence of the future mother on the religious education of her child. More white-collar than blue-collar parents send their children to Catholic secondary schools, presumably because the parents perceive parochial

---

[9] *The Church and the Public Schools: An Official Statement* (Philadelphia: The Board of Christian Education, Presbyterian Church in the U.S.A., 1957).
[10] *Ibid.*, p. 19.

schools as a more favorable ladder for social mobility than public schools.

That parental interest in public schools becomes minimal when the children are in parochial school is borne out by studies. Where the parochial school group becomes large enough, this fact can become highly significant in the politics of school-board elections.[11]

In summary, while most of the population is educated through a massive public education system, significant minorities attend private or parochial schools. Although the elite private school still retains its image as a gentlemen's school and a path for social mobility, the shift in the college emphasis, even among the Ivy League group, to intellectual achievement has tended to reduce the value of this preparatory experience. It would appear that the social consequences of attending or not attending these schools are no longer as crucial for individual success as they might once have been. The parochial school, on the other hand, bids fair to become a major competitor of the public schools for public financial support and public interest. This has already happened in some communities. Since the struggle for support has widened to include more of the country, it will inevitably continue to be a major national issue. Whether students educated in parochial or private schools differ significantly from the rest of the population in terms of their democratic commitment cannot be established.

LOCALISM VERSUS NATIONALISM IN EDUCATION:
an American Obsession

We have described the impact of society on educational processes and, in particular, have shown how local variations produce variations in the schooling provided. These variations, in almost all cases, can be attributed to the local character of American public education. This localism is engrained in the American tradition. To challenge the right of a local community to run its own schools is akin to blasphemy. Yet, there are increasing pressures upon local schools to seek outside help and support.

As was pointed out, local schools vary in their ability to support education. Despite strenuous efforts, many communities lack the tax resources to provide education at desirable levels. Many states, in response to pressure, have established equalization funds, the purpose of which is to make up for local educational deficiencies. This trend in state financing has become highly significant over the past few years. In over half the states during the years 1959-60, 60 per cent or more of state money for schools was in the form of general-purpose equalizing funds.[12]

Increasingly, rural, urban, and suburban schools will have equal state financial support. What they do with their resources will vary. In suburbia, for instance, proportionately less will have to be spent on remedial reading programs than in the big city; in rural areas, money will be spent for

---

[11] Peter H. Rossi, and Alice S. Rossi, "Some Effects of Parochial School Education in America," *Daedalus*, 90 (Spring 1961), 300-328.

[12] Albert R. Munse, *Revenue Programs for the Public Schools in the United States, 1959-60*, United States Office of Education, Misc. No. 38 (Washington, D.C.: Government Printing Office, 1961), p. 17.

more teachers to teach more subjects in order to provide an adequate all-around program.

Interestingly enough, however, local resistance even to state support has been noted. In order to overcome such resistance, states hold out additional funds as carrots, so that the school district will be tempted to add the new facility because it does not have to pay for it. If the state told the district what to do with the money, resistance could be expected. State department of education personnel often have to plead, cajole, and entice districts to make changes in the direction of better education as perceived by the state department.

Federal assistance to the local school is another matter. For over twenty years federal aid has been a legislative issue. Three major conflicts have served to defeat major legislation for the schools: (1) There is resistance by wealthy states to supporting education in poorer states. No acceptable formula has yet been found to provide support for all children regardless of the wealth of the state. (2) Parochial school interests have insisted that any federal aid be provided for nonpublic schools as well as for public schools, while non-Catholics in the main have strongly opposed any kind of legislation that permits church schools to use public money in any way they see fit. The churches, even if such money were provided, insist on the right to dispose of it without federal intervention. (3) Finally, there is a question whether federal money for public schools should or could be provided to districts where no effort is being made to move toward genuine racial integration.

These major differences have split the public to the point where little educational legislation can obtain enough support to pass through Congress. These issues are highly significant. They reflect deeply felt interests that have sectional or personal bases.

Beyond this, there is a general and pervasive disagreement in respect to centralization of control. Here the educators themselves are far from agreement. Even if the above barriers to federal aid could be overcome (and we believe that in time they will be), a deeper feeling must be changed, too. Despite the fact that Americans believe they have the most stable and effective democratic government, there is a folk fear of federal power. Deeply engrained in the American tradition is a faith in the efficacy of state control. Every demand for federal intervention in some area is met with counter cries of "control by Washington." Although most interest groups in America derive benefits from some type of federal intervention or control, in any other area they see the menace of federal domination and the loss of personal liberties. Few areas arouse such fear of federal control as the schools. Since education has been a local matter from the beginning, the specter of the federal bureaucracy appears to be ever more horrible.

Yet, some sharp critics of education have called for some kind of national program with federal support as the only way to bring schools in general up to the standards of the best. These critics are met with a recital of the dangers of ever letting the central government get control. Nazi Germany and Communist-dominated countries are cited in evidence. Thus the argument continues.

Although formal ceding of power over local programs to the federal government may not come about for many decades, the differences that we have enumerated are slowly being eroded by several forces. Not the least of these is the very fact that federal spending on education has increased a great deal, thus supporting some efforts to raise standards and put into operation programs that local communities cannot afford. The National Defense Education Act is a good case in point. Through federal support, local schools can now install science and language laboratories. Teachers can be trained for science, mathematics, and foreign language, and other teachers can also obtain further training. Between 1957-58 and 1959-60, federal funds provided for states increased an average of 45.6 per cent. This phenomenal growth, in just two years, suggests the trend of the future.[13]

Although the federal program is voluntary, there are few states that are not using NDEA funds for their schools. In one sample of schools studied, every school had participated in one or more phases of the NDEA program.[14]

Other forces tending to nationalize school programs, particularly at the secondary level, are the college entrance examinations, the Merit Scholarship examinations, and other nationally distributed tests for assessing college preparatory ability and achievement. Most colleges today expect some standardized test scores to accompany admission applications.

Another nationalizing force has appeared in the form of new programs in science and mathematics. These programs, supported in part by private funds and by the quasi-public National Science Foundation, have markedly influenced mathematics and science teaching. A large proportion of mathematics and science teachers have participated in NSF summer institutes. Local differences in mathematics and science will undoubtedly fade away as all teachers come under the influence of these institutes.

Accrediting by nongovernmental regional associations tends to support conformity to a common program. These regional associations typically take in a number of states, and though autonomous, appear to share similar standards. Such a document as *Evaluative Criteria* published by a national board and utilized by the various accrediting associations provides a common base-line leading toward similarity in programs.[15] Although the foreword to *Evaluative Criteria* explicitly states that the criteria are to be used to promote the idea that schools that differ markedly can be equally good, the net effect is to suggest those practices that are better, and thus to lead toward eventual standardization of programs and facilities.

67

[13] Munse, *Revenue Programs*, p. 5.
[14] Roald Campbell, "Nationalizing Influences in Education," paper read at American Educational Research Association annual conference, 1962. (Mimeographed.)
[15] *Evaluative Criteria* (Washington, D.C.: National Study of Secondary School Evaluation, 1960).

The schools are big spenders. They purchase millions of dollars worth of products of many kinds. The producer who hopes to have a wide sale of school products must have something that is appealing on a national scale, because here, of course, is where the largest profits lie. In one field, textbook publishing, the influence of a national market can be most keenly detected. Pictures of racially mixed groups in textbook illustrations are conspicuous by their absence. If any were to appear in a textbook, that book would automatically be excluded from a sizeable group of states. Thus, regional sensibilities tend to creep into national programs and to establish a national pattern.

It costs money to produce films; therefore, people in the educational film business produce those films that will sell most widely. It costs money to produce and tape television programs. The airborne television experiment, covering seven states, provides extensive standardization of programs in this area. We can expect more, rather than fewer, standardizing activities.

Some critics of education have supported a "conspiracy theory" regarding the national control exercised by teacher education institutions, particularly centering on the purportedly evil influence of Teachers College, Columbia University. For many years, Teachers College has attracted a large group of educators seeking higher degrees. Many of these educators have subsequently become professors of education in other institutions. Some have become superintendents of schools. Some have written school and college texts. If this indicates a conspiracy, the evidence is lacking. That some Teachers College leaders stood for a certain approach to education cannot be denied; however, the divergence of opinion now evident among educators, many of them Teachers College products, indicates that their training was perhaps more liberating than conforming.

The effect of national associations of educators is hard to assess. While educators themselves may attribute some influence to such associations, their pronouncements have had less ripple effect than a book by such a non-public-school observer as Dr. James Conant. The foundation-supported programs tend to be obscured from the public, but the public figures associated with them are seen and heard.[16] The influence of foundations is detected by many educators in their support of certain programs that may thereby gain national scope, and in their withholding of support from other programs that do not fit into the pattern of the foundations.

Finally, a most powerful force for standardization is the very movement of people themselves. Families today move rather frequently, as the statistics show. They bring with them particular expectations regarding the schools. If the district they left had a good elementary science program, articulate parents may insist that the new school system do all it can to produce a similar program. Parents may be understandably bewildered, not to mention the distress of their young ones, if the mathematics taught in their new school system is way out of phase from that taught in the one from which they have moved. Enough cries from enough parents and enough trouble trying to fit children into a school program press the educational leadership to seek common emphases and curricula.

[16] Campbell, "Nationalizing Influences in Education."

The American pattern of education may remind one of a crazy quilt. The variations among schools are innumerable. These variations result from the local character of public education. But we have also, in effect, a triple school system—public, private, and parochial—which infuses additional elements of difference.

On the subject of establishing uniformity among schools, the American people are particularly sensitive. They suspect state interference in local affairs, and are almost paranoid on the subject of federal intervention. Though more money is needed, the local nature of education is bitterly defended, even at the cost of poorly supported, inferior programs.

Despite this insistence on the local nature of education, nongovernmental forces are slowly, perhaps irresistably moving the schools toward national conformity. The tests we use and the very materials we buy are made for a national school market. Also, the mobility of student and family is spreading the educational message from one part of the country to another: "Do not be *too* different!"

BIBLIOGRAPHY

BEACH, FRED F. AND ROBERT F. WILL, *The State and Nonpublic Schools*, United States Office of Education Misc. No. 28. Washington, D.C.: Government Printing Office, 1958. A summary of state provisions and a state-by-state report on legislation regarding nonpublic schools.

BRICKMAN, WILLIAM W. AND STANLEY LEHRER, *Religion, Government, and Education*. New York: Society for the Advancement of Education, 1963. Ten essays on the church-state issue, past and present.

EHLERS, HENRY AND GORDON C. LEE, *Crucial Issues in Education: an Anthology*, rev. ed. New York: Holt, Rinehart & Winston, Inc., 1959. Articles on both sides of a number of educational issues, including censorship, loyalty, religion and education, and federal support of education.

HACKETT, ALLEN, *Quickened Spirit: A Biography of Frank S. Hackett*. New York: Riverdale Country School, 1957. A biography showing the problems of founding and establishing a private school.

HANNA, PAUL R., "A National Curriculum Commission?" *NEA Journal*, 49 (January 1960), 25-27. The case for an advisory body on the national level to guide national curriculum development, with comments by those who disagree.

KOHLBRENNER, BERNARD J., "Some Practical Aspects of the Public Character of Private Education," *School and Society*, 86 (October 11, 1958), 348-51. A succinct statement summarizing the control exercised by states over private education.

LIEBERMAN, MYRON, *The Future of Public Education*. Chicago: University of Chicago Press, 1960. See Chapter iii for a ringing attack on local control of education.

MALLERY, DAVID, *Imaginative Teaching in Elementary Schools*. Boston: National Council of Independent Schools, 1962.

———, *New Approaches in Education*. Boston: National Council of Independent Schools, 1961. Both of these volumes document some of the lively deperatures from standard educational programs that private schools are attempting.

MAYER, MARTIN, "The Trouble with Textbooks," *Harper's Magazine*, 225 (July 1962), 65-71. A discussion of the impact of national sales on textbook production.

MCCARTHY, MARY, *Memories of a Catholic Girlhood*. New York: Harcourt, Brace & World, Inc., 1957. An evocative account, by a gifted writer, of a variety of educational experiences.

MCCOLLUM, VASHTI C., *One Woman's Fight*. Garden City, N. Y.: Doubleday & Company, Inc., 1951. The story of the woman who achieved a Supreme Court decision regarding religion and the schools, complicated by the fact that she was an atheist.

MCLOUGHLIN, EMMETT, *American Culture and Catholic Schools*. New York: Lyle Stuart, Publishers, 1960. An analysis and interpretation by a former Franciscan friar.

PACKARD, VANCE, *The Status Seekers*. New York: David McKay Co., Inc., 1959. The role of the elite preparatory schools in social mobility.

POWELL, THEODORE, *The School Bus Law*. Middletown, Conn.: Wesleyan University Press, 1960. A case study in education, religion, and politics in Connecticut.

ROSSI, PETER H., *Why Families Move*. New York: Free Press of Glencoe, Inc., 1955. A study in the social psychology of urban residential mobility.

SALINGER, J. D., *The Catcher in the Rye*. Boston: Little, Brown & Company, 1951. The modern classic about a private-school adolescent in contemporary society.

Institutions create expectations, and expectations create institutions. Students come to school expecting to learn to read, to be prepared for college, or to find a mate. Teachers come to school expecting stimulation, plodding routine, work with alert and responsive individuals, or struggle with hostile or indifferent students. These expectations on the part of the major players in the drama of the school have a significant impact on the process of education. In this and the next three chapters, we shall examine some of the expectations and experiences of the school as perceived by children, youths, and young adults, including how students tend to react to these influences. In later chapters, we shall examine the role of adults in this institution and assess their impact on the institution and its forms.

A WORLD OF PEERS

The elementary school is the child's first significant world outside the home and neighborhood. Here he is on his own. He is considered as a person only tenuously attached to his family and its social location. Here he begins the process of proving himself.

HOW SEPARATE AN ISLAND? THE CULTURE OF THE ELEMENTARY SCHOOL

8

This process, however, takes place in the company of 25 or 30 others of approximately the same age and often of homogeneous racial, ethnic, and socio-economic backgrounds. Thus, the proving process occurs with an audience of potential peers.

In the older one-room schoolhouse, where grades one through eight were taught in one room with one teacher, the child might find himself the only one in his "grade." Many teachers in such schools allowed children to read with others in grades ahead of them or to do arithmetic with those who were younger and in lower grades. Valuable learning may take place when older students help younger or when those with a developmental advantage work with the less-advantaged in a classroom.[1] The student in the one-room school had, in a sense, a view of child development always with him. He could see what he himself had been the year before and could look ahead to see what it would be like to be older.

Today's graded school cuts the child off from this view of past and future. In some schools the playgrounds are separated, with the primary grades allotted one area or time for recess and lunch and the upper grades a different time. Being cut off from any vertical view, the child has only his chronological peers for comparison. The work he does is carefully age-graded. The teacher's efforts are directed toward having most of the children progress along the age-graded sequence at about the same pace. His focus is on keeping up with all the other little Joneses; deviation may be treated with kindliness and understanding, but it is clear to all the children that there has been a deviation. The push toward conformity starts early.

THE PERILS OF DEVIATION

Most children do not have to face the perils of deviation because they are in the great "middle" for which school materials are prepared. The laggards, however, are conspicuous. Perhaps they are failed or nonpromoted, as it is called by school people (as though changing the name deflected the blow). The classroom is oriented toward achievement and success. Yet, both achievement and success are unevenly distributed. Some children experience more of both. They are those who enter school with more. The more intelligent children, those who feel loved and secure; children with superior backgrounds (richer in school-related experiences—books in the home, trips to museums and zoos, parents who converse with them and tell them stories) succeed and achieve more.

Deviation occurs not only through lagging but also as a result of excelling.[2] Research evidence shows that highly creative children and highly intelligent children tend to become isolated through the years because their behavior may be bizarre and nonconforming.[3] Their sense

[1] Ronald Lippitt, "The Learner and the Classroom Group," in *Human Variability and Learning*, ed. Walter B. Waetjen (Washington, D.C.: Association for Supervision and Curriculum Development, 1961), p. 60.

[2] Harper Lee, *To Kill a Mockingbird* (Philadelphia: J. B. Lippincott Co., 1960), pp. 23-25.

[3] George Kaluger and Ruthe Martin, "The Loneliness of the Gifted Child," *The Elementary School Journal*, 61 (Dec. 1960), 127-32.

of humor may not coincide with that of the group, nor will their answers be standard answers. Highly intelligent children learn, just because they are highly intelligent, to behave like everyone else. In fact, punishment for deviation, if it comes as too sharp a shock at a vulnerable time in the child's growth, may result in highly intelligent or creative children's effectively hiding their talents in order to gain acceptance from teacher, parents, and peers.

The classroom code must be learned by the students. It is learned quickly. Within a few weeks of the opening of school, even the first grader knows who has failed, who is a good reader, who does not behave, who is older or younger.

Schools are increasingly grouping children on the basis of ability, achievement, or teachers' judgment of the child's potential. These groupings reinforce publicly the differences between individuals that the teacher helps the children perceive. What it means to children to be put in a "slow group" or a "fast group" is being debated violently by educators. It is beyond question that, whatever the effects, children know how they are labeled.[4]

A common practice in early elementary grades is having a "sharing period," or a time to "show and tell." The educational basis for these activities appears sound: the children gain poise in telling about some event at home or something significant they have seen on the way to school. Each child who wishes has his place in the sun among peers. Anyone left out is so because of his own desires.

What is the effect, however, on children's judgments of others through such an activity? They may vie with each other as to the number of Christmas presents reported (how many distort the truth in order to "keep up"?). Private lives are laid out for all to see and comment about. The way the teacher responds to what is shown or shared can be devastatingly revealing. Studies of these class exchanges to show the shift in content over a period of time of teacher and peer responses are lacking. It would be interesting to know more.

Peers as audience and as measuring rod grow in potency in the very early school years of the child. He sees on the wall the drawings of other children and thus, by indirection is compelled to compare his own work. Friendship choices are asked for in a subtle fashion by today's teacher through the means of sociometric tests.[5] An older school might have seated the children alphabetically or by size or sex. The sociometric choices in the past were crudely (and cruelly) displayed in public through the "choosing of sides" for a spelling bee or a dodge-ball game. Today's technique pervades the classroom as a more covert atmosphere of acceptance or rejection by peers; however, potential rejection is still always there, and is made

73

---

[4] Maxine Mann, "What Does Ability Grouping Do to the Self-Concept?" *Childhood Education*, XXXVII (April 1960), 357-61. See also Margaret Rasmussen, ed., *Toward Effective Grouping* (Washington, D.C.: Association for Childhood Education International, 1962).

[5] David Riesman, *The Lonely Crowd* (New Haven, Conn.: Yale University Press, 1950), pp. 61-62.

the most of by the children in their social sniffings as to who is "in" and who is "out."[6]

The children's definition of who is "in" or "out" accords to varying degrees with the teacher's value system. In the typical elementary school (in suburbia, small city, and town) the teacher's values are the community's values. The children respond by judging their peers in terms of the cues provided by the teacher: "John is a good boy; he is sitting up tall and straight. David, don't slouch so; we don't do that, do we? See, class, the neat paper Janet made for me. Yes, I like the way Sue put all her books back just where they belong." As groups fall away from grace, however, the uneasy war between student norms and teacher-adult norms begins.[7] Where the teacher's values are at variance with out-of-school values as in the case of slum children, the teacher's chosen few have to develop an almost neurotic isolation or persistence in order to achieve and to succeed in school.

Within a few years, the battle between those who have accepted teachers' norms and those who have rejected them becomes stylized. Names are found for the teachers' favorites: "teacher's pet," is dated; today they are called "brownies" or "noses." A teacher's favor can safely be sought (depending again on the social environment on the outside) by most children through fifth or sixth grade; after this time it is dangerous.

74   **JUDGMENT DAY COMES EVERY DAY**

The interaction between student and teacher in the elementary classroom provides continual bases for assessment. As noted, the teacher is quick to point out deviates, to express satisfaction with normal progress, to approve those who "try." In addition, the children continually face and respond to ratings of learning and behavior as good or not good. Recitations, tests, report cards, and teacher-parent conferences provide data regarding the degree to which the child has conformed to the school's expectations.

The recitation is a classroom procedure whereby the students provide the teacher, too often, with the teacher's answers:

> Miss Manton tells a story to her second-grade class. . . . Before completing it she asks, "How do you think this story ends?" So far, so good. The children eagerly pose conclusions. To Tommy's response, Miss Manton answers, "No, I don't quite see how that could be." To Susan's, "No, I don't think so." To Mildred's, "No, that's not *what I'm thinking of*." [8]

The teacher's interest here is not in the ideas the children have, but in their ability to guess what she has on her mind. Observations of many

---

[6] Ronald Lippitt and Martin Gold, "Classroom Structure as a Mental Health Problem," *Journal of Social Issues*, XV, No. 1 (1959), 40-49.

[7] Willard Waller, *The Sociology of Teaching* (New York: John Wiley & Sons, Inc., 1932), pp. 339-74.

[8] John I. Goodlad, "Pressure to Learn Can Be Blocks to Learning," *Childhood Education*, 36 (December 1959), 162-65.

classrooms provide innumerable examples of this revealing phrase, "No, *that isn't exactly what I had in mind.*" The child who is apt at guessing what the teacher has on her mind gets an A. Girls seem particularly gifted in this guessing game with women teachers. This may be a matter of the differential perception of persons on the part of the two sexes.[9] Perhaps if the task were shifted from guessing to analytic thinking, the girls might not fare as well.

Thelen, however, has diagnosed the classroom as a place in which achievement has triumphed over inquiry. Tests, particularly objective tests, tend to tell the student that academic status—the grade—is more important than learning.[10] It is not only that marks are more significant than learning, the end becoming more important than the means, but also that a *wrong* answer becomes equated with a *bad* answer, and failure equated with evil. Yet, as Kelley so aptly states it, this is a fatal trap:

> Children should learn to enjoy and appreciate the fact that what they do may turn out wrong and have to be revised. . . . To be always right, if that were possible, would be deadly dull, and one would never learn anything. We only learn when our set of responses fails to take us where we want to go. Instead of following our children around to keep them from making mistakes, we should help them learn that making a faulty try is not a sin. It is the way, and the only way, that new doors open to growth. If a child gets the idea that to make a mistake is to sin, so great is his fear of error that he refuses to try, and retires into inaction. His capacity to act becomes inhibited, and he loses contact with the reality to be gained through action. The only sin involved is on the part of the adult who deprives youth of freedom to make mistakes.[11]

Test situations expose children of average intelligence, who should do well on tests, to shattering experiences of anxiety that effectively reduce their test performance in a number of cases.[12] Testing starts early (reading readiness tests for entering first graders are common practice) and continues forever. Children who are motivated by parental values and pressures to do well on tests, tend to do better than children not so motivated, regardless of intelligence. Test-practice sessions have been shown to improve the performance of children deficient in home coaching. Rewarding children of lower socio-economic levels improves their test performances far more than similar promises of rewards for middle-class children. The test-smart person has a long headstart over others. The overpowering thing about test results, however, as far as children are concerned, is their finality of judgment. The seeming infallibility of the objective and standardized test replaces fallible teacher judgment with a remote and unimpeachable authority. Even with teacher-made objective tests, there is something

---

[9] A. Robert Kohn and Fred E. Fiedler, "Age and Sex Differences in the Perception of Persons," *Sociometry*, 24 (June 1961), 157-64.

[10] Herbert A. Thelen, "The Triumph of 'Achievement' over Inquiry in Education," *The Elementary School Journal*, 60 (January 1960), 190-97.

[11] Earl C. Kelley, *Education for What Is Real* (New York: Harper & Row, Publishers, 1947), p. 90.

[12] Seymour B. Sarason, *et al.*, *Anxiety in Elementary School Children* (New York: John Wiley & Sons, Inc., 1960), Chap. x.

remarkably persuasive about the apparent "realness" of a child's score. The right and wrong answers can be added up. Anyone can count. What appeal is there against such omnipotent judgment?

The threat of failure and nonpromotion is familiar to all who remember school. That such threats work with some children and not with others is beside the point; teachers use this weapon indiscriminately. The significant fact, of course, is not only the threat of failure, but that the standard against which one is measured is one's classmates. What a powerful injection of hatred for others is thus administered, particularly for those who appear to be succeeding. Furthermore, there is no place to hide. Failure and success become everyone's knowledge. Teachers often resort to public reporting of scores, but whether out of laziness in not having recorded them already in their grade books or from mistaken assumptions about motivation is not always clear. Such reporting propels the student into the full glare of his classmates. How does he feel?

> Mrs. Logan, who was recording the grades, said, "Let's see the hands of those who didn't get 100."
> 3:08 Raymond sat there for a moment.
> He then very slowly and reluctantly raised his hand.
> The teacher called out the name of each child whose hand was raised, asking in each case for the number missed.
> After hearing from the first child, she said pleasantly, "Raymond, you missed two, didn't you?"
> Raymond mumbled in embarrassment, "Yes." He looked very unhappy and blushed again.
> He looked blankly at his desk for a moment. While Mrs. Logan went through the rest of the names, Raymond continued to appear somewhat crestfallen by his failure to get 100.[13]

The above excerpt is from a minute-by-minute account of life as it was experienced by one little boy in a small midwestern town. Sounds familiar, does it not?

It is hardly any wonder that boys, who fail far more than girls, dislike school, distrust intellectuals, and in later life find it hard to accept women as equals when as men they can get their revenge.

Despite the call for competitive situations in classrooms "because they prepare one for life," no work situation is as cruel as an elementary classroom. At least at work an adult competes with peers in an occupation he has selected because he feels fairly sure of success. The classroom is nothing like this. Here one may well be compared to and thrown into rigorous competition with those who always will excel, having been born with more of the intellectual and social equipment schools prize, or having selected the right parents in the right income bracket. The utter unfairness of this type of competition is quite lost upon those who demand more of it for children: adults who are probably most protected on their own jobs from any public invidious comparisons. Adults are so careful with each other: a person is not fired; he is permitted to resign. A child cannot resign; he is failed.

[13] Roger G. Barker and Herbert F. Wright, *One Boy's Day* (New York: Harper & Row, Publishers, 1951), p. 274.

Public failure in the classroom is probably one of the most destructive shocks to the individual's self-esteem that life can deliver. A study of matched groups of delinquent and nondelinquent boys reveals that:

> one of the most meaningful differences is that the delinquents much more frequently have a record of early failure experience in elementary school, and of having become alienated from the adult socialization culture through failure in the classroom group in relation to the teacher.[14]

School failure delivers a direct message to the child that he is not good, and this message comes across with exceptional clarity from the most powerful figure in the child's world after his parents. It is impossible for an individual, even a child, to sustain for long massive doses of self-dislike, which is engendered by being told how inadequate he is.[15] One obvious dynamic is to turn in hatred upon those others who have succeeded, those other "good" children. With increased increments of failure, eventually the child must turn on adults and later on all of society. The relationship between school failure and delinquent behavior has been known for some time.[16] It is interesting to speculate on the tenacity with which parents and probably most educators insist on liberal doses of failure throughout schooling.

Trauma is attendant upon report cards. Over the years a casual collecting of school cartoons shows them projecting an adult's view of the devastation that has been wrought by report cards. The comments of the cartoonists are wry, and not funny. In the view of the cartoonists—hurt children grown up—the assessment somehow seems to have missed the inner glory, the true soul, the person in the pupil.

77

When the report card comes home, the results can be catastrophic. Children report beatings, and being deprived of privileges and allowances for poor report cards. Others are given monetary rewards for good grades. Children are not always quite sure what the report card means, except that it is a highly significant judgment.[17]

Today's modern elementary school staffs often prefer a more roundabout procedure: the parent-teacher conference. The assumption here is that the meeting will cause parents to become the supporters of the teacher's efforts. The parent can be told how the child is progressing, and why she should help. The parent in turn informs the teacher about any trouble at home that might affect the child's performance. Children do not always view the interview so benignly. To the child, it is a secret and threatening meeting of the power figures in his field. They are potentially ganging up on him to restrict his freedom of movement, to exchange and share the dismal view both probably have of his talents—the ultimate invasion of privacy.

[14] Lippitt, in *Human Variability and Learning*, p. 57.
[15] Daniel R. Miller and Guy E. Arvanson, *Inner Conflict and Defense* (New York: Holt, Rinehart & Winston, Inc., 1960). See especially Chapters ix and x about responses to failure.
[16] See, for example, Sheldon Glueck and Eleanor Glueck, *Unraveling Juvenile Delinquency* (New York: The Commonwealth Fund, 1950).
[17] Lois Williams, "Teachers and Parents: Did You Know That Your Children Feel This Way?" *Childhood Education*, 35 (October 1958), 60-64.

My mother says she likes conferences but she is always so cross at me when she gets home. (Grade 4)

Some people don't like them. They say, "You must be stupid if your mother has to have a conference at school." (Grade 5)

The teachers fix up the rooms so the parents will think it's always that way. (Grade 7)

They talk about PTA and how to get money for it. Teachers and parents joke about how different you are at school and at home. They talk about what we'll have to wear for graduation and never ask us. And about how much studying we ought to do. (Grade 8)

They talk about the good points first and the bad points last so your parents won't forget. They get the good points out of the way in a hurry because all your parents remember are the bad ones. (Grade 8)

I don't know *what* they talk about. Maybe business 'cause that's what grownups talk about. (Grade 1)

I just hope our teacher won't compare us with last year's class at conference time. They were much better in reading. It's discouraging when the teacher brags on other kids, and what will your mother think? (Grade 4)

If they have time, I think parents like conferences. I don't mind, just so they don't discuss me. (Grade 3)[18]

Achievement is measured in terms not only of skills and information, but of proper behavior. The definition of what behavior is proper is up to the teacher. Rarely does an elementary school child feel that the development of self-control is a goal the school has for him or that he can or should establish for himself.[19] The child's achievement of compliance with the teacher's behavioral expectations is a complex and subtle process. Henry, in an analysis of the ways in which the teacher develops and then reinforces docility among middle-class children suggests that this is accomplished at the cost of intense hostility toward the school that becomes redirected towards other children. Furthermore,

> . . . the mental docility . . . achieved in these middle-class schoolrooms is a peculiar middle-class kind of docility. It is not based on authoritarian control backed by fear of corporal punishment, but rather on the fear of loss of love. . . . This kind of docility can be more lethal than the other, for it does not breed rebellion and independence, as struggle against authoritarian controls may, but rather a kind of cloying paralysis; a sweet imprisonment without pain.[20]

Fortunately, perhaps, girls succeed better at *this* task than boys! The use of emotional blackmail, as it has been aptly termed,[21] does not work with the culturally deprived child. No one has ever loved him much, so

[18] *Ibid.*, pp. 60-61.

[19] Mable C. Purl, "Children's Perception of Adult Behavior," *California Journal of Elementary Education*, 27 (August 1958), 22-27.

[20] Jules Henry, "Docility, or Giving Teacher What She Wants," *Journal of Social Issues*, 2 (1955), 33-41.

[21] George Sheviakov, Fritz Redl, and Sybil Richardson, *Discipline for Today's Children and Youth* (Washington, D.C.: Association for Supervision and Curriculum Development, 1956).

the teacher's threat to withdraw loving approval leaves him quite cold. Respect, rather than love, makes sense to such children.[22]

ANTISEPTIC CONTENT

The view of life provided by the materials of study in the elementary school classroom is a very special one. Studies of school textbooks show the antiseptic quality of much that is provided for the student. Recent outcries against "Dick and Jane" type basal reading books has focused attention on the banality, triviality, and unreality of the content whereby basic skills are to be learned. As has already been mentioned, the typical textbook is lily-white (unless the stories are about foreigners, who may be dark-skinned) and middle-class. "Textbook town," as one study of textbooks pointed out, is one where mothers have babies without being pregnant, and nothing bad ever happens (except when a favorite pet dies). Daddy comes home from work carrying a briefcase, and all are happy.[23] Another study supports the thesis that sex makes a difference in elementary textbooks, as elsewhere. An analysis of third-grade readers found that female characters are typically portrayed as "sociable, kind, and timid—however, inactive, unambitious, and uncreative." Males, on the other hand, are portrayed as bearers of knowledge, as well as the active doers and thinkers, when any thinking is done. Another finding is the unrealistic optimism of the content. Hardly anyone ever fails at anything. Activity is usually physical, not intellectual. Independent action, particularly on the part of children, is apt to be punished, unless this action takes place under the direction of a superior. In fact, the only autonomous characters in these texts appear to be animals or supernatural beings.[24]

79

Shifts in content emphasis in recent years may reduce some of these effects. For example, science, with a built-in appeal to boys is now a standard subject in most elementary schools. Rote learning and memorization in arithmetic is giving way to teaching that emphasizes number concepts and insight into number relationships. Basal reading series, through which all children marched at more or less the same pace, are giving way to individualized reading programs whereby the elementary teacher, with the help of a perceptive librarian, can provide varied and nonstandard reading fare for children.

The content taught, however, still fails to meet the criticism made by Allison Davis, who 15 years ago saw little justification for the excessive time devoted to written communication, when so little is given to helping students draw inferences from the analysis of their own experiences.[25]

[22] Frank Riessman, *The Culturally Deprived Child* (New York: Harper & Row, Publishers, 1962), p. 46.

[23] Abraham Tannenbaum, "Family Living in Textbook Town," *Progressive Education*, 31 (March 1954), 133-41.

[24] Irvin L. Child, *et al.*, "Children's Textbooks and Personality Development: An Exploration in the Social Psychology of Education," *Psychological Monographs*, 60 (1946), 1-53.

[25] Allison Davis, *Social Class Influences Upon Learning* (Cambridge, Mass.: Harvard University Press, 1948).

The remoteness of content from the concerns of childhood is pointed out by Havighurst and Peck, in their assessment of what is known about the development of character:

> The idea of giving any formal place to the phenomena and laws of human behavior in the curricula of elementary schools as yet seems to strike many people as bizarre. If only because of tradition-bred familiarity, it seems more "sensible" to spend years studying the geography of foreign lands, the construction of sentences, and the mysteries of the multiplication tables, rather than spend some time each day teaching children how to understand and reason about the behavior of themselves and others. They *must* cope with human behavior, all day, every day. They care passionately about making sense of it. Yet we leave them mystified, confused, and ignorantly inept at it.[26]

Perhaps these criticisms help us understand the seeming great lack of learning, despite the earnest efforts of so many, which teachers and parents complain about when children advance to the next rung in the educational ladder. The school demands of children that they deny what their own sense experiences tell them and accept instead the school's version of reality. They may be making such an effort to meet this demand that in the process they have little energy left with which to learn the content that is offered them.

Another educational dilemma revolves around sex. On the one hand we are told: "For the main business of the classroom, [learning to learn] the difference between boys and girls is of little or no consequence. . . ."[27] On the other hand, we learn: "In his social clique, his school, and his formal organizations, the child gains prestige if he learns the sex-appropriate code, behavior, and goals, but meets extreme social—and at times physical—punishment if he does not," because "sex-inappropriate behavior, social or physical, is still one of the most severely punished infractions of our social code."[28] An analysis of the research on sex differences shows that, truly, boys and girls differ in some educationally significant ways, that school practices covertly recognize this, but that for some inexplicable reason, educators on the whole prefer to ignore not only their own response to sex differences but also that of the children.[29]

80

SUMMARY

Willard Waller, over 30 years ago, in his brilliant and perceptive analysis of the sociology of the school, identified what he considered the "separate culture of the school."[30] In this chapter, in discussing the

26 Robert F. Peck and Robert J. Havighurst, *The Psychology of Character Development* (New York: John Wiley & Sons, Inc., 1960), p. 195.

27 Solon T. Kimball and James E. McClellan, Jr., *Education and the New America* (New York: Random House, 1962), p. 289.

28 Allison Davis, *The Psychology of the Child in the Middle Class* (Pittsburgh: University of Pittsburgh Press, 1960), pp. 38, 41.

29 Walter Waetjen and Jean D. Grambs, "Sex Differences—a Case of Educational Evasion?" *Teachers College Record*, 65 (December 1963), 261-271.

30 Willard Waller, *The Sociology of Teaching* (New York: John Wiley & Sons, Inc., 1932).

culture of the elementary school, we have asked ourselves how separate an island is this institution?

To say that the school is not very separate from the cultural mainland is to suggest some of the reasons for the failure of the school to educate most children as well as we would wish and as our society and our children need. It is apparent that the dominant values of the culture are conveyed to the classroom, including the folk notions of how children are motivated, and what ought to be the true content of learning. Cultural confusions, distortions, and imbalances are the daily diet of modern man. It is no wonder that the school to which he sends his children presents them with impossible problems and inadequate solutions. The school, in truth, is probably doing the best it can.

Most elementary school children appear to like teachers and to like school. Children are being treated in school more and more as individuals having social needs, with kindness and attempts at understanding.

For most children, the modern elementary school is a welcome experience. For many children, too, it is a happier place to be than at home. However, we are apt to become sentimental when we view young children and view the school that we have structured for them. Such a view may crowd our vision of what is really going on. And it is important not to substitute what we wish to know for what is out there in actuality.

The dilemma is one of ends and means. Our goals are fine; our wishes for children and youth are pure and altruistic. The question we must continually ask is whether the means we have devised and the practices that result will help our children achieve these ends.

81

BIBLIOGRAPHY

AUSUBEL, DAVID P., "Learning by Discovery: Rationale and Mystique," *The Bulletin of the National Association of Secondary School Principals,* 45 (December 1961), 18-58. A carefully organized discussion of the educational implications of the point of view of Bruner and others.

BRUNER, JEROME S., *The Process of Education.* Cambridge, Mass.: Harvard University Press, 1961. This discussion of the learning process in relation to the organization of content has had a stimulating effect on current curriculum planning. See Ausubel, *op. cit.,* for a critique.

DEUTSCH, MARTIN, *Minority Group and Class Status as Related to Social and Personality Factors in Scholastic Achievement,* Monograph No. 2. Ithaca, N. Y.: The Society for Applied Anthropology, Cornell University, 1960. Report of a research study in slum schools, comparing white and Negro classroom activities and responses, and differences between boys and girls.

EPSTEIN, JASON, " 'Good Bunnies Always Obey': Books for American Children," *Commentary,* 32 (Feb. 1963), 112-22. Morality as it is preached in children's literature.

FLEMING, ROBERT S., ed., *Curriculum for Today's Boys and Girls.* New York: Charles E. Merrill Books, Inc., 1963. Outstanding elementary school educators spell out their prescriptions for modern education. Makes an interesting comparison with Rafferty.

FRANK, LAWRENCE K., *The School as Agent for Cultural Renewal*. Cambridge, Mass.: Harvard University Press, 1960. A stirring answer to the pessimism expressed in Jules Henry's book, *Culture Against Man*.

GOODLAD, JOHN I. AND ROBERT H. ANDERSON, *The Nongraded Elementary School*, rev. ed. New York: Harcourt Brace & World, Inc., 1962. Excellent summary of literature about effects of nonpromotion on learning; suggests a more appropriate organizational pattern.

JOHNSON, MARTHA C., "Let's Get Rid of Report Card Jitters," *Parents Magazine* (June 1962), pp. 40-41. An example of a popular approach to the problem of the report card.

MAC DONALD, JAMES B., ed., *Research Frontiers in the Study of Children's Learning*. Milwaukee: The School of Education, University of Wisconsin, 1960. Four papers describe some of the conditions under which learning takes place. Of particular interest is the statement by Walter Waetjen regarding the findings on child development and sex differences that are particularly relevant to the school.

MAYER, MARTIN, *The Schools*. New York: Harper & Row, Publishers, 1961. A journalist's tour through some of America's school rooms. Not a complete picture, but a vivid one.

MEYER, W. J. AND G. G. THOMPSON, "Sex Differences in the Distribution of Teacher Approval and Disapproval Among Sixth-Grade Children," *Journal of Educational Psychology*, 47 (1956), 385-96. Teachers punish and praise boys more than girls; both teachers and girls perceive boys as more aggressive. Teachers respond to boys' aggression with counter-aggression.

MURPHY, GARDNER, *Freeing Intelligence Through Teaching*. New York: Harper & Row, Publishers, 1961. A noted psychologist presents a spirited and challenging view of the teaching process and how it can release human potential if appropriately used.

PARSONS, TALCOTT, "The School Class as a Social System: Some of Its Functions in American Society," *Harvard Educational Review*, 29 (Fall 1959), 297-318. A theoretical discussion by a leading sociologist, with particular reference to the continuing selective function of classroom and school procedures.

RAFFERTY, MAX, *Suffer, Little Children*. New York: Devin-Adair Co., 1962. The author, elected state superintendent of schools of California in 1960, slashes away at what he considers the evils of modern education. (Compare to Fleming, *op. cit.*)

TABA, HILDA, *School Culture*. Washington, D.C.: American Council on Education, 1955. See especially Chap. II, a case study of an elementary school.

It is better to be young than almost anything else. It is better to be young in the United States than almost anywhere else. Being an adult means being burdened with decisions, duties, and dullness. This, in part, is the message that the young appear to be getting via the mass media and their parents' complaints about the world and themselves. Despite the obvious advantages of being young, today's youth seems incredibly irresponsible and ungrateful, gets into all kinds of trouble, and obviously is not of the caliber of previous generations; at least this is the view of a number of distressed adults. In response to this kind of valuation, what is youth doing? How does the school fit into the picture?

INSTITUTIONAL ARRANGEMENTS

Adolescent culture has grown in and around the secondary school. Before we can see what youth has made of its place in the institution, we must take a brief look at how the school itself is organized.

The American high school is coeducational, comprehensive, and free; attendance is compulsory until at least age 16. Secondary education

EDUCATION FOR LIMBO:
ADOLESCENT CULTURE
AND
THE SECONDARY SCHOOL 9

includes the junior as well as the senior high school. The typical pattern today is for a two- or three-year junior high school, followed by a three- or four-year senior high school. Most of our discussion in this chapter is devoted to the typical educational experiences of adolescents in the senior high school but many of these comments will also be applicable to many junior high schools. Though the junior high does differ in some ways from the senior high, it is indubitably a staging area for the significant adolescent experiences of the senior high school. Secondary schools range in size from 70 students to 5,000. Although there are many small high schools, they enroll only about 20 per cent of high-school students. Most large high schools are found in big cities; the small public high schools are found in rural areas or small towns or villages.

The school year is approximately 180 days long. Nearly all schools recognize four holidays in common: Thanksgiving, Christmas, Washington's Birthday, and Easter, two of them uniquely American and two historically Christian. The school day is usually divided into periods of equal length, varying with the school from 45 to 55 minutes. A student is required to take certain courses and elects others so that he has a "full program." Each class usually meets five times a week for one period a day. The school typically has a principal, assistant (or vice-) principal, guidance counselor, clerk, nurse, and librarian. Hot lunches are provided, as is bus transportation for students who need it. The faculty is made up of about equal numbers of men and women. They generally teach subjects in which they have had college training, although many may teach in fields where they have had little preparation. If the school is large enough, the faculty is divided by subject fields into departments each with a head. The school sponsors various clubs and activities and cosponsors others with community- and youth-serving agencies. Athletics are the major interscholastic activity. There may also be interscholastic debates, speech contests, music festivals, and science fairs. Most schools have some kind of student government with student-elected officers.

This institution, with some variations, can be seen almost anywhere. The differences tend to be relatively minor variations rather than extensive departures from the pattern.

The structure of the high school we know today was fairly well established by 1900, and there have been no major modifications since. Course content has shifted, new courses have been added, some old ones dropped, and the aims of the school have broadened. But the structure itself has remained rigid. One of the major forces sustaining the structure has been the Carnegie unit, a measuring device whereby a school gives credit for work done. One Carnegie unit is earned by a student for 180 days, an hour each day, of a single course in which outside preparation is required. Fractions of a unit are earned for courses without outside work of an academic nature. A Carnegie unit presumably means the same thing in one part of the country as it does in another. The unit was developed by the Carnegie Foundation during the years 1908-1910 as a method of distinguishing a high school from a college for the purposes of giving pensions to college professors to be paid for by the Carnegie Foundation. A college was defined as an institution which accepted so many units of work for admission from a "lower" institution. Thus the Carnegie unit came to be tied in closely with college admissions.

The course requirements for college admission have remained relatively unchanged, although Latin and Greek have given way to modern foreign languages and increased amounts of science and mathematics are now expected. College admissions requirements, initially set by college entrance examinations, dictate what the high school will offer. This is done through accrediting associations made up of high school and college representatives. The major purpose of such nongovernmental accreditation is to be sure, when a school tells the college on a student's transcript that he has, say, four Carnegie units of French, that these units represent courses that are up to the standard defined by the accrediting association.

Since the schools are financed on the basis of numbers of students in attendance, there is intense interest in child counting. Compulsory attendance laws also make it mandatory that the school district know where every schoolchild is at every moment of the school day.

The pressure upon the secondary school to know where every student is at every moment has resulted in a whole pyramid of controlling devices. In most secondary schools, for instance, no student is permitted out of his assigned class without a "pass." This form must be signed by the teacher liberating him, and usually shows the reason for his departure from class and his destination, and notes time of departure to circumvent any untoward loitering. Time between class periods is carefully limited to the minimum amount required so that students must hurry lest they be late for the next period. As a result, secondary school hallways are apt to be dangerous places for an unwary adult as the students hurtle around corners and down corridors. There appears to be tremendous pressure to get students from one classroom cubicle to another with a minimum of unsupervised interaction among them. In some schools, hall monitors stand at intersections to see that students remain on the designated side of the halls; stairways are labeled "up" or "down." Teachers are often asked to stand outside the doors of their rooms during the passing period to see that students move along. Rules forbidding students to go to lockers except at designated times during the day—before school, at lunchtime, after school —mean that many students carry a heavy load of textbooks much of the day. In order to check on illegal departures from classes, students are sometimes stationed in the hall during periods to see that each out-of-class student has a legal pass. Sometimes teachers are assigned such duty. Honor students may be given a permanent pass which entitles them to come and go without asking special permission.

As one views these regulations he can only ask how they are perceived by the adolescent. Most students appear to take them as part of the way things are done, and ask no questions. At some time almost any adolescent may try to "get away with something" by flouting a school regulation, and certainly weak teachers are the target for many students who are thus trying to defy authority—although in a relatively safe fashion. Some students, most often boys, do get into trouble by violating the rules. It is more noteworthy how few students even think about rebelling.[1]

[1] Edgar Z. Friedenberg, *The Vanishing Adolescent* (Boston: Beacon Press, 1959).

Viewed from the outside, these controlling devices, although based on the necessity for accounting for each student, appear also to contain elements of adult hostility toward and fear of adolescents. At the extreme, some secondary schools tend to treat the students as inmates of a restrictive institution; the school is more like a prison than a haven for intellectual activity. In more benign schools, the hostility and fear are veiled, but still may be seen in ingenious restrictions on student freedom. These restrictions tend to convey the feeling to students that their own decisions are not to be trusted. Given little independence, students are certainly not encouraged to develop any on their own. The apathy of many students towards decision making within the school may be a result of this kind of institutional control. Such apathy unfortunately tends to spread, and contaminate other areas of decision making and the whole process of learning.

Increased population and pressure from such an eminent critic as Dr. Conant,[2] have resulted in the ever-increasing size of schools. Schools of 2,000 students are common. It is argued that too small a high school cannot offer the rich curriculum needed to provide for development of many kinds of talents and abilities. But a study of Kansas high schools suggests that, even if intellectual needs are better cared for in the large school than in the small, certain aspects of the large school environment may be less helpful to the adolescent. In the small high school more students participate in activities, even though the range of choice may be smaller. More students have access to leadership roles. Fewer students drop out of school, and more students feel well-known by the faculty. As the authors state:

> Although there has long been evidence from industrial psychology that the larger and more bureaucratically efficient the organization the greater the degradation of the individual, this knowledge has had little influence upon schools, and the widespread concern for the organization man has not been accompanied by a similar concern for the organization child.[3]

The organizational features of our secondary schools have a significant impact on adolescence. The kinds of behavior we observe among adolescents are to some extent a response to these institutional arrangements. The adolescent culture, which has been dissected, analyzed, deplored, condemned, and emulated at great length and on numerous occasions in recent years is, I suggest, in large part *reinforced if not molded by the students' reactions to their schools.* The adolescent, while also being acted upon by the out-of-school forces described in Chapter 2, works out his mode of behavior within the social milieu of the high school.

[2] James B. Conant, *The American High School Today* (New York: McGraw-Hill Book Company, 1959).

[3] Roger C. Barker, *et al.*, *Big School—Small School* (Oskaloosa, Kansas: Midwest Psychological Field Station, Cooperative Res. Project No. 594, University of Kansas, 1962), p. 232.

The secondary school differs from the elementary school; and secondary school students differ from elementary school students. For one thing, age has brought physical growth changes of great significance. In addition, each secondary student brings with him a significant school history. He has had at least six years of classroom experience, and he *knows* school. He may look forward to the new freedom and intellectual stimulation of the secondary school. Or he may feel that this new, bigger institution just offers more of the same defeating drudgery.

Although many news stories and feature articles about adolescents recount their ingenuity, inventiveness, and appeal, many more concentrate on the lurid and the disagreeable. Stories of such aspects of youth culture seem to be more saleable to the mass media. Tales of youthful violence may also provide the adult reader a vicarious re-entry into a world that he outgrew before he knew it existed. And yet these same adults may live in daily proximity to one or more adolescents, in a relationship that is only too often uneasy or hostile. "Are *our* kids able to do these awful things I read about in the newspapers?" the agitated parents ask each other. One notes with alarm the pervasive fear of the adolescent, which communicates itself even to prospective teachers.

The adolescent himself is not immune, of course, to the bad image that he appears to convey.[4] Being seen as evil does not encourage one to be good. Being perceived as someone to be feared may enhance one's feeling of possessing power which ordinary mortals cannot (and perhaps should not?) exercise.

Adolescents are subject to almost all of the stresses and strains and contradictions of American life that impinge on adults, but with an added irony: adolescents are neither expected nor asked to concern themselves with these pressures and problems. Not only is the adolescent not asked, but when he evinces interest, he finds that no one particularly cares for his opinion, and certainly he is not expected to be the least bit helpful. There are a few places and a few programs where youths are taken seriously, notably the American Friends Service Committee field programs of work and study. Such programs, exciting as they may be to the reader, enlist very few, and have had little spread into the larger institutional context. One can only wonder why. Are we afraid that youth will find out too much about the cracks in the adult world? Or do we want to protect them during the golden years of youth? Or are we just entangled in institutional inertia which prevents our heeding the recurrent messages from the larger community?

The failure to enlist the talents and energies of youth in concerns of the larger community has furthered the development of a separate community of adolescents with its own vigorous culture (which is extremely profitable to the producers of fad items). This culture has its own rites of passage, language, etiquette, dress, and morality. Adults, noting the evi-

87

[4] Roy Sorenson, "Youth's Need for Challenge and Place in Society," *Children*, IX (July-August 1962), 131.

dence of this separate adolescent culture, are alternately appalled, angered, and envious. The adolescent, working within and against this adult ambivalence, attempts to achieve some personal equilibrium through the creation of his own inner world, where the cues are known, where there is safety, and where there is acceptance.

This separate culture seems to be not only a response by adolescents to the way society treats them, but an attempt to cope with their own developmental problems in the modern world. Young people have always had to grow up. They have always had to exchange the ways of childhood for those of maturity. In the complexity of an industrial society these growth efforts are made infinitely more difficult.

As observed today, the developmental problems of youth may be briefly summarized. First, a youth faces the problem of identity. How does one learn who one is when roles and values regarding roles change so swiftly? Second, he has the problem of self-esteem. How can anyone like me, asks the adolescent, when I am not sure I am worthy of being liked; I hardly like myself. Third, there is the problem of privatism. This is a term used by David Riesman to denote a turning away from social concerns and the larger world to find one's own self-gratification. One feels that most important experiences are those which have purely personal meaning. After all, why not have fun today when the future is in the lap of the bombs? Fourth is the inability of adolescents to gain commitment to adult goals and values. In fact, to many adolescents, to be an adult appears to be one big headache.[5]

These then, are some of the major developmental dilemmas of modern youth. Does the school help or hinder the resolution of these dilemmas? What, in effect, is the outcome of the meeting of youth and secondary school for 3, 4, 5 or 6 crucial years?

The answers to the above questions cannot be simple ones. We offer here a sociological interpretation; a look at the process within the context of interacting social forces. As in the case of our examination of the elementary school, what appears to be of great sociological significance may often lie hidden beneath the institutional facade. It must be repeated, again, as discussed in Chapter 2, that each society supports the kinds of schools it wants. Our inquiry here is to see whether the institution we have created serves or impedes the realization of our avowed social goals.

THE LOST LEARNING

THE SORTING PROCESS

Most people rather simply assume that the major function of the school is imparting knowledge. The secondary school, however, by its very processes, may make the acquisition of knowledge very difficult for many of its students. We have already noted how the elementary school rewards those children most who come with most, and who have learned best how to give teacher what she wants. The secondary school contiues this process, but the means used are somewhat different. Students who

[5] *Ibid.*

have learned how to "read" teachers do better in school; those who are more docile and conforming tend to do better, which works to the advantage of the girl, and the middle-class child.

The secondary schools employ two methods whereby students receive differential rewards. One method is the sorting of students into so-called homogeneous groups (sections, levels, tracks, etc.) and the other is the organization of separate curricula (college preparatory, general, commercial, vocational).

The sorting is based on achievement measured by teacher's grades or standardized tests, and ability measured by group intelligence tests. The theory behind "homogeneous" grouping is that students will perform better when not competing against their intellectual superiors, or when not held back by their intellectual inferiors. Research can be cited to give comfort to those who support this theory as well as to those who deny it.

This sorting process produces a status system. The top group, intellectually, is the same as those who are college-bound. There is no comparable top ability grouping for those who are not college-bound; the intellectually able student is accorded this designation only when he selects the academic, college preparatory program. Thus the academic value system assumes that to be a good person, one has to be "smart," and plan on going to college. An attempt to break this pattern is to be found in the nongraded high school, an institution still so new as to be found in only a few places in the United States. An examination of the curricula at Melbourne High School in Cape Kennedy, Florida, a well-publicized pioneer in nongrading at the secondary level, shows that the highest level of inquiry is available only in academic subjects. The shop, industrial, homemaking, and business courses are either not given a phase or level designation, or are at the most basic level of offering. It would be interesting to examine the status system, here, too.[6]

What are the implications of this sorting process? Suppose a student is highly gifted in terms of any IQ measure utilized. Despite this endowment, he knows that his parents cannot afford to send him to college, and are not interested in such a course of action even if they could afford it. Besides, his own interests lie in auto-mechanics. He can think of nothing more desirable than obtaining a job as a mechanic, earning enough for his own car, and saving money after this to the point where he can eventually run his own repair shop. On the basis of these goals, he selects the vocational program. His schedule is then organized so that his academic classes —English, United States history, mathematics—are taken at the same time period with other vocational students. In the status system of the school such students are labeled as inferior.

Teachers perceive those not in the college preparatory program or the "top" sections as generally less good. "I have a class of commercial girls and they are the deadliest class I have all day," is a typical remark from an academic subject teacher. Similar comments are made by teachers who have vocational boys, or that vast middle group, "the general course" students. In the status system of the school, the college preparatory sec-

[6] B. Frank Brown, *The Nongraded High School* (Englewood Cliffs, N. J.: Prentice-Hall, Inc., 1963), pp. 138-41.

tions dominate. "Around here you're nothing if you're not college prep," was the way one boy summed up the feeling of the vocational group in a large comprehensive high school.[7] "These boys were almost obsessed with a feeling of social isolation from the rest of the school," Mallery continues in his report. All of the elective posts in school government appeared to go to the college prep bunch. They won the honors and ran the school. Studies of social class and participation in school affairs show that these two are positively related. The higher the student's socio-economic status, the more likely he is to be in a college-bound program and the more likely to participate in school-related activities. This is no minor coincidence; it costs money to participate in such things as the school band, the science fair, even the 4-H Club. The more interesting the activity in terms of youth culture, the more often does it appear to be out of reach of young people because they lack the money to pay the price—dues, travel expenses, cleaning bills for uniforms, special entrance fees or equipment fees.

During adolescence, most individuals pass through a period of great self-doubt and feeling of unworthiness. The sorting process of the school reinforces this sense of being unworthy for a large number of students. For some students the process whereby the school indicates that he is less worthy starts in elementary school. The children most likely to evoke this labeling from the school are those from culturally deprived homes or low socio-economic levels, boys, members of minority groups, late-maturing students, and the intellectually poorly endowed.

What are the social consequences of lumping all of these kinds of persons together in one group and labeling them as less good? The most obvious consequence is that students take on themselves the label of not good and are convinced that they cannot succeed at school tasks—cannot learn. Therefore they do not learn. They sit, usually politely, sometimes not so politely. Some remain in school for the whole course, despite continuing assaults upon their self-evaluation. That they remain is probably due to certain other aspects of the school program which we shall discuss later. Many do not choose to remain, however.

The problem of school dropouts has caused considerable and increasing concern. These individuals, who leave at the earliest legal moment—or earlier if a pretext can be found—are typically those in the lower tracks, though not necessarily the least able intellectually. Studies of dropouts indicate that they leave for financial reasons (which can be interpreted, "I needed a job to get a car to do the things I think are fun"), or to get married, but a large proportion in every study report that they have left school because "they were not interested." Our question would be whether they left school or were psychologically and socially pushed out. The fact that boys outnumber girls in all studies of dropouts is due, research seems to indicate, to the greater trouble boys have with the school as an organized institution. Girl dropouts are typically involved in disturbing situations which involve their own personal-emotional life outside of school. For boys, however, the school

[7] David Mallery, *High School Students Speak Out* (New York: Harper & Row, Publishers, 1962), p. 113.

appears to provide "a special culturally determined focus for rebellion and conflict formation." [8]

The result, whatever the motivating impetus, is typically that those least able to cope with the complexities of modern society, being less agile with ideas and things, and not motivated by middle-class goals, are those who earliest appear on the doorstep of the adult world. But the door is not open for them. Convinced of their own lack of value, without the necessary job and social skills to obtain or keep a job, these youth are, as Conant has aptly termed them, potentially the most explosive segment of our society.[9]

If achieving an adequate view of self is one of the crucial tasks of the adolescent, the secondary school makes this difficult, if not impossible, for thousands of youngsters.

If the view from the bottom appears to be dismal, there is some reassurance, we are told, in the fact that the able and the bright are now getting the education they deserve. Let us examine the situation as objectively as possible from the sociologists' vantage point. First, however, the reader must be on guard. Most readers of this book were themselves always in the top or bright or fast section. Thus, they have been imbued with the self-concepts and views of an elite. For an elite is exactly what the sorting process tends to produce in the secondary school. Few members of an elite view those who are subordinate with compassion. The rationale for being one of the elite (in an egalitarian society) is that one is, really, better. An elite position is, however, vulnerable. The lower classes might rise up in wrath, or they might be impolite, or stage freedom marches, or refuse to vote for school bonds. The subordinate group might not like being subordinate. They might seek ways of getting even. In any event, the sorting process of the schools has worked already upon the perceptions of most of those who are reading this volume, and most of them have been sorted into the "good" bin. It may be difficult for them to follow the discussion without becoming defensive.

Let us return to our examination of the sorting process examining it now as it affects the able student. The "best students" are those who are college-bound. Some of the girls are exceptions, but they must pretend to be going to college in order to be with their social peers.

These bright students know they can learn—the school has told them so. It has put them in sections labeled "academically talented" or "accelerated" or "honors." From this vantage point they can look down upon the intellectual cripples below them. The leadership of school activities falls into their hands; by no coincidence, we may remark. There is a very high correlation between father's occupation, socio-economic status, and the ranking of a student in the top sections of a secondary school. Just as was noted for the elementary school, in the secondary school also, those who come with more, get more.

[8] Solmon Lichter, *et al.*, *The Drop Outs* (New York: Free Press of Glencoe, Inc., 1962), p. 61.

[9] James Conant, *Slums and Suburbs* (New York: McGraw-Hill Book Company, 1961), p. 2.

However, all is not completely rosy for the academically able student. Lest his high status go to his head, his position is made carefully insecure. We do not want to develop intellectual snobs, says the school. These able students are not to think that learning is easy. Students are reminded that if their performance slips, they may be removed from these advanced and special groups and placed with ordinary mortals (read "slobs").

One teacher was quoted as saying:

> I hope you boys and girls will be as excited about this new math program as I am. By the end of the year you will have gone through 30 books.
>
> As one of the top 7th grade classes, you should know that we're going to shove a lot down your little throats. If it's too much, you holler and we'll slow up a bit. But we won't slow up till you yell real loud.[10]

Larger high schools, particularly in upward mobile suburban communities, may add accelerated programs on top of college preparatory or upper-level-track programs. These are open only to the student who the faculty feels can do the demanding work required. It has been remarked by observant adolescents that, if one really wants a good record, it is better to stay in the regular college preparatory program with the more mediocre students, than stand the stiff competition of the real "brains."

The insecurity of the very able student is one of the more noticeable mental health hazards existing in today's secondary schools. The prod of uncertainty and anxiety and always potential public failure pushes the students on and on and on. Academically talented students do not appear to be better adjusted than their more mediocre companions. In fact, one careful study pointed out that "they were equally as prone to feelings of personal inadequacy and self-dissatisfaction" and "they experienced inner conflicts and ambivalences to the same extent as adolescents of average intelligence."[11]

The significant question to ask is whether these students are being pushed to more depth of intellectual searching, or to learning how to win the teacher's approval, make the grade, and retain the status of special selection.

It is highly probable that many adolescents do become intellectually interested by richer offerings. But many do not. Within their own value system the student who succeeds best in secondary schools is the one who obtains the mark of high achievement without appearing to put out much effort or evidencing much involvement. Of able students, the one ranking lowest in the esteem of his fellows was the high-achieving studious nonathlete.[12]

While the school takes an active part in some aspects of the sorting

[10] *Washington Post and Times Herald*, September 6, 1962, p. 131.

[11] Donald C. Smith, *Personal and Social Adjustment of Gifted Adolescents* (Washington, D.C.: Council for Exceptional Children, NEA, CEC Research Monograph, Series A, No. 4, 1962), p. 55.

[12] Abraham J. Tannenbaum, *Adolescent Attitudes Toward Academic Brilliance* (New York: Teachers College, Columbia University, Bureau of Publications, 1962), p. 46.

process, other parts of it are up to the student. He may select the curriculum he wishes to pursue. Typically the high school offers three or four curriculum sequences: college preparatory, general, vocational, and commercial (secretarial or business). Theoretically the student has freedom of choice among these, yet the function of teachers and guidance counselors is to help get each student in the right slot. The obviously bright student from an upper socio-economic level who selects a vocational or commercial course will be viewed with alarm and he may be closely questioned as to why he or she did not choose the college preparatory program. Likewise, a not-so-bright student who selects the college preparatory program, particularly if from a lower socio-economic level, may be questioned regarding the practicality of his academic choice.

If the assessment schools made of the potential of each youth were valid one might at least accord them this function. But the assessment is apt to be neither valid nor reliable. Achievement tests and intelligence tests are biased against children from deprived and restricted backgrounds. Teachers' judgments are swayed by factors other than achievement. Creativity, as we pointed out earlier, is not correlated with intelligence; thus, many highly creative individuals may, at the crucial point of adolescence, be forever shut out from realizing their own unique ability. Society, too, is the loser.

Can schools meet the problem in any other fashion? Abilities do differ. Intelligence and creativity are not equally distributed to all men alike. The school in a democracy proclaims its devotion to individual differences. An industrial society has room only for those educated enough to deal with its complexities. Since most youth cannot find work, they are increasingly being forced to go to school and stay in school. The solution to the problem of how to deal with individuals and their differences in a mass institution has so far eluded us. The very sorting procedure that is designed to meet individual differences merely exacerbates the problem. But this is not seen by the interested public, and only reluctantly admitted by educators. Differences are not only accentuated, they are labeled, and organized into a status hierarchy. It is no wonder that so many young people (all those classified and found wanting) feel that in many respects the secondary school is not for them.

GETTING THE GRADE

Grades and marks begin to assume importance in the eyes of the child as he progresses through elementary school. In the secondary school, grades are the constant companion of his days. The last four years of secondary school are those whose grades are recorded on the official record for transmission to colleges, and it is these grades which count in determining who is admitted where.

The students are quite candid about the relationship of education and marks: "Our real aim—to grow intellectually—is blocked by this terrific marks-for-college hassle," was the way one boy put it.[13] The new anxiety about getting into college, and getting into a good college, has made the

[13] Mallery, *High School Students Speak Out*, p. 73.

pressure on the students to get good marks more severe than it has ever been before.

The sorting process into tracks or levels or ability groupings of one sort or another has an effect on the grading system. In a number of schools, the students in the lower tracks or levels are not permitted by school policy to receive anything more than a "C" or passing grade. In some schools the "D" sections are not permitted to obtain very many "C's." In other words, the grade has already been determined when the student is put in the slower section. School personnel almost invariably complain about the lack of interest and motivation in the slower ability groups. The students shrug their shoulders and say, "Why work, we can't get any kind of a grade anyway." It seems odd that the educational profession does not see the inherent irrationality as well as tragedy in the situation.

On the other hand, the bright students in the top sections are not guaranteed anything. They find themselves running, running, just to keep within sniffing distance of the carrot which is always kept just beyond their noses "so that they will be really challenged to put forth maximum effort." This maximum effort requirement, for five "solid" subjects a day, sets a killing pace for adolescents. For the accelerated sections, teachers boast about the college level work they require, often using college texts. Forgotten is the fact that the college student has many free hours during the day to study, absorb, think and talk about his classes (if he so desires). Not so the high school student. He rushes from class to class on a schedule carefully devised to reduce loitering in the halls. And what is it all for? To get the grade.

It has been noted that Americans have a deep distrust of genuine intellectual inquiry. Nowhere is this more clearly seen than in many a secondary school classroom. We might add that contrary to what some of our critics say, this is not unique to America, but seems to be true of the arid classrooms of other countries as well. It is hardly the fault of the students that they appear to work only for grades or, in Europe, to pass examinations. Repeatedly one hears, "You must take notes on what I am saying (or what is in the movie, or what is in this student report, or what you are reading) because it will be on the examination." And this in turn will partly determine one's grade. The teachers who can motivate students to want to learn without recourse to the "grade carrot" are rare indeed.

It is of more than passing interest that there is a minor flood of books (some paperbacks) on the market designed to help the parent help the child do better in school. Some of these are indeed useful, such as the volume by Mary and Lawrence Frank, *How To Help Your Child in School*.[14] Of interest, though, is the spate of volumes typified by that of Harry Shefter, *How to Get Higher Marks in School*.[15] Note that the emphasis is not on how to learn more, but how to get better grades. But even the grade motivates only those to whom it has some significant meaning, primarily those who are concerned about getting into college. "How

[14] Mary and Lawrence Frank, *How To Help Your Child in School* (New York: Signet Key Book, 1954).

[15] Harry Shefter, *How To Get Higher Marks in School* (New York: Washington Square Press, Inc., 1962).

do you motivate students to want to learn when they don't even care what grade they get?" is a recurrent complaint of teachers.

The loss of significance of the grade started early for many students, as we noted in the preceding chapter. The pattern of discriminatory grading continues throughout the secondary school. Boys still fail to get as good grades as girls. Is it because girls are smarter? Or is there some bias in the system? In any event, to many youths, both boys and girls, there appears to be something phoney about the grade. It seems to be an evaluation by the teacher of his liking for a student as often as it is a genuine appraisal of what the student has attempted and achieved.

CONTENT

Part of the failure of the grading mechanism as a motivator for a great many students resides in the emptiness of the content presented, the mastery of which determines the students' grades. In today's world it appears as an anachronism that students still read such nonclassics as *Silas Marner, Ivanhoe, Evangeline.* The diagramming of canned sentences strikes innumerable students as just not worth the effort; the grade isn't worth it and the teacher isn't nice enough. The third time around on United States history (5th grade, 8th grade and 11th grade) does not seem to enliven the increasingly massive parade of facts.

A man who is a school superintendent made this comment on high school learning:

> I almost failed high school algebra and geometry. I barely squeezed through high school at all. Sometimes I wish my old high school would burn down, and with it all the records. I completed two years of Latin by grace of a special tutor employed by my parents. I also completed two years of French, and the required two years of history, English, math, and science. When I say completed, I mean completed. The object of American education is to complete learning. At the end of each course I closed my books, those that I had bothered to open, and put them out of my mind.[16]

95

When queried, young people indicate that they are vitally interested in learning about themselves, the world of work, and the social reality around them, and in facing the major ethical and moral problems of the day. When one examines the curriculum, one finds only some of these ingredients included, and then in a fashion designed to offend nobody. In terms of ethics and values, the public secondary school is particularly hesitant: Whose values? Whose ethical system? Since, as was pointed out in Chapters 4 and 5, there are as many answers to these questions as there are organizations and groups in the community, the school perforce chooses to stay neutral. Avoiding the whole area, the school fills the students' days with increasingly irrelevant activities.

Another missing dimension is suggested by Kubie:

> Perhaps above anything else, the adolescent needs not only to be exposed to human suffering, but also to be given the responsibility of ministering

[16] Charles H. Wilson, *A Teacher Is a Person* (New York: Holt, Rinehart & Winston, Inc., 1956), p. 24.

to it. Yet instead of this, the educational years cultivate in each student a maximal concentration on himself. Moreover, we know that the essence of maturity can come only through the insight which arises out of the interaction between living and blundering, and then of studying and dissecting our blunders. Neither living without self-study nor study without living is enough.[17]

One abortive effort to do something about the secondary school was the so-called Life Adjustment Program sponsored by the United States Office of Education in the late 1940's. This effort was a vulnerable target for the savage critics who saw all the failures of the United States in the race with Russia as stemming from a watered down, child-pampering school program. As a result, the attempt to relate school to life was shunted aside. More generations of youth have thus continued to slip through the high school untouched by significant learning experiences which might equip them to deal with a monstrous adult world.

For only two groups is the curriculum clearly related to their goals: the student seriously intent on college knows he must take a prescribed course and do well; the vocational and business student thinks he sees clearly and prepares for the world of work ahead of him. Others just drift. Take girls, for instance. Most of them will be married within a few years of leaving high school. Their major responsibilities will be in child-rearing and home management. The secondary school offers little that is of value to these highly important and socially useful activities. Practically no child psychology is offered; it probably should be required. Budgeting and consumer education are units in courses taken as electives by a minority of girls. The same is true of home management. The school curriculum makes the assumption that its student body is either job- or career-oriented, and that these are the primary goals to be served. Such simple goals were outmoded by 1930, yet the school program has remained virtually unchanged.

LEARNING REGAINED: the Fun Way

In one area only has the school succeeded in putting learning goals first; this area is the extra-curricular activities which it sponsors. Here students, without fear of grade or examination, may join an Astronomy Club, or Stamp Club, or Hot-Rod Club, or Future Nurses. Here young people are often encouraged to decide upon their own activities, as a group, and carry them out with a minimum of adult supervision. The high level of interest and involvement in these activities on the part of many students indicates how meaningful the activities are for them; the difference in the very faces and attitudes of students who are thus involved is noticeable.

The learnings achieved through these informal means are not, however, reflected on report cards. They do become part of the college-bound student's record. Some of these students appear to hunt for activities and

[17] Lawrence S. Kubie, "Are We Educating for Maturity?" NEA *Journal*, XLVIII, 1 (January 1959), 68.

seek office so that they will have an impressive roster to show admissions officers. The evidence shows that those who participate in activities are those who make the better grades and come from the better homes. There are more girls than boys among them.

Some of the in-school activities share the elements of the club program. Typically these are the school paper, yearbook, band and orchestra, debate club, and varsity athletics of all kinds. As Coleman has suggested, there is a sense of identification with the school team which propels the athlete forward to victory, and also produces the proud support of the hundreds of loyal and nonathletic members of the student body.[18] It is our army going forth to conquer the enemy.

Members of the team—whether it be an athletic team, or the band or the newspaper staff—are cooperating for goals greater than their own individual achievement. And they are working for the School: The Greater Honor and Glory of the School. To these students, the high standing of the school name is something of significance, since what they do (winning, putting out a good paper, marching with precision at half time) contributes to this prize. Thus the adolescent attains a feeling of self-worth. He has found a place in his school milieu in which his efforts count towards a greater good. Noteworthy is the fact that similar feeling about the value of the end result does not occur in the classroom.[19]

Science fairs have become quite popular, but they generate only mild interest in the nonscience student because (we can hypothesize) the awards and rewards are for *individual* achievement, and are not perceived as achievement in whose glory the nonwinners can share. The science fair, too, has in some instances become a chore ("you had better enter something or you will get a lower grade in the course") or another entry in the all-important record of activities to impress hardhearted college admissions officers.

Some schools forbid participation in activities if a student's grades are not good. The reasoning is that if the student cannot work hard enough to do well in his regular classes he obviously does not have time for any "extra" activity. One can see the irony of this in track plans where certain sections are doomed to low grades, no matter what, and are thus automatically excluded from the kind of adolescent activity which might be positively motivating. One might also wonder whether academic, class-oriented achievement is a true measure of what the student can produce when out from under the examination-grade syndrome. It is a common report that the student who refuses to read the history text, may, in the privacy of his own life, be an avid collector of pictures of old guns, and an authority on the same. Or the student who cannot read *The Tale of Two Cities* is able to translate the most esoteric language in electronic magazines and build his own robot.

Yet high school is a magnet for young people. They may scorn teachers and studies, but something is there that keeps them coming: athletics and

97

[18] James S. Coleman, *The Adolescent Society* (New York: Free Press of Glencoe, Inc., 1961), p. 320.
[19] *Ibid.*

social affairs. Here, indeed, is where the "fun morality" of the American scene gets institutional approval, closely followed, we might add, by the modern church social calendar.

If students are less than absorbed in their studies, what are they absorbed in? The highest degree of involvement for most of the student body occurs in that activity which is least intellectual: sports. The passion with which students respond to their school teams indicates something about the lack of any other suitable object for such feelings. Although the image of the athlete is somewhat tarnished in the public mind since it has become fashionable to get good grades, the good athlete and the good student are the individuals who are at the peak of peer approval. But even if he is not so bright, it is better for a boy to be a good athlete than a good scholar.[20] For girls, being a drum-majorette is an equally enviable position. Observing the gyrations of these young maidens at football games suggests some interesting parallels to the speculative mind. After all, if games are a substitute for war, as William James once remarked, then like armies, teams must be accompanied by their camp-followers, now dressed in skimpy costumes and flourishing sparkling batons, a rather interesting symbol. The ritual of the games, and their accompanying release of feelings—hate and triumph, despair and achievement,—reinforce the significance to the adolescent of his own private world of self-indulgence. The adults around approve and participate. Most of the space given to school news in the local newspaper is devoted to high school athletic contests.

Arthur Miller, in *Death of a Salesman*, has poignantly and painfully identified some of the consequences of this value system. As Benne says:

> Willy Loman had taught his son, "Don't worry too much about what you learn or what you think in school; learn to be liked by other people." The proudest day of his life was when Biff, playing in a high school football game in Brooklyn, made a touchdown and the whole crowd stood up and cheered.[21]

What defense has youth against this kind of adult involvement? Some of the most important decisions made by student councils have to do with the kinds of dances to put on, who shall sponsor them, what shall be worn, how they shall be policed, etc. These become the true concerns of youth. Nor is there much in the adult culture of the school which suggests to adolescents that their preoccupation with games and dances is anything but right and normal. In fact, students who show a lack of interest in athletics, who want to read extra books, who do not attend school dances or parties, are considered by many teachers to be odd-balls, immature, eccentric.

The central position of social interaction in the secondary school is very obvious when the problem of school desegregation is debated. The difficulty is not that Negro and white youngsters cannot learn in the same setting, but that this setting is a *social* one, in which finding friends of both sexes

[20] Coleman, *The Adolescent Society*, p. 308. See also Tannenbaum, *Adolescent Attitudes*, p. 80.

[21] Kenneth Benne, *The Quest for Identity and Community* (Columbus: The College of Education, The Ohio State University, 1962), p. 9.

is a highly important and valued activity. Also, the whole community participates in the games, so that desegregating the student body could mean desegregating the adult community as well.[22]

ARE TEACHERS PEOPLE?

Students stay the same age, but teachers keep on getting older. After only a few years of teaching 16-year-olds, a whole cycle of change has taken place. Zoot suits have been replaced by black leather jackets. Skirts have climbed above the knee. Hair has been cut to a half inch above the scalp, and so forth. With each year, the real world of the adolescent recedes further from the teacher's view. While this is also true of the elementary school, the significant world of child and teacher still are in essential communication: the child wants and needs recognition and support and a sense of achievement from adults; teachers still feel that these are valuable goals, and thus they can develop a community of interests.

Are the adult goals and the needs of adolescents the same or congruent in the secondary school? As we have noted, the adolescent faces some crucial developmental dilemmas. Many adults have not themselves fully worked out these dilemmas. Observing adolescents struggling for self-definition, and perhaps noting that it takes the shape of denial and resistance, the teacher may be understandably annoyed. It is the teacher's requests that are being resisted, it is the teacher's goals that are being rejected.

Most crucial, adolescents in their explorations of who they are inevitably run into sex. It is terrifying for the average teacher to face realistically the obsession with sex which is part of the normal adolescent state of mind. Some adults have achieved satisfactory sexual identities; many have not. All kinds become teachers.[23]

The gap between the generations has its advantages, when viewed from the adolescents' side. Having found out that he is supposed to be struggling to gain independence from home (and he usually is) he can successfully ward off attempts of the high school to bring parents more into the act. The less he lets his parents know about school the better, is the view of the average adolescent. Since teachers are often very uneasy in the presence of parents, this desire on the part of the youth is rarely challenged. The teacher therefore can operate in ignorance of the real world of the adolescent outside of school, and the home can remain ignorant of the peer culture which governs the life in the school corridors and playing fields during the interstices of school routine.

In many nonclassroom activities the teachers are viewed by the student as allies and sometimes as friends. The relationship between student and teacher in extracurricular activities is often warm and helpful. The teacher in the classroom, however, is another animal. Typically, a student is one of 120 or 150 students who pass through the teacher's classes daily. It is often weeks before all the names are learned, and even then the student

---

[22] Don Shoemaker, ed., *With All Deliberate Speed* (New York: Harper & Row, Publishers, 1957), p. 200.

[23] Arthur T. Jersild, *When Teachers Face Themselves* (New York: Teachers College, Columbia University, Bureau of Publications, 1955), Chap. v.

may feel he is merely a name in a roll book. For those on the fringe, the quiet, the mediocre, the teacher is remote indeed. The very bad and the very good attract the major part of the teacher's fractioned attention, and even these get only bits and pieces.

The teacher, as unremitting judge of achievement, as the gatekeeper to success or failure, the holder of the higher mysteries of the grade, is hardly in a position to attract trust from his students. The emptiness and remoteness of content only serves to increase the distance from the teacher's world felt by students. The code of the peer group works to keep the separation sharp and clear. Grades are so omnipresent and crucially important to teacher and student, and also so subjective and dependent on teacher whim and favor, students work upon each other to keep teachers at arm's length. The student who really likes a teacher, who is genuinely interested in a subject, or fired by an idea, is either so popular that he can defy the code, or so outside the world of his peers that their judgments of him do not matter. Students respond with fervor and interest to those teachers who seem able to teach significant subject matter with evident regard for the world of youth and the struggles of the individual student. What is distressing is that so many enter the profession of teaching with such hopes in mind, but are early defeated by a system which not only makes it difficult to keep such a view of teaching and students, but actually establishes a code for teachers (in the teacher's lounge) that says that they, too, must reject youth.

Much has been written about the process of identification as one of the ways in which the individual finds his role, finding and identifying with a role model. In previous generations there was some evidence that the teacher provided such a model for many young people. The teacher-model appears in the autobiographies of many prospective teachers today; teachers do not appear as significant models in the lives of many other youth. To them teachers just do not represent a way of life, either personal or otherwise, that they choose to emulate. That the system itself interferes with such model identification is already clear. Who can identify with one who has the power of life or death? whose love is conditional on "performance?" who appears to be aligned with the enemies, the other power figures in the field? Most secondary teachers, who are honestly attempting to teach and help students, are tolerated if not liked; few are admitted into the magic circle of students' confidences. Students who do end up with a teacher-friend tend to be deviants from the peer code or the better students who are complying with the school's norms in satisfactory fashion.

THE DOSSIER

A recent element has been added to the modern school: guidance. Every high school which can possibly afford it has a guidance and counseling office. Here the record-keeping activity takes place. With the increased use of electronic scoring devices, more and more scores can be more inexpensively recorded. We can confidently look forward to a time when most students will be tested at frequent points along the educational ladder.

Included in the student file are not only scores, but other items of information. If a student has been suspended, or otherwise been in trouble with the authorities, this is recorded. Referrals to clinics or special testing are put in the record. Incidents involving individual teachers may be recorded. Facts about the family find their way into the record. Recommendations for college or employment are put on file.

What is the significance of this record? For one thing, it is there. It may be used as a threat: "This kind of behavior will be entered on your permanent record." The record follows the student: If he moves, his school is begged to send the record along. With the many "security" jobs in both government and industry, the record is a source of great interest to investigative personnel. The aberrations of youth have followed many a person into middle age, because they were in the "permanent record." [24]

How secure is the confidential file? In some schools a distinction is made between that file which is in the outer office where grades and absences are recorded, and that file in a separate office (of the principal or guidance counselor) where test scores and other personal matters are kept. Where student clerks and clerks from the community may have access to any of these files, their relative security is open to question. Because of this fact, some systems refuse to release psychological test reports to the schools. Some schools refuse teachers access to confidential files, fearing that they may make nonprofessional use of the information, or may not have the professional training necessary to interpret test findings. What then is the value of the testing or interviewing?

A further complication has been added because of the legal question regarding the confidential nature of school records. A New York court recently upheld the parent's right to see his child's test scores, even though the school authorities felt that these were of the same nature as a doctor's medical records which are not available to a patient or his family.[25]

Despite the cloudy issues that surround the student file, the fact is that we are in the era of the dossier. Its purposes may be pure and the motives of those who administer the records above reproach. Unfortunately, the system does not guarantee that good motives coincide with good judgment; or that high purposes take into account a multiplicity of value systems.

SUMMARY

The social valuation of learning will inevitably dominate any kind of institutional manipulation. If grades continue to be more important than learning, then no matter how the task is presented, nor how amiable the personnel, the adolescent will respond to the implicit valuations that are conveyed by both in-school and out-of-school forces. If the school can remove itself sufficiently from the culture to enthrone learning as a desirable outcome, then some serious social consequences may have to be faced. Too many tales of teachers and systems constrained by public pressure to keep

[24] See comment by David Riesman in Friedenberg, *The Vanishing Adolescent*, pp. xii-xiii.
[25] Martin L. Gross, *The Brain Watchers* (New York: Random House, 1962), p. 167.

students from genuine confrontation with significant learning experiences suggest that the task is difficult. We believe it is not impossible.

BIBLIOGRAPHY

BARRY, RUTH AND BEVERLY WOLF, *Epitaph for Vocational Guidance: Myths, Actualities, Implications.* New York: Bureau of Publications, Teachers College, Columbia University, 1962. The guidance function is dissected and some significant questions raised about what is being done.

FINDLEY, WARREN G., ed., *The Impact and Improvement of School Testing Programs,* Sixty-second Yearbook, National Society for the Study of Education, Part II. Chicago: University of Chicago Press, 1963. Articles by experts evaluate the issues and problems in the widespread use of standardized tests and testing programs.

FRIEDAN, BETTY, "The Sex-Directed Educators," *The Feminine Mystique.* New York: W. W. Norton & Co., Inc., 1963. A modern feminist view of the role of women, blaming modern education for distorting the woman's role.

FYVEL, T. R., *The Troublemakers: Rebellious Youth in an Affluent Society.* New York: Schocken Books, 1961. An English author contrasts delinquency in America with that in several European countries.

GINZBURG, ELI, JAMES K. ANDERSON, AND JOHN L. HERMA, *The Optimistic Tradition and American Youth.* New York: Columbia University Press, 1962. Unusually well-written analysis of how contemporary values and social practices affect youth.

GOODMAN, PAUL, *Growing up Absurd.* New York: Random House, 1960. Essays by an astute observer regarding the situation of youth today confronting the conflicting pressures and expectancies of our society.

GORDON, C. WAYNE, *The Social System of the High School.* New York: Free Press, 1957. This research study describes the status and prestige system of the school, on both the formal and informal level.

GROSS, MARTIN L., *The Brain Watchers.* New York: Random House, 1962. A somewhat overstated and intemperate discussion of current testing practices; however, it contains criticisms well worth pondering.

HAVIGHURST, ROBERT J. et al., *Growing Up in River City.* New York: John Wiley & Sons, Inc., 1962. Reports a ten-year study of youth and their education in a midwestern community.

HENRY, JULES, *Culture Against Man.* New York: Random House, 1963. See especially Chapters 6 and 7 on teen-age culture and the school as seen by an anthropologist.

LOTT, ALBERT J. AND BERNICE E. LOTT, *Negro and White Youth.* New York: Holt, Rinehart & Winston, Inc., 1963. A psychological study in a border-state community.

PATTERSON, FRANKLIN et al., *The Adolescent Citizen.* New York: Free Press of Glencoe, Inc., 1960. Chapters written specially for this publication discuss the secondary school and aspects of today's social world that impinge on the awareness of the adolescent and influence his role as a future citizen.

SMITH, DONALD C., *Personal and Social Adjustment of Gifted Adolescents.* Washington: Council for Exceptional Children, NEA, Research Monograph No. 4, 1962.

"Teen-Age Culture," *The Annals of the American Academy of Political and Social Science*, 338 (November 1961), 1-136. Twelve reports on various aspects of teen-age culture by competent authorities.

The High School in a Changing World, Thirty-sixth Yearbook. Washington, D.C.: American Association of School Administrators, 1958. Reports ways in which secondary schools are adapting to new demands with new instructional and organizational procedures.

TIPTON, JAMES H., *Community in Crisis*. New York: Bureau of Publications, Teachers College, Columbia University, 1953. A case study of a community and a school when segregation was eliminated. Particularly pertinent today.

WATSON, GOODWIN, ed., *No Room at the Bottom: Automation and the Reluctant Learner*. Washington, D.C.: National Education Association, 1963. Five experts provide different views of how automation may affect the reluctant learner and what might be done about his education.

WILLIS, MARGARET, *The Guinea Pigs After Twenty Years*. Columbus: Ohio State University, 1961. The follow-up of a group of students whose high school education was radically "progressive."

Like American education generally, the American college or university is a unique institution. One of its unique features is that there is little that one can call typical about this institution. True, its student body usually has completed a high school education, but beyond that there are almost as many kinds of institutions for higher education as there are kinds of students seeking such an education. This diversity in institutions appalls foreign visitors. It also makes it extremely difficult to make generalizations about higher education in America. But with the increased dissatisfaction with the products of all educational institutions, the American college has also experienced a wave of critical scrutiny, in some instances backed by sophisticated research. The impetus for today's examination of the college was spurred on by the finding that going to college for for four years appeared to have little effect on students' values. They entered college with certain attitudes, feelings and beliefs, and left college with them relatively unimpaired. If college was to be liberating, the only visible evidence was that the young man or woman was now free to be more like everyone else.[1]

[1] P. E. Jacobs, *Changing Values in College* (New York: Harper & Row, Publishers, 1957).

STAINLESS STEEL IVORY TOWERS: THE CULTURE OF THE COLLEGE

10

Why does the college appear to fail in its task? Are students really apathetic and indifferent? Are colleges as non-intellectual as observers have claimed? What forces are operating on the college population to make for intellectual liveliness or intellectual death?

The questions are sharpened and made more perplexing by the contrast between the few very effective colleges and the mass of higher educational institutions. What is that makes the educational experience at colleges like Reed, Antioch, and Swarthmore, so impelling and persuasive, when equally small and equally serious colleges seem to have little intellectual impact on most of their students? [2]

The college is a complex social institution. To gain insight into its operation we will examine the college, first as it is perceived by students, then the college that is the domain of the professors. Next we will consider the administrator's college, and finally, the college that the public sees.

THE STUDENT'S COLLEGE

The college-bound student today differs in some significant ways from his predecessors.

College education in the nineteenth century was primarily for those of high status, or those who were seeking such status. The latter group was not exceptionally large, since for the common man college was usually too remote and too expensive. More significantly, upward mobility could be achieved without the patina, burdensomely acquired, of a college education. In fact, in some spheres, a college education might be a distinct handicap to mobility, since the graduate might be perceived to be too "smart" or too "refined" for the hurly-burly of the market place. Most of the population was engaged in agricultural pursuits, and there was little perceived relationship between higher education and better farming. Few women were expected to pursue education beyond secondary school, and few did.

How the times have changed! In October 1960, nearly one of every two high school graduates was attending college.[3] Of course not all of these would stay in college. Less than half could be expected to complete a four year program and earn a bachelor's degree. Still, not only have the absolute numbers of individuals who desire a college education increased at a great rate, but the percentage of the college age group enrolled in college has increased tremendously. Instead of being a real goal for a few, a remote and improbable goal for many, and an impossible one for still more, a college education is now quite routinely expected by an ever growing portion of the school community.

The factors that have impelled this change are several. First, the population itself has increased. Second, the status to be achieved via a college

105

[2] *Ibid.*, Chap. 6; see also Burton R. Clark, "College Image and Student Selection," in *Selection and Educational Differentiation*, Report of a Conference, Field Service Center and Center for the Study of Higher Education (Berkeley: University of California, 1959), pp. 155-68.

[3] *National Education Association Research Bulletin*, XL, No. 2 (May 1962), 42.

education is now clear; lacking this certificate of achievement, the *average* individual today can not be sure that he has a chance to acquire a middle class job, or rise above such a job. Third, there are few places where even the very *able* young person can find satisfying employment unless he has a college degree. Fourth, there are more colleges, more of them within commuting distance of more students. Fifth, parental income has increased to the point where maintaining a non-contributing member of the family for a longer period is feasible. Sixth, prejudices against the educated woman have declined markedly. Finally, the culture of the adolescent peer group suggests that there are many personally rewarding features about the years at college which, over and above the economic aspects, makes this experience desirable.

Once college has been accepted as a goal, comes the question "Which college?" Preceding college admission the individual today goes through a complicated series of tests, interviews, and visits. Then a period of intense anxiety and waiting occurs. In suburban America thousands of tense parents and their offspring wait the fateful missive which announces their acceptance or rejection by the college of their choice. Not to get into the college of one's choice is almost worse than not going to any college at all. Those colleges which are the first choice of able students get the cream of the student crop: the Big Ten, the men's and women's Ivy League, and a select number of small but reputable liberal arts colleges. The second-choice colleges—state universities, state colleges, junior colleges, subsistence level private schools—tend to have second-rate student bodies. Or at least the members of the student body tend to think of themselves as such, which amounts to the same thing.[4]

The diverse interests that bring a student to college determine to a large extent the kind of college he will find.[5] Every college and university is made up of many sub-systems, populated by like-minded students. To be sure that like meets like, colleges and universities sponsor various kinds of organizations. The fraternity or sorority provides the basic social group identification. Here members are elected who appear to be the right "type" for the brotherhood. They must appear to share similar backgrounds, tastes, attitudes towards college and towards the opposite sex.[6] If fraternities are too few to sort everyone out, clubs will provide base-groups. Every campus has its special interest clubs, and spawns new ones with each new generation of students.

A number of clubs with varied social activities are sponsored by religious groups. Their hope is that young people, meeting others of like religious convictions under the chaperonage of a kindly, folksy and understanding cleric, will resist the secular influences of higher learning, will marry some-

---

[4] Clark, "College Image," in *Selection and Educational Differentiation*, pp. 155-68.

[5] C. Robert Pace, "Interactions Among Academic, Administrative, and Student Subcultures," in *The Study of Campus Cultures*, ed. Terry F. Lunsford (Boulder, Colorado: Western Interstate Commission for Higher Education, 1963), pp. 129-38.

[6] Gene N. Levine, and Leila A. Sussmann, "Social Class and Sociability in Fraternity Pledging," *American Journal of Sociology*, XXV, No. 4 (January 1960), 391-99.

one met under the religious tent, and remain among the faithful when graduated.

Clubs are particularly appealing to students who do not seek or are not chosen for the organized living of the fraternity or sorority, the day students and dormitory residents. The dormitory student often lives in rather bleak and impersonal buildings; the newer they are the larger they are apt to be. His friendships may grow along the same corridor or among those in adjacent rooms; the other residents are slightly familiar faces in a sea of strangers, no more. Neither the dormitory nor the mass dining halls for thousands of students provides a small familiar group. Thus the club comes into its own. Club life and student activities provide opportunity to find friends, and without friends in college one's education is empty.

In the dormitory as in the fraternity house it is highly unlikely that two or more students will have the same classes, except in a very small college. There is thus a significant lack of common intellectual experiences to be talked over in the informal group. The larger the college the more will this be true. Multiple sections of a given course may meet throughout the week, taught by different instructors who provide different intellectual experiences. "Consequently it is difficult for [students] to communicate about intellectual problems outside class, and the common concerns which become the basis of social communication are football, the student newspaper, dating, and the dormitory food." [7]

The intimacy and continuity of the small group—the club, fraternity, or sorority—thus provide compensation for the otherwise fragmented college experience. If the talk is trivial, the relationships at least are real and supporting.

The commuting student is seen as a special case, to be pitied and helped if possible. This student lacks the basic experience of college life—to be away from home on one's own with several thousand of one's age mates. The college and university strive manfully to make up to the poor commuters their loss of this vital aspect of higher education, through special groups "just for commuters."

All students are appealed to when the big intermural games are played. The football games in the fall, and increasingly the basketball games in winter and spring, are the object of a total college interest. Here, at least, the diverse groups are welded together, in their common support of "our" team against "theirs." While sports on the campus have been denounced and decried as shifting the focus of student attention from the proper function of the college or university, it is not the students who are worried. To them the massive activity program of the campus, and a sporting chance to win a championship, are essential elements in the college they have come to attend. For a moment at least, all are children of the alma mater.

Of course not all the time at the college or university is spent in fun

[7] W. J. McKeachie, "Research on Teaching at the College and University Level," in *Handbook of Research on Teaching*, ed. N. L. Gage (Chicago: Rand McNally & Co., 1963), p. 1163. See also Theodore M. Newcomb, "Student Peer-Group Influence and Intellectual Outcomes of College Experience," in *Personality Factors on the College Campus*, pp. 84-85.

and games. Some time is devoted to study. The educational aspects of the college are highly organized. The typical college requires certain sequences and selections of courses of all students in a so-called "general education" block, regardless of what a student's major aim might be. The pre-law student takes a prescribed number of math or science units, and the art student does likewise. The freshman and sophomore programs usually allow for only a minimum of elective courses in line with a student's major, or selected area of concentration. The sequence leading to a degree in any given field is usually prescribed.

Like the high school, the college dictates what appears to be in the student's best interests. Most of the students are mildly annoyed by the restrictions that hedge their intellectual life. Do we know how many come to college with a burning desire to take a course in philosophy, or elect something in art, or try out a different scientific field?[8] Were they so motivated, they would soon find that there is usually no room in their program for these luxuries. And, even if they did want to sample a subject outside their own field, they would find that most courses outside of the general education "block," are designed mainly to produce future philosophers, artists or scientists, and woe betide the casual student who just wants to find out.

There is nothing in the process of moving toward a baccalaureate degree that requires the student to be intellectually stimulated to arrive at his goal. The student who attends college in a persistent effort to rise from lower class to middle class, who must work grueling hours on a job for long and tedious years, is usually far from being involved with the college as an intellectual arena:

> . . . these students, for whom college is an adjunct to the world of jobs, are also resistant to intellectual demands on them beyond what is required to pass the course. To many of these hard-driven students, ideas and scholarship are as much a luxury (and distraction) as are sports and fraternities. If the symbol of the collegiate culture is the football and fraternity weekend, the symbol of this vocationally oriented college culture is the student placement office.[9]

The junior college serves as a mid-way institution whose function has been aptly named a "cooling out" process [10] in which guidance personnel turn students from visions of a baccalaureate degree to goals more within their range, namely two-year terminal vocational courses.

It might be futile to suggest that lack of intellectual involvement in fraternity men, working part-time students, and failing junior college students may be caused as much by the arid classroom as by their own resistance to ideas or their lack of intellectual capacity. How many under-

[8] Agatha Townsend, *College Freshmen Speak Out* (New York: Harper & Row, Publishers, 1956), pp. 35-37.
[9] Martin Trow, "Student Cultures and Administrative Action," in *Personality Factors on the College Campus* (Austin: The Hogg Foundation for Mental Health, The University of Texas, 1962), p. 206.
[10] Clark, "The 'Cooling Out' Function in Higher Education," in *Selection and Educational Differentiation*.

graduates remember their classroom hours as scintillating and exciting and how many as intensely boring or impossibly difficult to undertand? Few studies tell us whether the professor teaches well enough to be stimulating to the awake or understood by the dutiful. The available research suggests that most college instruction ranges from mediocre to poor.[11]

The larger the institution the more likely it is that hurdles to graduation have been set up. However, small schools can be just as rigid. Foreign languages are being required in more and more general education courses, with a corresponding loss of students who have neither interest nor aptitude in languages. A mathematics and science hurdle is usually established, irrespective of the student's abilities or interests. If a student cannot write, even though he may paint or sing marvelously, he probably is not college caliber. However, if he plays ball marvelously the college or university will provide special coaching to help him in his weak areas. The game must be won, though the great song or the new formula may be lost forever because of a fatal weakness in English I.

Whatever the defense of these requirements may be, many students view them less as intellectually liberating and challenging experiences and more as requirements to be gotten out of the way as early and as painlessly as possible. The passive acceptance of what appears to be extremely unreasonable can be detected as the mark of the mature sophomore; the freshman may find it jarring, disconcerting, and, in a number of instances, simply not acceptable—*ergo*, the bright student who flunks courses for no apparent reason. The students who survive the "required" courses have managed to do so by learning the system.

The system is relatively simple; you find out what the professor wants and give it back. If the English instructor favors rich hyperbole, that is perforce the kind of writing that you will do in your theme. If, however, you were given an instructor who prefers the terse, direct, Hemingway style of writing, then the obliging student learns to write that way.[12]

It is soon quite apparent that the instructor not only knows the answer, but can enforce it. College, the student finds out, is very much like high school only more so. In high school, the unfair teacher was at least vulnerable to massive frontal attacks by aggrieved parents, often followed (or preceded) by the directives from the principal to be able to document the evidence for student evaluations. Not so in the college. It is a rare student who would dare bring his parent into the fray. It is just not done (though deans can testify that attempts are made from time to time, which—unless the college is financially very weak—are tactfully turned aside after a solemn discourse on academic freedom). The system upholds the judgment of the instructor, no matter how patently biased or even downright incompetent he may be.

Being away from home serves to increase the student's feelings of being a victim, albeit a willing one. To remain away from home (itself a great relief), one must endure. To complain about the system might bring

---

[11] Nevitt Sanford, ed., *The American College* (New York: John Wiley & Sons, Inc., 1962), pp. 365-77.

[12] McKeachie, "Research on Teaching," in *Handbook of Research*, ed. Gage, p. 1119.

parents into the picture to question one's ability to make a go of it. One might be snatched out of college and the security of an allowance, and pushed into the real world of work.

Since he cannot beat the system, the student joins it. He learns how to study professors. By the time he is a venerable senior he has an acute sense of which instructor to trust and which not to trust.

The student who has found his niche in academic work, who finds that he can most nimbly perform the experiments or learn the theorems or the chronology of battles, may be particularly adept at a special kind of agreeing while seeming to disagree. This particular skill is of value for graduate school and further work for advanced degrees. The student learns that his professors are gatekeepers to still further education. A bad letter of recommendation can keep one out of graduate school, no matter how scintillating the record: "He shows brilliance, which may indeed be productive when he can overcome some personal handicaps." The best students are disciples, and the atmosphere of the college is well designed to promote this kind of response in those who choose to continue advanced study.[13]

Having survived those courses which are not related to his major interests, the student is then free to specialize.

Some programs are seen to be "better" in the eyes of the student college community, usually reflecting faculty valuations. Who is at the top of the academic status heap varies from generation to generation. Not so long ago the classicists and philosophers were considered the intellectual elite of the campus; today it is the pure physicists, the mathematicians, and students in other "pure" scientific fields. Engineering is not as high in status; the humanities are taken over by girls; agriculture is way out, and such fields as nursing, home economics, and public school teaching are relegated to low rungs on the ladder.

These valuations may affect the student's occupational choice. A boy who chooses secondary school teaching prior to college entry, may find that his professors show only thinly veiled contempt for school teachers.[14] If the student is fairly good in an academic area, and sensitive to these social valuations, he may relinquish his initial interest in school teaching. As in the case of the student's residence, the field of study he chooses provides him with a separate, and often isolating, intellectual arena, where he acts and interacts with like-minded persons, and develops and shares their snobberies and self-concepts, and internalizes the valuation of the campus about his chosen field.

It is practically impossible to explain to students before they come to college about the process of "registration." After the first experience with a procedure which ranges from bad to excruciating, the student becomes sophisticated about his program. He finds out that one does not select a

[13] Edgar Z. Friedenberg and Julius A. Roth, *Self-Perception in the University*, Supplementary Educational Monographs, No. 80 (Chicago: University of Chicago Press, January 1954).

[14] David Beardslee and Donald O'Dowd, "Students and the Occupational World," in *The American College*, ed. Nevitt Sanford (New York: John Wiley & Sons, Inc., 1962), p. 619.

course because it is interesting, but because it furnishes two easy credits, or it meets at 10 o'clock on Monday, Wednesday and Friday. Technically, a student has an academic adviser with whom he works out a program of courses each semester. The experienced student studies the class schedule, finds the required courses he must take, notes the hours given, and then tries to build up the rest of his schedule so that he has maximum free time on convenient days.

The student finds, also, that credit-counting is very important. The rules and regulations typically set out the numbers of credits required for graduation in this or that area. Failure to fulfill the credit requirements to the letter usually results in failure to graduate, even though the omission may be as significant as one-half unit in "health."

Counting credits, which started in high school, continues through college, and pursues the student into graduate school. Most universities stipulate a minimum number of credits which must be in a graduate student's record before he can possibly apply for the degree, no matter how much competence he may have otherwise demonstrated.[15]

It should be of surprise to no one, therefore, that the students absorb the valuation of intellectual activity which is conveyed to them via these devices. It is not content, but credit, that counts. It is not competence achieved but requirements met.

Because of the irrelevance of what they are taking to their major concerns, their lack of involvement in the ideas conveyed by their instructors, and the need to return to the teacher what he wants, students find it not only easy but in some cases necessary to cheat. It is a rare campus in which most students do not cheat at least once if not oftener in the course of their college careers, with few feelings of guilt or remorse. They do not even blame the system. If professors are sufficiently myopic to give the same exams year after year, or the same topics for themes, or the same reading assignment, then they are fair game. One of the more bitter sources of envy in day students and dorm students for fraternity members is that the House, in the interests of its survival, (most colleges demand a minimum grade average to remain in the House) keeps a careful collection of themes and term papers, of past exams and tests, in every course obtainable. The urgency to obtain these is so great that major security measures are invoked at the time of final exams on some campuses; themes to be written in class must be put down in bluebooks especially provided by the instructor so that prewritten themes cannot be sneaked in.

Earlier we noted that there is an institutionally defined gulf between high school student and high school teacher which is particularly useful for the student, although often galling and frustrating to the teacher. The same condition permeates the college. Students tend to perceive their professors as somewhat remote persons, who lead barely normal lives, and are for consultation and advice only in narrowly defined academic

---

[15] Dietrich Gerhard, "The Emergence of the Credit System in American Education Considered as a Problem of Social and Intellectual History," *American Association of University Professors Bulletin*, XL (Winter, 1955), 662.

matters. The larger the campus the more likely is this to be so, and it is particularly true in metropolitan universities with many commuting students. Faculty members, however, hold power and authority over the individual's future, so are to be treated with care. It is best to be at least polite and to show some interest, even if feigned. It is well-known college folklore that the blonde in the first row who smiles so very responsively to the academic jokes of her professor may receive a grade out of proportion to her demonstrated achievement. To show a real rather than pretended interest in the class material is to cause peers to be suspicious and antagonistic. If the student makes it clear he is only exploiting the weakness of the professor, and does not really mean it, it is all right.

The average professor is uninformed about the happenings which are significant in the lives of his students: who is dating whom, who has broken up with whom, who has been nominated for Prom Queen, who has made the second team. The concepts, ideals, and concerns which are the burden of much of the classroom instruction rarely if ever are related to the actual life the students are experiencing on campus.

The culture of the student tends to isolate the very able student who gets the best grades. "D.A.R." (Damned Average Raiser) is one of the terms used to designate those who throw the "curve" out of line. On a large number of campuses the students are graded on what is known as "the curve." This is an approximation of the normal curve of distribution, which means that 7 per cent get A's, 24 per cent get B's, 38 per cent get C's, 24 per cent get D's and 7 per cent get F's. It can thus be seen that a DAR might push one's own grade further down on the curve; and this is not a very good thing to do. To be really liked in college (as is true in the high school) the individual must do well, but not too well, and must not strive too hard to attain success. For girls, collegiate success may spell personal failure. Too high grades may discourage dates.

Of the college personnel with whom the student has contact, the most significant persons are often those in the dean's office. The dean, and his or her assistants, who work with student groups, enforce rules and regulations, and live in the dormitories, are the major contact point of the administration with the daily life of the students. These individuals are indeed charged with a tremendous task; they must act *in loco parentis* to these students who are at a particularly ambiguous age. Are these students adults or aging adolescents? Are they able to discipline themselves or must they be guided and supervised, with clearly defined limits to their freedom? The typical residential college reflects the contemporary American double standard. Both boys and girls are expected to refrain from drinking on campus, and off campus to drink only discreetly and when they are of age. Boys are provided only nominal supervision in their living groups, usually having a graduate student or young instructor (who gets his room and board free) living with them "just in case." The girls are kept in purdah. Their hours of coming and going at night are carefully dictated. Quiet hours are enforced. Room checks are common. Even seniors are permitted only so many late evenings and week ends away.

Students appear to accept these restrictions with good grace; many, in fact, feel that it is "good for them" to have rules that regulate their study hours and tell them when to go to sleep. "I would never get my studying done," says many a woman student, "if I didn't have to be in by 10:30." The young man says wistfully, "I sometimes wish they ran the boys' dorms as strictly as the girls'; it is just too noisy and there are too many interruptions for me to get my work done, and I don't like the library."

The rules serve to provide some stability, at least for the women, and serve to keep most of them at an intellectual task which they lack the discipline or interest to pursue on their own. Similarly, the deans are responsible for protecting the chastity of their female charges who, presumably, without such regulations might find it hard to withstand the importunities of spring, passion, or drink. That many do succumb is wearisomely familiar to many deans of women, who are convinced they have no choice but to boot the offending girl off campus. Certainly the college could not in any way change the manner in which students are housed, treated, and supervised. That the students are getting smarter than the deans is apparent, however, in the statistics of the decreasing numbers of virgins, men and women alike—and decreasing faster among the women than the men—now graduating from colleges. It is only the foolish, the careless, or the ignorant who are caught. But the system carefully and sometimes even graciously preserves the outward *appearance* of the amenities; the girl can have her cake and eat it too, and her parents will be none the wiser, particularly if she comes home with a diamond ring before graduation.[16]

The differential motivations of men and women in going to college are part of what makes the college. The boys go primarily to prepare for a vocational future and incidentally to find a sexual or marital partner; the girls go primarily to find a mate, and incidentally to know what it means to go to a college class.[17] The truly fortunate girl is one who finds a husband in the college she attended; husband and wife then have something in common to talk about for the rest of their lives. The real disadvantage of going to a single-sex institution is that the most significant part of life—the college years—can never be truly shared with one's spouse.

There are innumerable variations of college life as experienced by students. Many colleges and universities deviate markedly from the foregoing description in one dimension or another. But by and large the significant college drama for students is played out not in the classroom, but in the House, the dorm room, the dark nook at the local bar, on the dance floor and playing field. That these experiences are incredibly significant is attested to by the power, strength, and tenacity of the old grad.

113

[16] Clifford Kirkpatrick and Eugene Kannin, "Male Sex Aggression on a University Campus," *American Sociological Review* No. 1 (February 1957), pp. 52-58; "Student Sex Standards and Behavior: The Educator's Responsibility," *Journal of the National Association of Women Deans and Counselors* XXVI, No. 2 (January 1963), entire issue; Milton I. Levine, and Maya Pines, "Sex: The Problem Colleges Evade," *Harper's Magazine*, No. 1337 (October 1961); Gloria Steinem, "The Moral Disarmament of Betty Coed," *Esquire*, No. 9 (September 1962).

[17] Elizabeth Douvan and Carol Kaye, "Motivational Factors in College Entrance," in *The American College*, ed. Sanford, pp. 199-224.

There is something rather poignant about the old grad. In some respects he has never ceased to be a sophomore, and as such is the object of satire and ridicule. He turns up regularly for the Big Game and grows embarrassingly sentimental as he gets happily drunk on the stands. He is the first to howl for the scalp of the coach when the team loses. He views with great suspicion any major changes in the conduct of the college or university.

If there is a patronizing public view of the old grad, college and university administrations and governing boards are deadly serious about him. He is appealed to for funds by even that immensely rich, state-supported giant, the University of California. Smaller colleges may live or die depending on alumni support.

Alumni are a fertile source of two things, new students and new money. The old grad often likes to send his children to his own alma mater, and if he is really enthusiastic about his own educational experiences, will proselytize his friends' children, also.

Getting money out of alumni is a full-time job on many campuses. Rich alumni are fair game, and every once in a while one succumbs to the lure of a building named after him, or an endowed professorship. Public support for higher education, although extensive, is only sufficient to keep most public colleges and universities alive on a starvation basis. The luxuries of higher salaries, better buildings, special programs, must come from generous alumni. There may be an interesting relation here: big donors who gain personal satisfaction out of seeing their names in marble tend to belong to that group most opposed to increased federal support for higher education. If the colleges were more amply aided by public sources, the old grad would not be nearly so important. No private institution today can subsist without generous infusions of new money from outside. Endowments just do not keep up with expanding needs. Private institutions thus cultivate a particularly warm interest in their old grads.

The power of alumni is exercised not only in endowing buildings and professorships, but in sitting on boards of regents, and listening alertly to all news about the college. The alumni choose to remain potent, and they are. Visiting alumni are treated with care and attention. Each alumnus speaks to a public, and the image of the college is conveyed by these individuals; the image had better continue to be a viable one or the college is doomed.

The conservative force of alumni groups needs assessing. They may well perceive themselves in this role, and be proud of it. What they are protecting and conserving in many instances may be excellent, or it may be outmoded and may actually interfere with the true function of the university. Were there less vociferous support by alumni for big-time football, many a college would long ago have shucked it off. The anachronism of nondemocratic social living groups, such as fraternities and sororities with restrictive clauses, is protected because of alumni involvement in their perpetuation.

The student's college is a very special entity. It not only engulfs him on entrance, it stays with him through life. The mark of the college is the result of *student culture* acting upon the individual rather than the impact of great ideas and great missions enunciated in the classroom.

THE PROFESSOR'S COLLEGE

Although teaching occurs at every point along the educational ladder, each institutional unit establishes a special cultural role for those doing the teaching. Professors are clearly identifiable as a special breed, both in their own perception of themselves, and in that of their students and the public.

The professor is seen as behaving in a manner rather different from people. He is entranced by remote and impractical concerns, like digging for ancient bones, editing obscure letters of obscure politicians, dissecting Shakespeare's sonnets for new meanings. These activities are pursued and defended with passion as right and proper pursuits for a professor. Others who are working on more obviously practical problems, such as how to find an effective poison for roaches, or a better method for hybridizing zinnias, or a way of mapping brain patterns of schizophrenics, are also apt to be single-minded in tilling their own particular fields.

This characteristic of the professor is probably the one which has the most effect on the kind of colleges and universities we have. It is clear to the professor that what he is studying, or teaching, is important and valuable. He does not always accord this valuation to the activities of his colleagues in other disciplines, although he is quite ready to let others live if they leave him alone.

In his own area of specialty, the professor becomes in all truth "the expert." If anyone knows, he knows. He knows enough to know how much more there is to know, and the limitations of his own knowledge.

The traditional areas of expertness in which the professor used to specialize tended to be those least useful in the ordinary pursuits of daily life. In decades prior to the New Deal, no one would have dreamed of asking a professor to help make political, economic, or "practical" decisions.

The expertness of today's professor, however, extends over the whole range of human activity. The result is that many a campus is split between those who pursue knowledge for its own sake, and those who pursue it because it will be useful. The applied and the practical have become fields of expertness and extra remuneration. The market-place professors are apt to be patronizing of or mildly amused by their other-worldly colleagues. The split in the campus personality between these two kinds of scholarship and professorial activity may result in bitter rivalries; budget for new staff, equipment, salaries and buildings may be at stake. With the business mind more apt to be represented on governing boards, as we shall see later, the university of today is more apt to favor the stainless steel tower than the ivory tower.

Although jealously interested in any special prerogatives gained by his colleagues, the professor, having carved out an area of scholarly interest, is apt to be phenomenally incurious about what happens to the students he teaches. Thus it is that the student culture noted previously can flourish in direct antithesis to the burden of the professor's instruction, and yet produce no more than mild dislike. Certainly the professor sees no call to relate classroom life to student life. If there is a separation between student and professor it is comforting to the professor that this is so. And indeed, how could the relationship be otherwise? The professor lectures to groups ranging in size from 50 to several thousands. He may face the nonaudience situation of the television lecture in which even the cues of bored or alerted students are missing. If he chaperones a fraternity dance, or appears at the dean's tea for new students, he may have no inkling whatsoever whether any of these students were or are in his classes unless they tell him so.[18] It is only with the few "major" students that a professor may have continuing contact, and even with them contact may be made only during the fleeting harried moments of registration. Professors who seek intimate contact with students flee the large universities, and in so doing typically give up involvement with their profession on a national basis for involvement wth their institution on a local basis. It is almost impossible to have it both ways.[19]

The actual arena of significant ambition for most professors is that provided by others in his own field. The historian seeks accolades more urgently from other historians than from his own college president. Psychologists write erudite articles for other psychologists, and have little interest in seeing that their findings are communicated to applied fields where they might be needed. Far better, in most areas, for the professor to be published in a journal of his own discipline, with, say, a circulation of 5,000, than to appear in the *National Education Association Journal* with a circulation of over 800,000.

Since only his peers can fully appreciate the delicacy required in carrying out some esoteric experiment, their plaudits ring sweetest. The net effect of this kind of closure to all but one's own reference groups has been to keep the world of discovery and intellect separate from the daily world of people. This is as true in our times as it has been for centuries. Though more students are going through college classrooms, more books are being read, and more symphonies attended, the world of many professors remains a cloister. Is it any wonder that there is little communication outward?

Another characteristic of the professor is his conviction that if he knows his subject, he can teach it. Few professors, after the sensitive first year or so of college teaching, are good listeners to their own lectures. Few are concerned with the methodology whereby they make their area of mystery known to 18-year-olds. Professors are notoriously uninterested in their own major activity—teaching—as a *process*. Professors of psychology

---

[18] Sanford, *op. cit.*, p. 354.
[19] Theodore Caplow and Reece J. McGee, *The Academic Marketplace* (New York: Basic Books, Inc., 1958), p. 85.

may give erudite lectures on the psychology of learning, on motivation, on levels of aspiration, on anxiety, yet see no implications for the way they teach. Most psychology courses violate every principle of learning the professors enunciate.

The standard teaching procedure is to have a 50-minute period, during which the instructor lectures. Students take notes silently. Sometimes there is time before the end of the "hour" when students may ask questions to clear up a point. Laboratory sessions supplement science lectures; other specialties may also have laboratory periods (speech, electronics, foreign language, surveying). Tests are given at mid-term, and there are two- or three-hour "finals" at the end of the semester.

As classes become more specialized, students may write papers, abstracting what their elders and betters have already said about something, and reorganizing it, with footnotes. Seminars, so-called because the professor is no longer lecturing, but acting as critic or moderator, are offered sometimes for seniors majoring in the subject and sometimes only for advanced graduate students. Here there are usually a few students who are beginning to approach some semblance of expertness in the field.

In recent years, and after much prodding, most universities and colleges have established some kind of "honors" program for bright, able, and highly motivated students. Interestingly enough, in describing the "image" of Swarthmore, where the honors program has had a very long history and is one of the aspects of the college that is typically pointed to with pride by interested parties, prospective students made little or no mention of the program as one of the college's most distinguishing features.[20] The honors programs, although designed to lift the intellectual lights of a few students, are also perceived to be a way of making one work considerably harder for the same end, namely a B.A. There does not appear to be great student clamor to participate in honors programs in many institutions. The separation of peer group from academic achievement, as noted previously, works against supporting honors programs, or any other *academically* based incentive. The peer group does not share in the program, and its interests are turned basically to other activities.

As in the high school, many of the large undergraduate courses, particularly those for the first two years, are dominated by a single text, or at most a text with related readings or a supplementary text. Only as the student progresses into his junior and senior year may he read widely, although again this may be in a selected list of books. The major intellectual activity for the college student as prescribed by his professor, other than laboratory work, is to read, sometimes to write, and once in a while to talk.

New devices, such as television and electronic grading machines, have had some impact on the classroom. The professor has found that it is much easier (and more efficient) to give 200 students an objective-type test which can be machine-scored, than it is to try to give the same number an essay examination. Just the thought of grading that many essay exams is enough to make the ambitious and dedicated professor

[20] Clark, "College Image" in *Selection and Educational Differentiation*, p. 162.

quail. With the increased size of colleges, more and more students are enrolled in large classes, thus feeding more students to the machine.

Between the professor and most of his undergraduate students there exists an anomalous creature known as a "graduate assistant." In smaller institutions these may actually have the rank of instructor. The professor gives the lecture, and the assistant or assisting instructor makes up the tests, grades the papers, listens to student complaints, proctors exams, and leads the discussion sections if there are any. It is conceivable that a student could go through four years on some campuses and never talk directly with any of his course professors, dealing and being dealt with only by the intermediate personnel.

Such assistants and junior instructors are apprentices, and their role is to learn how to become professors. There are few chances for such beginners to learn how to be better than their elders, except by accident. The prospective college teacher learns that the more like those above him on the ladder he is, the more likely are his chances to make his own gradual and necessary ascent.

The status system of the college or university is carefully structured by rank: instructor, assistant professor, associate professor, and full professor. Junior colleges and some deviant institutions such as St. John's and Sarah Lawrence do not have such ranks, but award salary on the basis of tenure. The typical pattern is for the faculty member, having acquired a doctorate in his subject field while working as a graduate or research assistant, to start as an instructor or assistant professor. Having dutifully served three to seven years at this rank he is either moved up or moved out. As an associate professor he has tenure, that is, a continuing contract, unless he is severely derelict in his duties. After quite a few years the average faculty member may eventually be promoted to full professor. Some persons never make it before retiring, due perhaps to lack of openings at the top (where the salary is sufficiently high that in order to balance budgets the number of positions must be limited), or to lack of appropriate productivity, or to incurring the hostility of those in power.

The promotions procedure varies from campus to campus, but is often a shared responsibility. That is, although the final approval of a promotion may rest with a dean or president, faculty committees make the initial recommendations. Such committees must be staffed by those who do not seek promotions for themselves: full professors. Those of lesser rank have their jobs cut out for them: to impress these senior staff members so that when the time comes, they will support one for the appropriate promotion. As can be seen, this procedure lends itself readily to the manipulations of politicians. Faculty members with wives who play on the "bridge circuit" (though not well enough to win too many times against the wife of a full professor) may do better on promotions than a faculty member not so fortunately endowed. The deviant, the odd-ball, the anti-social, either has to find the right campus and the right department, or retire and write his novel of professorial life. The promotions system rewards competence, scholarship, and the *right amount* of eccentricity. But even among intellectuals, to be too different is to be suspect.

Promotions for those who are striving and who behave are based in most schools on one criterion. Except in the small liberal arts colleges and in some state colleges and junior colleges that are avowedly only teaching colleges, almost all promotions are based on one's "contribution." [21] This can most clearly be seen in terms of publications; therefore, all prospective professors must publish something, somehow, sooner or later. The pressure to publish is so great that, as in the case of psychologists, professors personally pay journals for "extra pages" so that their articles, accepted for publication perhaps 12 to 18 months later, may appear at an earlier date. The proliferation of scholarly journals is made necessary not only because of the mass of research and thinking going on, but because publication in a journal is a necessary condition for the individual to get ahead. The relative obscurity and questionable value of much that is published is thus quite explainable. That it is also unnecessary to the advancement of knowledge is beside the point.

Books are as useful as articles in some disciplines, although a college text is rated below a research monograph. Obtaining government or foundation research grants is very helpful as are short term overseas assignments or Fulbright's. Obtaining such grants or awards takes special skill. For instance, it is better to apply for a Fulbright in a relatively unpopular area —such as Pakistan—where language is no problem (no one knows Pakistani anyway) than for the popular places such as London and Paris. It is getting overseas that counts, no matter *where*. It is important not to stay overseas very long, however. Two years is about the outside limit. Otherwise the promotions committee may forget one's existence.

Participation in professional organizations is useful, too, not only to further the interests of one's own field, but to further one's own interests. It is highly important to attend national conferences. One can find out what positions might be open which pay more or have increments of status beyond one's own. Also, if one is an advisor of a stable of doctoral students it is highly useful to place them in good locations. Some of the major national conferences appear more like a slave market [22] than a scholarly gathering. Invitations to read papers at such meetings are prized; such a platform brings one to the attention of one's peers who in turn may make one an offer at another institution. This can often be used neatly back home in obtaining a raise or promotion or both.

The teaching the professor does is always stated as his most important function, and his contribution to his discipline as secondary. In practice the two are reversed, and in some notable instances a very inferior teacher may move rapidly up the academic ladder because he is a productive researcher, a fluent writer, impressive to his peers as a scholar in the field, or because he or his wife has "connections." That thousands of students may therefore suffer at his hands in academically stultifying or intellectually empty situations is only regrettable.

What the professor does in the classroom is far less important to his career than what he does outside it. These outside activities, however, must

[21] Caplow and McGee, *The Academic Marketplace*, p. 82.
[22] Caplow and McGee, p. 116.

be within his discipline. The professor who chooses to be "popular," to go on the club lecture circuit, or to write trade books for general circulation, may be considered not quite solid. The professor who goes to Washington to take part in the actual functionings of government instead of trying for a research grant at home may likewise find himself somewhat under a cloud. Such activities, we must hasten to add, are forgivable if one has already attained his majority—his full professorship—but may be a handicap to one still climbing.

Problems of academic freedom are of great concern to the professor, although why this should be is somewhat hard to tell since actually few professors are engaged in anything which would cause anyone to make protests. The remarkable thing is not that academic freedom is invaded but that so few professors provide a target for those who would limit freedom. It is better to be safe in any ivory tower than out of work in the market place.

Characteristic of professors is a profound distaste for and distrust of all administrators. These persons understand budgets and personnel problems having to do with lesser persons, like clerks and secretaries. Disdaining to participate in administration, although nearly all college administrators of rank have themselves been professors or college teachers, most professors have unwittingly rejected other major functions also. Who determines course requirements? Who enforces them? When and how can a course or program be changed? What shall be the policy regarding student failure? When is a course "good enough" for seniors or easy enough for freshmen? These and thousands of other decisions regarding the intellectual fare of the college must be made. The average faculty member may fret and fume when his own pet area is mangled by an administrative decision, but he is silent, apathetic and usually uninformed regarding other decisions that affect the student's intellectual life. It is not that administrators do not establish machinery whereby faculty may, in most instances, participate in such decisions. It is just that the job is too vast, and it means working at it full time. And only administrators have full time to work on such matters. While faculty may advise and review, rarely are they the effective channels whereby major changes occur.

College faculties are a favorite of novel writers. The picture that is painted may be bleak, focusing on intrigue, gossip, petty personalities and strangling provincialism. Yet the accuracy of the over-all picture cannot be completely denied. Every college and university has its areas which correspond only too well to the novelists' pictures. Yet they also have their areas which correspond to the ideal held by the distant public and the wide-eyed freshman. Here are persons of spirit, energy, indignation, and inspiration. It is fortunate that so many professors of this kind survive, since the institution and its arrangements do not make it necessary, and, in many instances, make it very difficult indeed. It is also noteworthy that almost every professor has each year a coterie of students who are devoted, interested, and affected by what he is and what he professes. Yet thousands of students spend four years on a campus and never have this experience. One cannot wholly blame the professors.

College administration offers something of a paradox. The presidents of great colleges and universities are supposed to be scholars, and most of them have been, but the task of the administrator does not depend on those qualities and skills which make for the brilliant scholar. College presidents may be selected for their broad erudition and genuine scholarship, but they must be backed up by a full field of administrators, who survive from administration to administration much as civil servants survive the periodic upheavals in Washington. The major difference is that, unlike the President of the United States, a college president is appointed until he retires or finds a better job, so there is no guarantee that a mediocre president can be voted out (or removed) from office.

The college or university is organized into separate departments, schools or colleges. Administrative responsibility for these subdivisions is delegated to various individuals. In the case of a department, this person may be known as the department head or department chairman. A school, such as a school of dentistry or a school of engineering, will have a dean. So will a college. In addition to departments or other administrative units, most lively colleges and universities have various institutes. These are usually semi-autonomous groups of research specialists who have rank on the faculty of the university, but whose main work is supported not by university funds but by special research grants or consulting fees. Professors gravitate towards these bodies like bears towards honey; there they are seldom bothered by routine teaching assignments, can work on research of their own devising, more or less, and can evade the onerous burden of faculty committee work. The purpose of university administrative units is to establish a smaller faculty group for the purpose of making decisions about the area of instruction. The faculty meet with the department head or dean and decide which courses are to be dropped, which added, what changes in requirements or sequences are to be made, and other such vital matters. Since many faculty groups are too large to make these decisions as a group, committees are appointed. There are many such matters to be decided, so every department or school worth its salt has literally dozens of committees which must meet and deliberate.

Despite their scorn for administrators, professors cling tenaciously to their committee prerogatives. Although incredibly time-consuming, faculty groups do not willingly give up any power which they think they can exercise through committees.

That this power is more apparent than real is, however, a well kept administrative secret. Actually, no one really governs a college or university. The president, although given high status and impressive offices, and often a mansion, car, and household staff as well, cannot in actuality tell his faculty very much. A good proportion of them are usually on tenure: associate or full professors. In a successful college or university these individuals may have national reputations in their fields, and by the time such eminence has been reached they are afraid of no one, college presidents

121

included. Although they may keep silent on the great moral and social issues of the day, having less than a burning interest in them, such professors may well flex their muscles if any administrator dares intervene in the affairs of the department in any but the most tangential fashion.

But the president does not need to worry. The bureaucracy which is so readily spawned when any group of persons tries to organize to get a job done is very apparent in the college or university. It is the miles of red tape, of forms and regulations, of transcripts and class reports, that effectively enmesh college personnel. So much time and energy may be devoted to unsnarling one piece of red tape, that another one becomes snarled in the meantime, and the whole thing goes back to committee.

Divided as the governing of the university may be, a part of the essential weakness is that the power of university administration is in the hands of amateurs. Neither presidents nor professors are trained in administration. Despite this, so distrustful are academic persons of the bureaucratic mind, that most colleges and universities appear to prefer the chaos of amateurism to the efficiency of the expert. There is a theory, not tested, that the goals achieved by efficiency may be contrary to the goals sought by an intellectual community.

It is possible that inefficiency in university administration should be protected and prized. The research engineer is apt to be far happier with the freedom from surveillance and the opportunity to pursue his own goals in the university, even if he must work on a pittance, than with the luxurious support provided in the mass electronics industry where he works on what he is told to work on.[23] As Clark states it: "The loose, meandering, overlapping structure of authority we often find in colleges may be there because it is in the service of rationality rather than of madness." [24]

The president of the institution must apply his own charm and wiles to govern others' inertia, although the institution is too large for close supervision. Most faculty members, concerned with their own college, department, or school rather than with the institution as a whole, leave over-all decisions to the president. But even if he sees his mission as serving the total institution, he is not free to act without reporting to, and taking directions from, a board of regents or trustees.

As was noted in discussing the government of the public school system, higher education is also effectively directed by lay persons. The public school board is typically elected by the people. A board of regents for a college or university is appointed, or is self-perpetuating. In the case of public colleges and universities, the governing boards are usually appointed by the governor, the legislature, or the state board of education, which is itself appointed by the governor. Private institutions usually replace members by vote of the board itself, thus keeping control within a group of like-minded persons.

The public at large knows little about such boards, and is unable to

---

[23] Jules Henry, *Culture Against Man* (New York: Random House, 1963), Chap. i.
[24] Burton Clark, *Educating the Expert Society* (San Francisco: Chandler Publishing Co., 1962), p. 162.

influence their deliberations since it has no hand in selecting those who are to serve. The average citizen would have no chance to serve on such a board even if he were interested. The persons selected for this service are almost all from the worlds of business, commerce, and the professions. They are persons of power in the state or community, and usually of independent wealth. Serving on these boards takes time, and pays nothing.

Board members find a business background very useful, since one of their major functions is directing the investment of endowment funds. Most private colleges are financed in part by income from endowment, and this income consists of returns on investments. A corporation president will understand the problem of investment far better than an educator. A university is big business and auditors must be kept happy. If public funds are involved, cost accounting is elevated to a major role. The board of regents approves the budget, which gives the board the power to implement the educational policy which it favors.

The traditional composition of boards reflects an interesting American distrust of the educator. Faculty members are rarely represented on the boards which determine their fates, and students never.[25] In a few instances an alumni representative is elected or appointed.

Communication between faculty and board is practically nonexistent. Information on faculty needs is channeled to the board via deans and presidents.

The net effect of these provisions is to make the college or university basically a conservative institution. The nature of alumni is to resist change, and this is true of boards and regents. Faculty members exercise little power, and the president, despite his title, has few means other than the influence of his own personality to make his leadership felt throughout the institution.

Thus the college or university, despite the concentration of the educated intellect of the community in one small area, performs its functions today in even less effective fashion, and with many more students, than ever before. Perhaps this is the way the American public wants it.

THE PEOPLE'S COLLEGE

If colleges change little, and if there is no great outcry against them for failures in the public sector, the public has only itself to blame. As has been noted, the picture of the college professor conveyed to the public via popular literature is not a particularly attractive one. No one really envies these men of knowledge since in gaining their expertness they have lost their threat as men.[26] One can afford to let the professor spout, within limits, because no one has to take him seriously.

While scorning the educators, the public has a mystical faith in the process of higher education. In the minds of the public, anyone who wants to and tries hard enough should be allowed to go to college. Statistics on

[25] Walter P. Metzger, *Academic Freedom in the Age of the University* (New York: Columbia University Press, 1955), pp. 141ff. and 182ff.

[26] Edward Albee, *Who's Afraid of Virginia Woolf?* (New York: Atheneum Publishers, 1962).

who does go to college show that the most significant single factor is income. It appears that high income is invariably associated with college aptitude; almost 100 per cent of those whose fathers have upper-middle-class incomes and above manage to attend college.

This folk belief that anyone can succeed in college if he can get there is attested to by an advertisement of a local bank. Anyone who came to the bank could fill out a card for a drawing. The lucky winner would get a college scholarship.

The belief in the efficacy of a college education is maintained as long as the students are peaceable, the faculty are quiet, and the football team wins. Even the usual spring riots on campus are associated with nothing more harmful than exuberant good spirits and warm weather, and are viewed with only moderate disapproval. However, if students become seriously involved in current happenings—participate in sit-ins, picket for peace, demonstrate against or for something controversial, invite Communists to speak on campus—then the public becomes indignant and calls for investigations. If a professor speaks out loudly enough to make the headlines, challenging a locally held conviction, there may be public cries for his head.

This view of the role of the college or university helps to keep the academic world from having an effective influence on the world of everyday people and everyday decisions. It keeps the campus itself a relatively harmless place for most students to be. Between the time they enter and the time they leave they are merely four years older.

And this is the way the public wants it. Not for Americans the college as a seed-bed of revolution, as is true in South America and the Middle East. Higher education is so safe one can even trust one's daughter to it.

With higher education becoming more and more available for more and more students, there has been an inevitable growth of public awareness. When only a few individuals were affected by college programs, no one cared very much if ideas were somewhat radical or deviant. Although the fight for academic freedom in America has always been waged against intransigent conservatives holding firmly to parochial beliefs and insisting that all conform, the achievement of today's *relatively* free academic atmosphere appears to be the result of the colleges' having less and less to say that is important. The bland educator and the equally bland educated appear to have adjusted to this intellectual wasteland.

But there is evidence of discomfort regarding this kind of empty education. Whether or not change can be achieved by deliberate planning remains to be seen. Paul Goodman describes the power of teaching of the medieval university. He goes on to say:

> This spontaneous quest by the anarchic early community of scholars to understand their culture and take responsibility for changing it should be ours as well. Our children not only grow up in a civilization immeasurably more confused and various than any before, but they are now prevented from undertaking the quest itself by foolish rules, meaningless tasks, and an absence of responsible veterans to guide them. We must restore to them the chance to discover their culture and make it their own. And if

we cannot do this within the universities, it would be good for the universities themselves if we tried to do it from without.[27]

[27] Paul Goodman, "For a Reactionary Experiment in Education," *Harper's Magazine*, 225, No. 1350 (November 1962), pp. 61-72.

BIBLIOGRAPHY

ANDERSON, KENNETH E., ed., *The Coming Crisis in the Selection of Students for College Entrance*. Washington, D.C.: American Education Research Association, 1960. Seven authorities point out current problems and dilemmas in college admission policies.

BOROFF, DAVID, *Campus USA*. New York: Harper & Row, Publishers, 1961. Lively journalistic portraits of a variety of American colleges and universities.

————, "St. John's College: Four Years with the Great Books," *Saturday Review* (March 23, 1963), p. 61.

CARMICHAEL, OLIVER C., *Graduate Education*. New York: Harper & Row, Publishers, 1962. Graduate programs come in for some critical appraisal.

CLARK, BURTON R., *The Open Door College*. New York: McGraw-Hill Book Company, 1960. A case study of a public junior college with liberal admissions policies and no tuition.

CORSON, JOHN J., *Governance of Colleges and Universities*. New York: McGraw-Hill Book Company, 1961. Astute dissection of the internal workings of the university.

DeHUSZAR, GEORGE B., ed., *The Intellectuals*. New York: Free Press of Glencoe, Inc., 1960. A collection of comments, from a wide range of sources, on the intellectual life and those who practice it. Controversial.

EVANS, M. STANTON, *Revolt on the Campus*. Chicago: Henry Regnery Co., 1961. Describes the conservative movement that has taken place during the late 50's and early 60's among college students.

GOODMAN, PAUL, *The Community of Scholars*. New York: Random House, 1962. A radical educator dissects the university of today and proposes his unique solution.

HOFSTADTER, RICHARD, *Anti-intellectualism in American Life*. New York: Alfred A. Knopf, Inc., 1963. Traces the development of American attitudes toward intellectualism from early days to the present, with a critical assessment of the contemporary scene.

KINKEAD, KATHERINE T., *How an Ivy League College Decides on Admissions*. New York: W. W. Norton & Company, Inc., 1961. Fascinating report by a journalist regarding the workings of admissions programs today.

LAZARSFELD, PAUL F. AND WAGNER THIELENS, JR., *The Academic Mind*. New York: Free Press of Glencoe, Inc., 1958. A field study of a sample of colleges and college faculty members and their responses to attacks on academic freedom.

MECHANIC, DAVID, *Students under Stress*. New York: Free Press of Glencoe, Inc., 1962. Research study of a group of students preparing for and taking doctoral exams. Do not read it if you have any interest in doing graduate work.

MILLER, DELBERT C., "Town and Gown: The Power Structure of a University Town," *The American Journal of Sociology*, LXVIII, No. 4 (January 1963).

MUSHKIN, SELMA J., *Economics of Higher Education*, Bulletin No. 5. Washington, D.C.: United States Office of Education, 1962. Extensive treatment of all aspects of higher education as it affects the individual, institutional, and national economic interests.

ORLANS, H., *The Effects of Federal Programs on Higher Education*. Washington, D.C.: The Brookings Institute, 1962. Federal money has had a marked impact on what universities and faculties are doing today.

RIESMAN, DAVID, *Constraint and Variety in American Education*. Garden City, N. Y.: Doubleday & Company, Inc., 1958. Perceptive essays on the sociology of intellectual life with particular attention to higher education.

SELDEN, WILLIAM K., *Accreditation: A Struggle over Standards in Higher Education*. New York: Harper & Row, Publishers, 1961. A little-known aspect of the forces leading toward common programs in higher education.

VEBLEN, THORSTEIN, *The Higher Learning in America*. New York: Sagamore Press, Inc., 1957. Originally published in 1918, this criticism sounds remarkably pertinent today.

WAKIN, EDWARD, *The Catholic Campus*. New York: The Macmillan Company, 1963. A sympathetic report, once over lightly, of eight different Catholic institutions.

WEDGE, BRYANT M., ed., *Psychosocial Problems of College Men*. New Haven: Yale University Press, 1958. How students adjust or fail to adjust to college demands, and how they are helped.

The actual school experience of children is in the hands of teachers. Whatever kind of schooling takes place is that which goes on under the direction of a teacher.

For a great number of children and youth the significant adults outside the family will, for many years, be their teachers.

In this chapter and the next, we will attempt to review some of the major issues and confusions which surround the teacher, the teaching art, and the production and evaluation of teachers.[1]

THERE ARE ALL KINDS OF TEACHERS

During the course of his educational career, a student may be instructed by at least 30 teachers, and may know many more. Including college instruction, the individual may well have shared classrooms with 100 persons who were considered teachers.

To the nursery-school child the teacher is not even a person:

[1] For more extended discussion see: Willard Waller, *The Sociology of Teaching* (New York: John Wiley & Sons, Inc., 1932); Lindley Stiles, ed., *The Teacher's Role in American Society* (New York: Harper & Row, Publishers, 1957); Jacques Barzun, *Teacher in America* (Boston: Little, Brown & Co., 1947).

THE TEACHERS: PART I

11

The children were entering the elevator—girls first, then boys—a game started previously. One boy turned and said, "Teacher is a girl and should enter."

"No, a teacher is not a boy or girl," said Harry. "She's just a teacher."[2]

Slowly the picture of the teacher clarifies, and also changes. In the elementary grades, children perceive the teacher as a substitute parent, many even calling out "Mother" in moments of extreme excitement. In junior and later in senior high school the teacher is seen more clearly as a person with some special subject matter or skill competency. In college, the professor figure emerges as a person quite distinct from a "teacher" but still one who does perform a teaching function.

The vast proliferation of specialties in all professions has also occurred in education. There are teachers of the blind, the deaf, the spastic, the severely mentally retarded, the institutionalized, the delinquent, the adult illiterate, the foreign-born.

The schools provide many specialized personnel to supplement the teacher: counselors, nurses, librarians, audio-visual specialists, social workers, school psychologists, research and testing specialists, school building and maintenance personnel, public relations specialists, curriculum specialists, and all kinds of supervisors.

THE SCHOOLTEACHER'S MANY TASKS

Just as there are many people who teach all kinds of things to all kinds of peoples in almost any conceivable setting (there is a school for croupiers in Las Vegas we understand), so also is the task of the teacher many faceted.

The teacher:

Judges achievement
Conveys knowledge
Keeps discipline
Gives advice, receives confidences
Establishes a moral atmosphere
Is a member of an institution
Is a model for the young
Participates in community affairs
Is a public servant
Is a member of a profession
Keeps records.[3]

[2] Kenneth Wann, Mirian S. Dorn, and Elizabeth A. Liddle, *Fostering Intellectual Development in Young Children* (New York: Bureau of Publications, Teachers College, Columbia University, 1962), p. 77.

[3] Jean D. Grambs, "The Roles of the Teacher," in *The Teacher's Role in American Society*, ed. Lindley Stiles (New York: Harper & Row, Publishers, 1957), pp. 73-93. See also, Donald P. Cottrell, "Do We Need to Revise Our Concept of the Teacher?" *Rhode Island College Journal*, I, No. 3 (December 1960), 85-94.

It is the claim of critics of modern education that no one person can perform all of these functions and perform them with any measure of skill. It is, in fact, ridiculous to expect this of teachers. Partly in answer to this sad state of affairs, and certainly beginning before the critics found out about it, specialized personnel have been provided to take over some of the teacher's tasks. Counselors provide more expert counsel and advice; clerks do some of the record keeping, and so forth. Despite this, most teachers are still expected to perform most of these tasks.

The relative importance of a teacher's tasks differs with the individual student. For some, the most important thing a teacher can do is to receive a confidence, and respect it. Another student may respond only to a teacher who is erudite about outer galaxies. A team needs a coach who can inspire it to victory.

A newly documented truth, however, is that not all teachers are equally good at all things. A contribution of the research and experimentation conducted under the leadership of Lloyd Trump has been to emphasize the fact that some teachers do some tasks better than others.[4] Some teachers are especially good at organizing a bit of knowledge in an interesting, exciting, and understandable fashion. Others are better at working with small groups. Others are able to guide the creative interests of individuals on a one-to-one basis. Some secondary schools have begun to try out the notion that teachers are not equally capable; they are not the interchangeable spokes of a single wheel.[5]

The idea of the elementary teacher as the teacher of all subjects to all students for one year has recently been drastically challenged. The controversy is a hot one, and the fight has just begun. The issue is whether one teacher in a self-contained classroom should teach almost all the elementary subjects to a group of pupils who remain with her all day, or whether specialist teachers of various subjects, as in the secondary school, should be responsible for seperate subject instruction.[6]

Despite the claims of proponents of each approach to better organize teachers and use their talents, research is lacking to give either side comfort. In any event, it is apparent that we know relatively little about what good teachers do, or what results in most effective learning for most children. The one point of agreement is that it is impossible for today's elementary teacher to be, as one author noted, a modern "Encyclopedist." [7] A way out of this dilemma has not as yet been found to satisfy all.

It is now clear that there is an almost infinite variety of teachers, doing a great many different things all the time. There is a sneaking feeling, however, that despite the complexity of the situation, we ought to be able to find out what most teachers do most of the time.

Recent research reports what teachers are doing: by and large teachers

[4] Trump and Baynham, *Guide to Better Schools.*

[5] *Locus of Change: Staff Utilization Studies* (Washington, D.C.: The National Association of Secondary-School Principals, 1962), pp. 1-321.

[6] *The Self-Contained Classroom* (Washington, D.C.: Association for Supervision and Curriculum Development, 1960); George Stoddard, *The Dual Progress Plan* (New York: Harper & Row, Publishers, 1962).

[7] Johns S. Diekhoff, "The Last Encyclopedists," *Saturday Review*, XLV (September 15, 1962), 62-63.

are running the classroom. They do most of the talking, they establish control and keep it, and in many instances, although presumably they are teaching, little content is actually conveyed.[8]

The researchers are attempting to find out what it is that good teachers do, and teachers would like to know, also. The individual teacher may often feel pulled in contradictory directions. It is difficult to receive a student's confidence and at the same time be an objective judge of his behavior. It is a searing experience to empathize with a slow learner who is tearing his heart out just to learn the alphabet, and then have to fail him for the year. Yet these are the daily pressures on teachers.[9]

These multiple demands made on teachers have been viewed with alarm and pity but rarely with research tools. Jersild's study of teachers' responses to job demands is worth reading, particularly by those not planning to become teachers. It may discourage those so bound.[10] Jersild documents the multiple anxieties of the teacher. He does not, however, highlight the other face of anxiety, which is guilt.

The teacher's task, no matter how well done, is never completed; there is always the child not reached, the lesson this side of perfection, the word that should have been said and was not. Every aware teacher goes home daily with a sense of a task never finished, never perfect. Unlike the engineer, the surgeon, the poet, or the auto mechanic, the teacher can never stand off and view his job, and say, "That's a good job done." Compounding the guilt, of course, is the fact that the teacher never can see his finished product. And even if a student does achieve eminence, which of his many teachers deserves the credit, if any?

These are ghosts that stalk the teacher's days. Dealing with them requires resilience or immunity.

There have been many attempts to find out what methods of teaching may be most efficient. But for almost every experiment or research study proving one method to be better than another, there is another study that either shows there is no difference, or that the reverse is true.[11]

We actually know very little about what takes place in the classrooms of our country. Not only that, we know even less about how any given classroom activity or situation affects different individuals in the short *or* long run. It is no wonder that so much discussion about teaching and what teachers ought to do or be rests on wishful thinking or nostalgia,

[8] Marie M. Hughes, *Development of Means for Assessing the Quality of Teaching in Elementary Schools*, Cooperative Research Program, Project No. 353 (Washington, D.C.: U. S. Office of Education, 1959); David G. Ryans, *Characteristics of Teachers* (Washington, D.C.: American Council on Education, 1960); Ned A. Flanders, *Teacher Influence, Pupil Attitudes, and Achievement* (Minneapolis: University of Minnesota, 1960). (Mimeographed.)

[9] Grambs, "The Roles of the Teacher," in *The Teacher's Role*, ed. Stiles, pp. 73-93; J. W. Getzels and E. G. Guba, "The Structure of Roles and Role Conflict in the Teaching Situation," *Journal of Educational Sociology*, XXIX, No. 1 (September 1955), 30-40.

[10] Arthur T. Jersild, *When Teachers Face Themselves* (New York: Bureau of Publications, Teachers College, Columbia University, 1955).

[11] Donald T. Campbell and Julian C. Stanley, "Experimental and Quasi-Experimental Designs for Research on Teaching," in *Handbook of Research on Teaching*, ed. Gage, pp. 174-214.

and unconscious needs and wants. But whatever the teacher does, and whoever he is, he has a special relationship with his students because of two central factors: (1) students have to come to school to be taught; and (2) education is a necessary road for most people towards the good things in modern life. For those who fall by the wayside the world has little comfort or room. The teacher then, is an extremely important person.

THE TEACHER AS A POWER FIGURE

The teacher can promote or fail. He can reward or humiliate. He can encourage or ignore. He can help meanings become clear or he can irrevocably muddy the waters. No matter what else the teacher is or what the teacher does, he is a person of power.[12]

He is a gatekeeper to the world. All students are reminded of this fact by all teachers; and most parents, particularly those with ambitions for their children, are well aware of this. High grades may mean Harvard; low grades may mean ditch digging. The assessment of the student by the teacher may be unfair, biased, influenced unduly by nonacademic factors, but it goes on the transcript. This is power.

Power is derived from authority, and the authority of the teacher is very real. Legally he has rights which transcend those of children, whose only legal protection is against undue violence or subversion. The teacher acts *in loco parentis*. Actual physical punishment has been outlawed in most school districts by custom or by legislation, but the teacher has so much power anyway he usually does not need the strap.

Because of the way in which tenure laws are interpreted, the child is not even protected from ordinary incompetence. If this incompetence results in the child's not learning to read, being unable to do basic arithmetic, or even his dropping out of school, there is no recourse for the child or his parent. How can one *prove* that it was this or that teacher's incompetence that resulted in a student's failure in school or later in life? Thus the teacher's position is virtually impregnable to ordinary attacks for ordinary and even extreme lapses in competence. Occupying positions of such apparent invulnerability lends teachers the *appearance* of power, if not the internal satisfaction of enjoying power.

The power the teacher has over the student derives, also, from the fact that the student *has* to come to school. He does not choose his teachers; nor in most instances the subjects he will learn. He cannot say anything about the *way* he will learn either. These all depend on the teacher. If the teacher chooses the appropriate content and the effective method for teaching this child, then he may learn. If the teacher errs, then it is possible that the child will learn little or not at all. In any event the power to make such crucial decisions is the teacher's. Despite the surrounding bureaucracy, the teacher in actuality makes most of these decisions alone. He is alone in his classroom—with 30 subordinate and immature persons.

[12] David Jenkins and Ronald Lippitt, *Interpersonal Perceptions of Teachers, Students and Parents* (Washington, D.C.: National Education Association, Division of Adult Education Service, 1951), p. 79ff.

No matter what directives the superintendent has issued, what curriculum guides have been planned and published, what policy statements have been enunciated by the School Board, it is the teacher alone, behind the closed door of his classroom, who can exploit what is best with inspiration and talent, or subvert even the best with dullness or anger.

The teacher's power does not end with these basic ingredients: it is he who determines the nature of classroom relationships. If he can maintain order easily, with good humor, and can respond in proper fashion to student behavior or misbehavior, then learning can proceed. If his keeping order depends on sarcasm, temper, or seduction, then learning is distorted. It is not possible for the student to do anything about this. The atmosphere in the classroom is established by the teacher.

Students and parents may not agree with the valuations of the teacher, may reject his concept of good or bad behavior, may in fact differ on almost any subject, but the teacher is the final authority. He determines the grade that is recorded in the book. The teacher has many roles to play in the classroom, but in each one of them he wears this halo of authority and power.

There is a familiar adage that states, "Knowledge is power." The teacher, for at least half the student's school career, knows more than the students about the things he is teaching. He knows more subject matter, he knows more about how people learn, he knows more about the community, and he knows more about the lives of his students than they do about his. Such knowledge invests its possessors with power.[13]

Margaret Mead has identified one source of the hostility of parents toward teachers as an aspect of the "second generation" problem of American children. Because the culture changes so swiftly, most children today are in the same position as the children of immigrants; they inhabit a world which is strange and new to their parents, who do not even seem to speak the same language.[14]

The teacher operates within a peculiarly American tradition regarding the relationship of adults to children. As Borrowman has stated it:

> The dominant tradition might . . . be characterized as one of continuous tension between an explicit ideal of child submissiveness and implicit delight in the child's assertions of independence from adult authority.[15]

Thus parents enjoin their children to obey the teacher, to do as they are told, and at the same time show pride in the occasional "wild oats" or acts

[13] Kenneth Benne, A Conception of Authority (New York: Bureau of Publications, Teachers College, Columbia University, 1943), pp. 34-48, 70-113.

[14] Margaret Mead, And Keep Your Powder Dry (New York: William Morrow & Co. Inc., 1942), pp. 96-97.

[15] Merle L. Borrowman, "Traditional Values and the Shaping of American Education," in Nelson B. Henry, ed., Social Forces Influencing American Education, The Sixtieth Yearbook of the National Society for the Study of Education, Part II (Chicago: The University of Chicago Press, 1961), p. 145; see also Don Dinkmeyer and Rudolf Dreikurs, Encouraging Children to Learn: The Encouragement Process (Englewood Cliffs, N. J.: Prentice-Hall, Inc., 1963), pp. 117-19.

of safe defiance of such authority which shows that children have *spirit*. Those parents who feel particular insecurity in themselves or their world will be uneasy about classrooms where "the mantle of authority is lightly worn by adults." [16]

The power of knowledge may be perceived by parents as a threat rather than as an aid. Sure it is good for children to move out into a better world than the parents, except that they step on their parents on the way up and out. The facilitators of this process, teachers, are therefore in an ambiguous position.

A facetious discussion of the ultimate that may be attained in teaching machines by 1970 points out some of the reasons why they may be preferred by some students over some teachers:

> The machine gives a grade and the reasons for the grade . . . The machine is completely objective and consistent. This is a tremendous benefit—the elimination of argument. . . . It's absolutely no fun arguing with a machine.
>
> Furthermore, the machine gets along well with students. It is not in the least influenced by moods, illness, overwork, harassment by the principal, or financial worries. The machine does just as good a job no matter how late it was out the night before. The machine can do the same thing over and over without getting bored; therefore it never conveys any poisonous boredom to its students. Finally, in the thirty-five years the machine has been in widespread use we have never yet encountered a case in which the student is smarter than the machine; this has eliminated a lot of hostility on both sides.[17]

If teachers are worried that they will be replaced by machines, they might well ponder the above quotation.

The teacher as a power figure must, therefore, be dealt with by students and the public. There are several ways in which this can be accomplished. One method is to change the ways in which teachers utilize their power. Another is to reduce the concept of the teacher, and thus the person as a teacher, to manageable size.

The first line of attack, to reorganize the situation in which the teacher functions, is essentially the task of professional teacher education (which we shall discuss in another context later in the next chapter). Relevant here, however, is the major stress in such education on providing teachers with empathy for the students they are teaching. That is, when teachers see students as persons with significant and valuable human differences and needs, then the teacher must relate his behavior to these demanding realities. If punishment is to be administered it must be for the right reasons and for the right ends.

Teachers today are being provided increasingly insightful training in understanding what children are all about [18] but there is still abundant

[16] Borrowman, *ibid*.
[17] Hallett D. Smith, "How to Inspire a Teaching Machine," *The Key Reporter*, XXVIII, No. 1 (Autumn 1962), 2.
[18] Daniel A. Prescott, *The Child in the Educative Process* (New York: McGraw-Hill Book Company, 1957).

133

evidence that the findings of psychology are resisted by educators.[19] It is also true that the findings of psychology do not always provide a clear directive on which to act.[20]

Despite the great amount of study and research on motivation, learning and the behavior disorders, teachers still insist, in the main, on treating children the way teachers over the centuries have treated them: as immature persons to be driven or cajoled toward civilization, which means toward accepting the dictates of authority.

The second method of reorienting the authority of the teacher has been through the stress on "democratic classrooms." This concept infuriates the noneducator as much as it confuses the educator. Using the terminology of the political scientist conveys to the naive the idea that a democratic classroom is one in which students can vote on anything they want, even voting not to learn. It has been inferred too, that the teacher's authority is no more than that of an elected official who can, of course, be vetoed by an electorate who may vote him out of office. These concepts could hardly be more inappropriate, although it is understandable that the term itself leads readily to such conclusions. The hypotheses on which the idea of democratic classroom procedures is based are: (1) making decisions in a democracy is learned behavior; (2) this kind of learning can and should take place in a classroom; (3) if democratic behavior is not learned in the classroom there is no guarantee it will be learned anywhere else; (4) a democratic classroom requires a somewhat different definition of the relative roles of teacher and pupil.

It is at the last point that confusion and divergence occur. It is not that the democratic teacher is any less an authority but that it is recognized that students, too, have some authority. Students are able, for instance, to tell when they are confused; no one else can judge accurately. They can exercise authority by refusing to learn, as many do. The democratic teacher is one who clarifies his role as an adult authority, and also is clear about the role of the authority of the individual and the group. Since the teacher is always older (or at least knows more) than the students, his authority as one who knows *some kinds of things* is always fairly clear. But it is equally clear that there are other things he does not know. As has been stated, ". . . in a democratic society, expert authority can be derived from the democratic ideal," [21] but the ways in which a democratic expert behaves which distinguish him from a nondemocratic expert have not been clearly enough described to provide a model for the teacher to follow. Thus the concept of the teacher as a "democratic" leader has been difficult to rescue from the sentimentalists who wish to be "nice" to students, the

[19] Harry Beilin, "Teachers' and Clinicians' Attitudes toward the Behavior Problems of Children: A Reappraisal," *Child Development*, XXX (1959), 9-25; Roger Barker, "Difficulties of Communication between Educators and Psychologists—Some Speculations," *Journal of Educational Psychology*, XXXIII (September 1942), 416-26.

[20] Goodwin Watson, *What Psychology Can We Trust?* (New York: Bureau of Publications, Teachers College, Columbia University, 1961).

[21] B. Othanal Smith, William O. Stanley, and J. Harlan Shores, *Fundamentals of Curriculum Development* (New York: Harcourt, Brace & World, Inc., 1950), p. 152.

ineffective who cannot exercise any real authority, and from those who equate the concept with progressive education and John Dewey, and thus taint it beyond recovery.

Another major impediment to translating the concept of the democratic teacher into action is the teacher's own blindness. For example, a young man was sure he was being "democratic" in his classroom by being objective regarding achievement and the dispensation of the rewards at his disposal. He was found to be consistently overgrading and overrating those students at the upper end of the socio-economic scale, the docile and compliant. His relative power, and his freedom to exercise it as he saw fit, did not compensate for his inability to detect the bias in his judgment.[22]

We have just described two approaches that deliberate education of the teacher makes in attempting to cope with the power of the teacher and turn it towards humane and democratic ends. These attempts are only partially successful, as has been shown. Power viewed from the side of those who exercise it is one thing, however, and quite another when viewed by those who are acted upon. How does the student view those in authority and power over him? What can he do about it?

THE IMAGE OF THE TEACHER

Since few teachers have as yet been replaced by machines, it is necessary that something be done about teachers and their power. There are a number of ways of dealing with those who have power over one. One is to dethrone them, a second is to join them, and a third is undermine them. Since teachers are still necessary, they cannot be dethroned. Since they are on the other side of the barricade, one can join them only by going over to the enemy side, namely, by becoming a teacher. But until this eventuality occurs, the student, his parents, and the public can undermine them.

Americans have done an excellent job of cutting the power figure of the teacher down to size.

Even before they come to school, children may be exposed to the television version of schools and teachers, as described in Chapter 2. There are many more messages that convey to the public an image of the teacher.

Take novels, for instance. What kind of teacher do we read about in popular fiction? A careful examination of the teacher as shown in American novels discloses a grim picture:

> They grow older, but not happier, loving but unloved, wanting but unwanted, eternal strangers who devote their lives to the education of other women's children, graying, sharpening, harshening with the years, becoming autocrats in the classroom and recluses in the community, accepting their roles as old maids as they once accepted their roles as young schoolmistresses, dimly seeking some answer to all the pains and frustrations they can neither articulate nor understand . . . The male schoolteacher in the American novel is usually stooped, gaunt, and gray with weariness. His suit has the shine of shabby gentility and hangs loosely

[22] George D. Spindler, *The Transmission of American Culture* (Cambridge, Mass.: Harvard University Press, 1959), p. 31.

from his undernourished frame. . . . In short, to succeed as a teacher, one must fail as a man or women.[23]

A study of the stereotype teacher in movies is equally discouraging. Most movie teachers, both male and female, start out unmarried, and end unmarried, unless they do one of two things: leave teaching, or find a partner who is not in teaching.[24] If you want to stay in teaching, the message is, you had better be devoted to the muse, because no one else will have you. This stereotype is interesting, in view of the fact that 80 per cent of all men teachers are married, and 62 per cent of all women teachers, and most of these have children. The stereotype persists: in a study of stories dealing with teachers and schools in the *Saturday Evening Post* it was found that most teachers are represented as being different from other people. They are aliens and strangers in the community, and poor.[25]

College students also reflect this stereotype. While the teacher is seen to be self-sacrificing, interested in cultural and artistic things, he is not seen as a leader of the community, but as lacking strength, hardness, assertiveness and confidence. "According to students, the teacher does not play poker or become involved in activities that have a cast of vigorous masculinity." [26] Students at teachers colleges rated teaching and teachers as higher on desirable attributes; students at Ivy League colleges rated them much lower than they rated individuals choosing other vocations.[27]

This picture of the school teacher will certainly be protested by teachers, those going into teaching, and those who teach teachers. But, while it is true that many a campus queen is recruited from the students in elementary education, it is just such gorgeous girls who, if they do enter teaching, do not stay. The residue may indeed have a great deal to do not only with who enters teaching, but even more decisively, with who remains.

The stereotype serves to reduce the teacher in size, to make him or her appear to be less than adequately endowed with desirable characteristics, so that the teacher is no longer as fearful as an earlier generation perceived. Since the teacher has so much power, one gets even by demeaning this person behind his back, and in public giving him only a few grudging crumbs of esteem.

Behind a stereotype as we have seen there is some truth. Does the stereotype make the teacher, or does the teacher lend credence to the stereotype?

MANY ARE CHOSEN, FEW ARE CALLED

There are over 1,300,000 teachers in America. No one can question the fact that most of these individuals are very hard-working conscientious

[23] Arthur Foff, "The Teacher as Hero," in *Readings in Education*, eds. Arthur Foff and Jean D. Grambs (New York: Harper & Row, Publishers, 1956), p. 21.

[24] Jack Schwartz, "The Portrayal of Educators in Motion Pictures, 1950-58," *Journal of Educational Sociology* (October 1960).

[25] George Gerbner, "Smaller than Life: Teachers and Schools in the Mass Media," *Phi Delta Kappan*, XLIV (February 1963), 202-5.

[26] Donald D. O'Dowd and David C. Beardslee, "The Student Image of the School Teacher," *Phi Delta Kappan*, XLII (March 1961), 250-54.

[27] Wesley Allinsmith and George W. Goethals, *The Role of Schools in Mental Health* (New York: Basic Books, Inc., 1962), p. 267.

individuals, being paid at the lower end of the scale for professional workers. There is some evidence that, despite their best efforts, most of these teachers fall far short of being masters of their vocation. Many enter teaching; relatively few are great teachers.

If the stereotype teacher most often is a woman, this is, of course, borne out by the statistics. Most teachers *are* women. In the elementary grades, only 12.1 per cent are men. At the secondary level, only in the last few years have men had a slight edge in numbers. Men think that others consider elementary teaching a sissy profession for a male. That this is also true of secondary (and higher?) education we have the evidence of the stereotype. We also have some slight indication that men who choose public school teaching tend to have somewhat more feminine scores on standardized tests of masculinity-femininity than the average male college graduate.[28] Such evidence will be taken with a grain of salt when one considers that "femininity" scores result when one answers "yes" to such questions as: "I like poetry." [29]

Research studies have shown that the public school teacher ranks at the lower end of the group of professionals in terms of social status. The ranking is just above that of members of the major "female" occupations: nurses, librarians, social workers. The status of the teacher is not commensurate with the power he exercises.

Secondary school teachers are given a higher ranking than elementary teachers. One reason may be that their training stresses knowledge of subject matter while that of the grade school teacher stresses knowledge of children. Also, female occupations are typically rated as low, reflecting the lower valuation of women's activities and those interests which are associated with women. Despite much talk, enrollments of men in elementary school training programs have not expanded. For a man to be interested in young children (except as a pediatrician and then he is a doctor first and a baby doctor second) is to share in the preoccupations of women. And what self-respecting man would do that?

While Americans appear to value, indeed overvalue, children to the extent of letting them dominate many a household, this valuation does not extend to those who would minister to them. Housewives and mothers are accorded second-class status; so are teachers who devote their intellectual efforts to the young. Is it because, at heart, the American public really does not like its children? Feeling guilty about this, does it compensate by overspending on clothes, entertainment, and remote disease research? And then accord little recognition to those who deal with children in the hard and far more significant tasks of living at home and school?

An inquiry among 40 male elementary school teachers indicated their conviction that what they were doing was important, and that they were proud of their work, and felt they were better than the women teachers. On the other hand, they felt isolated among so many women, felt their status in the community was inferior, and thought that people looked on

[28] Anne Roe, *The Psychology of Occupations* (New York: John Wiley and Sons, Inc., 1958), p. 231.

[29] J. W. Getzels and P. W. Jackson, "The Teacher's Personality and Characteristics," in *Handbook of Research on Teaching*, ed. Gage, p. 536.

them as somewhat peculiar, if not downright sissy. They did not want a female principal, either. Elementary school teaching is women's work.[30]

It is difficult to assess the effect of the stereotype on teachers themselves. One notes, of course, the phrase that is meant as flattery, "Oh, but you don't look like a school teacher!" or "You don't act like a school teacher." The response, inevitably, is to feel secretly pleased. Is there something not good about looking or acting like a school teacher?

Actually, teachers are little different from other people. Part of the scorn heaped on teachers by more precious academicians arises because teachers fade almost inconspicuously into the bland features of American culture. They are not apt to be better read, more widely travelled, more in touch with the avant-garde than other people. In fact, teachers tend to reflect the conservative mores and beliefs of their communities. It is safer that way. And society above all wants its children safe. This is a perfectly rational and human desire, and if it works to select as teachers those who are ordinary and commonplace, the criticism can hardly be levelled against the teacher as a person.

If the teacher appears in the stereotype to be not very capable of success in the worlds of commerce and business, perhaps this rests on some basis in fact. Roe [31] reports research indicating that the lower the tested intelligence of teachers the more favorably disposed they were toward teaching. She also reports that research shows teachers tending to be less curious, slower in making decisions than other professional personnel. A study of men who had left teaching showed that these were the brighter persons. Those who left, interestingly enough, were making significantly more than those who remained in teaching. Only 1 out of 247 teachers had a monthly income of over $800, while 1 out of 5 of those who had left teaching had incomes of this amount.[32]

Dismal as the conclusion must be, the stereotype of the teacher in some of its dimensions does accord with reality: many teachers are less socially effective, less well endowed intellectually, and less well remunerated than their fellow professionals.

In view of both the reality and the myth, teaching will have drawbacks for a number of persons. Yet is it particularly attractive, too, to certain people. Teaching has always been one of the most available ladders for social mobility. In rural areas often the only college education available was a normal school or teachers college, which, state-supported, provided a cheap and easy way to get a college degree. A few years of teaching, and one could have saved enough for law school or advanced graduate work, or have acquired the maturity for politics or business.

The social background of most teachers for generations has been the upper-lower or the lower-middle class, with heavy rural representation. Today the picture is changed, but not much. The fathers of today's teachers

138

[30] Dorothy Rogers, "A Study of the Reactions of Forty Men to Teaching in the Elementary School," *Journal of Educational Sociology*, XXVII (September 1953), 24-35.

[31] Roe, *The Psychology of Occupations*, p. 231.

[32] Robert L. Thorndike and Elizabeth Hagan, "Characteristics of Men Who Remained in or Left Teaching," (Washington, D.C.: U. S. Office of Education, Cooperative Research Program, Project No. 574, OE23016, 1959-60).

are farmers (men, 20 per cent; women, 30 per cent), skilled or semi-skilled workers (men, 30 per cent; women, 20 per cent) or from managerial or self-employed categories (men and women, 22 per cent). Relatively few teachers come from the homes of professional, clerical or sales, or un-skilled workers. As has been noted about college education in general, the lower the socio-economic class of the student the more likely is there to be a demand that education pay off. Teaching certainly is a most visable means of immediate pay-off.[33]

That men see education as a way of getting a good start and moving on to something better is illustrated again by the statistics. The median age of men in teaching today is 33.6 years, with a peak at ages 30-35. At this point the young man with a family moves either up or out, and a great many of them move out. At about this age, however, women begin to move back in.

The median age of women in teaching is 45.5 years. While men may have nine years, on the average, of teaching experience to a woman's 15 years, the total experience of men has been continuous. Three-fourths of all men who enter teaching stay with it until they leave for good. Less than half of all women have had no break in their teaching careers.[34] That is, the older woman returning to teaching does so after her own children are able to fend for themselves. She may return with or without refresher courses, depending on the scarcity of teachers in her area.

This is only part of the picture. Education courses and teachers colleges are preparing a vast number of people who never will become teachers. Of 100 students who prepare to teach, and actually are fully certified at the end of the collegiate program, only about 60 will be found in the classroom the first year. Of this 60, only 85 to 90 per cent will return after the first year. After about five years, fewer than one third of them are still in the classroom, and after ten years only 12 to 15 per cent are still teachers.[35]

Many choose to enter education at some point along their vocational pathway, but few remain for the whole of their working lives. Some of the reasons may be defects in the school as an institution, lack of com-munity support, and the rigidity of community controls. In any event, somewhere along the line the education profession is losing more teachers than it or the country can afford. If, as we are told, there are 85,000 class-rooms in which substandard teachers are holding forth, it is not because of a lack of professionally educated teachers someplace in the community.

Part of the problem is money, of course. Although the teacher is better paid than ever before, salaries at every level are below those of persons of less or comparable education. If teachers appear poverty-stricken in the stereotype, there is ample basis in fact for this aspect of the picture:

According to the *West Virginia School Journal* (Jan. 1963) the average high school graduate can expect to earn $241,844 in his lifetime, and the

[33] *NEA Journal*, 52, No. 4 (April 1963).
[34] *NEA Journal*, 52, No. 4 (April 1963).
[35] Willavene and William Wolf, "Teacher Drop-outs—A Professional Lament," in *Teaching in America*, eds. Anthony C. Riccio and Frederick R. Cyphert (Columbus, Ohio: Charles E. Merrill Books, Inc., 1962), p. 327.

average college graduate, an additional $178,000. If I taught forty-five years at the maximum salary for an AB degree in my present county, I would earn $213,750—some $28,000 less than the average high school graduate.[36]

College professors' salaries are woefully below those of persons of like competence who are in business or government. The reluctance of the public to respond to continued pleas from teachers to raise salaries reflects, of course, American valuation of the teaching act. "Anyone can teach," is an unexpressed but probable sentiment. After all, at some time or another, all of us have taught something to someone. It is just a matter of knowing something. And since children know so little, the teacher logically does not have to know much, either. Therefore it follows that he need be paid little for the little he brings.

Another public image is the gay boatload of school teachers headed for a vacation in Europe. What more familiar character in fiction than the maiden school teacher, just this shade of 40, earnestly visiting the ruins of Rome and secretly looking for the last fading face of romance? If teachers have time for such luxuries, and the money to afford them, why pay more? There are few unstated issues that cause more confusion in the minds and hearts of educators than the summer vacation.

After nine months with 30 or more energetic American boys and girls any teacher, so the tradition goes, needs a rest. And if the teacher happens to bear the burden of 150 to 180 students at the secondary level, then he is even more in need of some relief. In addition, of course, teachers claim to be overworked during the teaching months, putting in many night hours, late after-school hours, and week ends on school tasks. It would be hard to prove the wear and tear on teachers. Certainly it is a demanding job, and its mental health hazards are real. But this can be said of many occupations which do not give their practitioners three months of vacation time as a result.

A further and much more devastating complication regarding the proper level of compensation comes as a result of paying all teachers the same. The brilliant, the good, the average, the mediocre, the bad, all get the same paycheck if they have taught the same number of years, and have the same amount of earned college credits. This strikes the public as downright odd. We will examine later proposed solutions to this dilemma.

SUMMARY

The emerging picture is of a vocation which is perceived to be of relatively low social status, as compared with other professions, followed by poorly compensated persons, mostly women, who probably could not compete too successfully in other occupations.

It is clear that the stereotype of the teacher tends to obscure the fact that there are many kinds of teachers, who do many kinds of tasks. Yet the stereotype persists, possibly as a way of dealing with persons whose power function is out of proportion to their social position.

[36] "Our Readers Write," NEA Journal, 52, No. 4 (April 1963), p. 6.

Because of the difficulty in seeing teachers and teaching clearly, some policy decisions regarding the education profession which we face at the moment are the subject of debate and confusion. We will examine these in the next chapter.

BIBLIOGRAPHY

ADELSON, JOSEPH, "The Teacher as a Model," *The American Scholar*, 30 (Summer 1961), 383-406. Perceptive analysis of the many ways in which the teacher functions.

BARZUN, JACQUES, *The House of Intellect*. New York: Harper & Row, Publishers, 1959. Biting analyses of the intellectual and the academic in American life, with special emphasis on the college level.

CHARTERS, W. W., "The Social Background of Teaching," in *Handbook of Research on Teaching*, ed. N. L. Gage, pp. 756-63. New York: Rand McNally & Co., 1963. These pages summarize most of the studies of the stereotype of the teacher in America.

HARRIS, RAYMOND P., *American Education: Facts, Fancies, and Folklore*, Chap. 5. New York: Random House, 1962. "Imaginary Teachers Everyone Knows" is a sardonic description of teacher "types," to illustrate the point that there are many views of the teacher, some derived from a by-gone era.

JACKSON, PHILIP W., "The Teacher and Individual Differences," in *Individualizing Instruction*, Sixty-first Yearbook of the National Society for the Study of Education, Part I, ed. Nelson B. Henry. Chicago: University of Chicago Press, 1962. Explores the fallacy of the "ideal" teacher and the "ideal" method.

JERSILD, ARTHUR T., *When Teachers Face Themselves*. New York: Bureau of Publications, Teachers College, Columbia University, 1955. The pressures upon the teacher are reported and discussed with particular focus on anxiety-producing aspects of the classroom.

———— AND EVE A. LAZAR, *The Meaning of Psychotherapy in the Teacher's Life and Work*. New York: Buerau of Publications, Teachers College, Columbia University, 1962. The psychological impact of teaching on the teacher is discussed in this research report.

MEAD, MARGARET, *The School in American Culture*. Cambridge, Mass.: Harvard University Press, 1951. Particularly interesting for descriptions of the different roles teachers can and do play.

RICCIO, ANTHONY C. AND FREDERICK R. CYPHERT, eds., *Teaching in America*. Columbus, Ohio: Charles E. Merrill Books, Inc., 1963. A superior collection of articles and research studies with particular emphasis on teachers and teaching. Many studies reprinted here are not usually available or known.

RIESMAN, DAVID, "Teachers as Countercyclical Influence," *School Review*, LXV, No. 1 (Spring 1957), 78-91. A distinguished social scientist analyzes the contemporary role of the teacher, and suggests a needed function for the future.

————, *The Lonely Crowd*, pp. 55-64. New Haven: Yale University Press, 1950. "Changes in the Role of the Teacher" is a stimulating discussion of teachers, teaching, and the contemporary emphasis on "other-directedness."

WHITE, RALPH K. AND RONALD O. LIPPITT, *Autocracy and Democracy*. New York: Harper & Row, Publishers, 1960. Reports in detail the famous experiments on social climates in boys' groups, and relates the resulting data to educational practice.

WRIGHT, BENJAMIN, "News and Comments: Love and Hate in the Act of Teaching," *The Elementary School Journal*, LXI, No. 7 (April 1961), 349-62. A perceptive analysis of the tyranny of teachers exercised through either hate or love.

The following are especially good reports on teaching and teachers, found in fiction, biography, or autobiography:

ALLEN, GEORGE N., *Undercover Teacher*. Garden City, N. Y.: Doubleday & Company, Inc., 1960.

ASHTON-WARNER, SYLVIA, *Spinster*. New York: Simon and Schuster, Inc., 1959.

BRAITHWAITE, E. R., *To Sir, with Love*. Englewood Cliffs, N. J.: Prentice-Hall, Inc., 1959.

COVELLO, LEONARD, *The Heart is the Teacher*. New York: McGraw-Hill Book Company, 1958.

HERSEY, JOHN, *The Child Buyer*. New York: Alfred A. Knopf, Inc., 1960.

HUNTER, EVAN, *The Blackboard Jungle*. New York: Simon and Schuster, Inc., 1954.

MACRAE, GORDON, *Dwight Craig*. Boston: Houghton Mifflin Company, 1947.

PATTON, FRANCES GRAY, *Good Morning, Miss Dove*. New York: Dodd, Mead & Co., 1954.

PETERSON, HOUSTON, ed., *Great Teachers: As Portrayed by Those Who Studied Under Them*. New Brunswick, N. J.: Rutgers University Press, 1949.

RASEY, MARIE, *It Takes Time*. New York: Harper & Row, Publishers,

SMITH, FRANC, *Harry Vernon at Prep*. Boston: Houghton Mifflin Company, 1959.

UPDIKE, JOHN, *The Centaur*. New York: Alfred A. Knopf, Inc., 1963.

The uncomfortable contemporary situation of the teacher is a result of social history. But the teacher's problem is also a result of confusions in the public mind regarding the teaching act itself. Is the ability to teach something that one is born with, like having perfect pitch? Or is it something that can be learned? Is teaching an art which requires certain inherent attributes or is it a skill which must be studied and whose operations are subject to experimental verification? These questions are the subject of continuous and increasingly acrimonious public debate.

PERSON INTO TEACHER: Professional Education

To the casual reader of popular discussions of education, there must be something rather disconcerting about the controversy over the education of teachers. The heat which is displayed appears to be more than the subject justifies. Teachers, like teaching, tend to set off highly emotional reactions. The current controversy over the education of teachers appears to derive some of its temper from the same social sources that make much of education a

THE TEACHERS:
PART II

12

target of public aggression: fear of the future, the threat of war, automation, and the inapplicability of the eternal verities. The teacher is aligned with those things in the culture which are fear-inducing. The power the teacher has to provide security (we must educate more scientists than the Russians), or produce fear (we would have enough scientists if we did not have so many stupid teachers), seems to work in the public mind. Schools have failed us (literally in many cases), which means that teachers have failed us. Something must be wrong. Lacking any method of analyzing the causes of the failure of teachers, the public tends to blame the most immediately available factor: namely, the education which teachers undergo.

Thus we see today the mounting of highly virulent and bitter attacks on the education of teachers. It is claimed that too much of the education of teachers is taken up with professional education courses. If, the argument goes, prospective teachers spent more of their time in "content" courses—that is, academic courses—they would be better teachers than if they spent the time in professional courses. Professional courses are typically derided by being called "how-to-do-it" courses ("Teaching elementary school reading"). Attaching the "home-made" connotations of the how-to-do-it fad to professional courses clearly puts teacher training at the handyman level. Once having made such courses appear inane, it is easy to convince people that very many of them are a menace to the production of good teachers.

Over the last several decades, two trends have been apparent. First is the continued increase in the number of years required to gain a certificate to teach. Today nearly every state requires a degree from a four-year college for an elementary teacher, and every state requires at least this for a secondary teacher. The additional time has been assigned to academic or content courses: those subjects that the teacher will teach. Thus a second trend is that the education courses have been slowly but surely reduced in proportion to the teachers' *total* preparation.

What part of a teacher's education should be related to the information, content, skill, that he will impart to students, and how much should be devoted to helping him know how to transmit adult learning to immature persons?[1]

It is interesting to note that, of all professional training, that of teachers requires the least amount of *purely* professional course work. That is, most of the program of an engineering student is in courses which are clearly related (or presumed to be) to what he will be doing. He takes rarely more than a semester of subjects such as sociology, political science, history, English or languages, whose relation to his future work is assumed to be tenuous. In fact, some engineering students have especially tailored courses such as "English for Engineering Majors." Medical education is also heavily weighted with professionally designated courses, and few medical

---

[1] Seymour B. Sarason, Kenneth Davidson, and Burton Blatt, *The Preparation of Teachers: An Unstudied Problem in Education* (New York: John Wiley & Sons, Inc., 1962), pp. 17-37.

schools give more than lip service to their pious hope that future doctors will have a good liberal arts background.[2]

The prospective secondary teacher, however, in his four years of preparation, may take a semester and a half of professional course work, and frequently not that much. The elementary teacher may spend one third of her time in undergraduate work in professional education courses, though this proportion is becoming smaller. The justification for the emphasis on academic course work is that it is more important for the teacher to *know*, than to *know how*.

To carry the argument to its logical conclusion, as many have done, is to argue that mastery in his field of knowledge is really all that a good teacher needs, and one can look forward to the golden era when professional schools of education will have withered away. As we have noted earlier, research does not tell us with any assurance just what it is that teachers do that makes it possible for students to learn. Lacking such surety, it is easy to fall into the trap of thinking that it really does not matter what method a teacher uses so long as we are sure he knows what it is he is going to teach. The fallacy here is unfortunately demonstrated by the ill-educated, half-literate, easily-fooled adults who are products of our schools. Obviously, teachers who just *know* are not thereby able to *educate*. A good case in point is the fact that educational level seems to make an unpredictable difference in the popular disapproval of fluoridation of water.[3]

The animosity between educational faculty and faculty in other departments of a college or university is well-known in academic circles.

145

The contempt that academicians seem to have for professional education programs also appears to be shared by the products of these programs. It is a typical experience for the beginning teacher (or even student teacher) to be told by the practitioners in the field to "forget everything you learned at the university." College instruction is considered unrealistic, theoretical, and impractical. In response to a poll, a sample of high school and junior college teachers stated their belief that the number of courses in professional education should be reduced, and that internships or experience should be substituted for education course work in qualifying a person for teaching credentials.[4]

The contradiction between what the university recommends as best practice and what the schools encourage throws many a beginner into conflict. After a few years, as can be seen from the poll cited above, a large proportion of educators reject their own professional training. There may be several significant reasons for this. The critics of professional education claim that the real reason is that education courses are poorly taught, and lacking in content. This may be true.

[2] Nelson B. Henry, ed., *Education for the Professions*, Sixty-first Yearbook of the National Society for the Study of Education, Part II (Chicago: University of Chicago Press, 1962), pp. 103-39.

[3] Wm. A. Gamson and Peter H. Irons, "Community Characteristics and Fluoridation Outcome," *Journal of Social Issues*, XVII, No. 4 (1961), 66-74.

[4] Gustav Albrecht, "A Survey of Teacher Opinion in California," *Phi Delta Kappan*, XLII, No. 3 (December 1960), 103-8.

Professional educators who teach these courses would advance other hypotheses. One, the time allotted to professional education is so limited that the new teacher is really not ready to teach, thus he starts his career scared and incompetent, and naturally blames the preparing institution for not getting him ready. This condition cannot be remedied by fewer education courses, but by more. Two, the professional program may indeed be teaching the right things but in the wrong way, as Sarason has pointed out when discussing how teachers learn to see and think about children.[5]

A third possibility is suggested by the problem facing newly graduated nurses employed in hospitals. Nurses appear to react in a way similar to teachers, feeling that in many respects their training did not fit them for real life in the hospital. There is a conflict "between school and hospital over allegiance to professional and bureaucratic principles." As a student, the individual was encouraged to think, to change, to show initiative. On the job, the nurse is expected to obey and to fit into an institutional niche. Even if it is a great responsibility, "It may be difficult for the new graduate to understand what is professional about filling out six legal forms for each patient admitted and completing pages of detailed charts and reports each day . . ."[6] Shades of the teaching profession!

Teacher education will continue to be the object of attack as long as the issues remain unclear, and as long as there continues to be lack of agreement as to what constitutes good teaching.

THE STAMP OF APPROVAL

146

Related issues which shake the academic community, but which are rarely noted or understood by the public, have to do with the accreditation of teacher education programs, and the establishment of certification requirements.

Accreditation is a necessary evil that occurs when one has to substitute negotiated consensus for folk consensus. It would appear the height of absurdity to consider accrediting Oxford University. Yet Albany State Teachers College must be accredited or its graduates are handicapped in getting a job. Accreditation is the seal of approval of the profession, and whether or not it is awarded means life or death to all professional schools, whether they train teachers, pharmacists, nurses, social workers, dentists, doctors, or librarians. In teacher training, a conflict centers around which shall be the proper accrediting group, one made up primarily of those who produce the teacher or of those who hire him. Currently, the National Council for Accreditation of Teacher Education includes professional teacher educators and nonuniversity personnel. The academic community, who feel that those responsible for academic, as against professional, training know what is best, consider themselves under-represented. Also, the organized education profession, represented by departments of the National Education Association, holds the most seats.[7] Implicit in many

---

[5] Sarason, Davidson, and Blatt, *The Preparation of Teachers.*

[6] Ronald G. Corwin, "The Professional Employee: A Study of Conflict in Nursing Roles," *American Journal of Sociology,* LXVI, No. 6 (May 1961), 604-5.

[7] James D. Koerner, "Teacher Education: Who Makes the Rules?" *Saturday Review,* XLV, No. 42 (October 20, 1962), 78-92.

criticisms of the current accrediting mechanism may be the fear that professional educators might some day get as firm a control over teacher preparation as doctors have over medical training. In the latter case this seems to be highly sensible; in the case of professional educators the idea makes many reasonable people violent. Why this is so remains unexplained and clouded over by polemics from either side.

There seems to be general acceptance and approval for having the medical profession control the professional education and activities of their colleagues. What doctors know is too esoteric, as well as too vital to be tampered with by ordinary men, no matter how knowledgeable in other fields.

Educators or teachers, however, are looked upon as half-educated fools who should not be trusted with anything as important as policy making for their own profession. It is a corollary of this position that academic personnel know better what is "good" education. Persons who have gained prestige in fields far remote from education often feel called upon to make pronouncements which, interestingly enough, may be given a respectful reception by the educated lay public. Admiral Rickover is a contemporary example of this.[8]

We can only wonder why this may be so. A number of hypotheses have been advanced, among them that educators do not talk sense. Another is that they do not talk English. A third is that education *is* public property, therefore the public should make decisions, even if wrong ones. If educators have failed to educate the public towards the right decisions then they have no one to blame but themselves. The reasoning is circular, and the circle is a vicious one.

Certification of *teachers* is another issue which rouses wrath and argument. The states do the certifying of teachers, and the rules that are established are usually those recommended by the professional educators in the state. Unlike law or medicine, there are no state examinations which establish the right to practice. Instead, the future teacher must submit evidence of having attended either an accredited teacher education program in an accredited institution, or must take specified amounts of courses in academic and professional work. The crux of the problem again lies in what constitutes appropriate training for teaching. People may become livid with indignation when they realize that many persons highly proficient in their fields may not be permitted to instruct children because they lack the stipulated professional education courses.

The difficulty involved in resolving this issue, again, rests on the inability of the interested parties to agree as to how competence for teaching can be assessed. Though certification by examination is currently being used in some states, it is clear that merely knowing something, and knowing the right answers regarding best educational practice, does not insure effective teaching. But then, neither does credit counting.

The academician who firmly believes that knowledge of subject matter is enough has a rude awakening when he attempts to transmit his specialized knowledge to children or youth. Such persons, after one or two

147

[8] H. G. Rickover, *Education and Freedom* (New York: E. P. Dutton & Co., Inc., 1960).

trials, often flee in terror to their laboratory or ivory tower, muttering that children are not as smart as they used to be, or convinced again that school teaching is a job best left to school teachers, who must indeed be peculiar to do it anyway.

The issues we have described are not new. What is new is the increased anger with which the issues are being discussed. The sociologist may well wonder why. Teachers, teaching, the education of teachers, appear to be caught up in the social revolutions that are engaging this country. One revolution is conservative, and wishes to change the status quo towards earlier patterns. There is distinct and clearly enunciated distrust of the professional educator, who is perceived to be either very stupid, power-hungry, or radical. That educators cannot be all these at the same time is irrelevant to the argument. Such persons as Admiral Rickover, James Koerner and the recently elected school superintendent in California, Max Rafferty, enunciate the current conservative position.[9]

Another group, less articulate, are the researchers in allied fields such as psychology, sociology and anthropology. As they build up ever-increasing bodies of information about learning, institutions, and culture it becomes clear that education could better serve society by making use of these findings in a deliberate fashion. However, these persons and groups typically talk only to each other, and rarely consider it either useful or necessary to communicate with professional educators. The noneducator in other academic disciplines tends, interestingly enough, to share the same view of educators as do those in the forefront of the conservative movement: that most educators are poorly educated, rather stupid, and more interested in keeping a job than making education significant.

The image of the teacher (and by contamination all educators) tends to influence public policy, public thinking, and academic evaluation.

The debate is fascinating, and the outcomes are serious, but one central key to the problem usually remains hidden: We do not agree on what a good teacher is, and we do not know what makes a good teacher.

WHAT IS A GOOD TEACHER?

The attributes of a good teacher depend on where you are sitting. The parent perceives the good teacher as one who fulfills the parent's own desires for his child—that he be disciplined, loved, and provided with saleable skills. The principal perceives the good teacher as one who keeps students in his classroom and parents out of the office, who gets his paperwork done on time and serves faithfully on faculty committees. The administrator also values teachers' participation in community affairs, far more than teachers do.[10] Teachers see good teachers as those who are like themselves—whatever that may be.

Research is of very little help. In commenting upon the problem,

[9] James Koerner, *The Miseducation of Teachers* (Boston: Houghton Mifflin Company, 1963); Max Rafferty, "The Seven Grim Fairy Tales," *Phi Delta Kappan*, XLII, No. 3 (December 1960), 114; Rickover, *op. cit.*

[10] C. E. Fishburn, "Teacher Role Perception in the Secondary School," *Journal of Teacher Education*, XIII (March 1962), 55-59.

Charters states: ". . . decades of empirical research have failed to identify unequivocally the *behaviors* which *define* 'effective teaching,' . . ."[11]

On the basis of a review of 61 related studies, one commentator makes this wry statement:

> It is worth noting that for all practical purposes, teacher competence is whatever people think it is. If Mary's mother thinks Mary's teacher is incompetent, then for her she is. If enough mothers agree, the teacher may be transferred or released. Similarly, if the principal's report says the teacher is effective, it is likely to be taken as so. When a school district adopts a check list on which to rate teachers, this, in effect, becomes the district's definition of an effective teacher.[12]

Now that we have identified the crucial problem in teacher education, namely that we do not know what a good teacher is, we can proceed to examine some further assumptions about and consequences of teacher training.

"Teachers are born, not made," is a favorite adage. Folk observation might well support such a view. Given two students with equally (on the surface) pleasing personalities and the same college grades, one will turn out to be a superb teacher (according to the standard of those who trained her) and the other will fail dismally. Predictions regarding who will or who will not succeed in teaching have not been markedly successful, although almost every known device has been tried, from Rorschach tests to interviews to academic achievement tests. The only factors which correlate highly in all such studies are the grade the student received in practice teaching and the subsequent judgments of those who hired him as teacher. Despite those who bewail the fact that many bright persons do not go into teaching, grades and IQ do not correlate highly with success in teaching. Experience shows that many college students with high grades prefer books to people, a handicap when it comes to dealing with 35 or 180 students. Principals are notably cautious when hiring a Phi Beta Kappa member. A high level of intellectual competence is often not accompanied by the patience to deal with duller, slower, less intellectually exciting minds.

However, many bright persons do become good teachers, and many not so bright. Research suggests that the "born" teacher is one who has had many personal experiences throughout his growing years in which he played a "teaching" or supporting role with dependent other persons.[13] Sarason has stated that the central problem in teacher education is communicating knowledge to children, and that an adult possessing knowledge is not guaranteed by this possession to be able to communicate it to children.[14] If he learned how to do so from informal early experiences,

149

11 W. W. Charters, "The Social Background of Teaching," in *Handbook of Research on Teaching*, ed. Gage, p. 726.

12 Robert B. Howsam, *Who's a Good Teacher?* (Burlingame, California: California School Boards Association and California Teachers Association, 1960), p. 15.

13 David G. Ryans, *Characteristics of Teachers* (Washington, D.C.: American Council on Education), pp. 363, 391.

14 Sarason, Davidson, and Blatt, *The Preparation of Teachers*.

well and good. If not, then someplace in his preparation this gap must be *effectively* filled, not by sitting passively in a lecture, being *told* about children.[15] One has to be in touch with the real thing.

In any event, the definition of the good teacher still eludes us, as well as the characteristics that this good teacher should possess before entering teaching or acquire during his preparation. Because of this lack, another controversy involving some major policy decisions is engulfing the educational profession.

MERIT PAY: A Case Study in Frustration

Teachers have always had salary troubles. In colonial times teachers were often paid in kind rather than cash, and were never paid enough. Until recent decades, men teachers were almost always paid more than women, and secondary teachers more than elementary. A major professional victory was won when salaries were finally equalized, and remuneration was made on the basis of preparation and experience. While the movement towards equalization of salaries was being won, the fight for tenure was also being successfully concluded. A good proportion of teachers today are employed in school systems where their jobs are protected by tenure, and where they are paid on the basis of preparation and experience. Salaries are still inadequate, however: 76.5 per cent of married men teachers hold a second job, 24.1 per cent of the single women, and 11.6 per cent of the married women.[16] It would be hard to match such dismal statistics in any other professional group.

Teachers in most school systems enjoy the benefits of a salary schedule. The salary schedule is a carefully worked out plan which provides for raises for teachers as long as they stay in the system. By a series of steps, the teacher moves up the salary schedule until, after 10 or 15 years in one system, he has attained the maximum permissible salary. He teaches at this level for the rest of his professional life.

To get these step increases, teachers in many school systems must meet added requirements which are presumed to upgrade the teacher. So many credits of college course work or educational travel must be earned during a given number of years in order to receive an increase. Typically, the course work taken is at the option of the teacher, as the person who best knows what he needs to know more about. It does not always work out this way; a third-grade teacher can take a course in Secondary Curriculum not because it will do her any good, but because it is offered at a nearby center on Wednesday evenings when she can get a baby sitter.

The reasoning behind the requirement of additional in-service education for more pay is clear. New knowledge accumulates, and teachers need to keep informed so that they can transmit such new knowledge to their students. Recent upheavals in the mathematics and science curricula have

150

15 Prescott, *The Child in the Educative Process* (New York: McGraw-Hill Book Company, 1957).

16 *NEA Journal*, 52, No. 6 (April 1963), p. 51.

exposed the fact that many teachers of these subjects although accumulating the requisite credits, rarely took them in the subject field they were teaching. To meet this problem, the federal government, through the National Defense Education Act, established special summer workshops for teachers in fields such as mathematics, science, and foreign languages, which would bring new information and skills to teachers at the level at which they could understand it.

The assumption is that participation in such workshops will make for better teachers. Are they, in fact, better teachers? Who should decide who is the better teacher? Should the better teacher be rewarded with a higher salary? These are the central issues in the fight over merit pay.

The public has become restive. Many tales of inadequate teaching have produced demands that something be done to discriminate among teachers. At least it seems highly unfair to pay weak Mrs. Smith and strong Mrs. Jones the same salary just because they each have an A.B. plus 30 college credit hours.

For the most part, the organized education groups are opposed to merit pay. Many critics of education are for it, and so are some educators. The goals are agreed upon: to see that good teachers are rewarded for their excellence, and thus to induce more and better persons to enter teaching and remain. How this shall be achieved is where groups differ.

One of the problems of the educational scene is that, in order to receive really good salaries—that is, over $8,000—the classroom teacher must leave classroom teaching. The biggest salaries are earned by a few superintendents and their assistants in large or wealthy school districts. Other school superintendents and principals of large schools earn the next largest salaries. Salaries above the maximum possible for a classroom teacher are earned by supervisors, school specialists of various kinds, and even college professors. Thus there is no salary inducement to the talented or ambitious or hungry to stay in the classroom if they have the wit or energy to complete the training necessary to get out.

At the college level one can advance up a four-step ladder (very slowly, but he can advance) from instructor, to assistant professor, to associate professor, to full professor. At all rungs on the ladder the college teacher can do essentially the same things: teach, counsel, do research, write books. The same situation does not prevail in the public school system.

True, there are hidden status rewards in being "promoted" from junior high to senior high, for some teachers, but the salary will be the same. The only way to get significant status and salary gains in public school education is to leave classroom teaching. As a result, many superb teachers become mediocre administrators—but how else could their talent be rewarded? Is it harder to teach first grade or twelfth grade? Is it more difficult to teach automechanics to potential dropouts, or instrumental music to a talented few whose eyes are on Julliard? Status differences are perceived, and the job demands do differ, but which is harder? Which ought to be paid more? Can you tell which is done better?

Such are the knotty problems on which the merit pay case founders. The impasse is reached on the question of who will decide, and on what basis. Rating scales of teachers exist by the hundreds. Every year more appear. As we noted earlier, there is so little agreement as to what constitutes good teaching, that it is not surprising to know that none of the rating scales have very wide acceptance.

Then, even with rating scale in hand, the question arises of who shall do the rating. Other teachers? The principal? A supervisor? A board member or other lay person? Some teachers become paralyzed when visited, yet are entrancing when there are no observers. Others are prima donnas for a select audience, but boring for just students. Can raters tell the difference? Which raters?

Thus the argument proceeds. A careful assessment of the basis for educational resistance to a rating system has not yet been made. The above objections are of course part of the picture, but not the whole story. In discussing adjustment to a work situation, Gross suggests that it is in the interests of safety and personal protection that work groups establish a means of controlling competition among members. If you let those with whom you work know your fears, weaknesses, and troubles, and thus establish a basis for mutual support, then these same confidants cannot be those whom you have to beat out for a higher place.[17] The introduction of a merit system is probably perceived as a threat to the noncompetitive basis on which teachers believe they must work.

A merit system, too, would encourage the Damned Average Raisers—those who are ambitious, work hard, and work overtime. The lazy and the mediocre would be shown up, and maybe spurred to action. If one has found a comfortable place to operate, without excessive effort, any attempt to jog one out of it or to make one work harder is bound to be resisted. Too, there is the horrible secret suspicion that even if one did work harder there would be no noticeable result, and no reward. In one's heart of hearts, one may feel he is *really* just about as mediocre as he acts. Industrial studies have shown clearly how workers resist payment by the piece since it makes all workers run faster; if there is such payment, they see to it that the fast workers are made to cease and desist, and produce only at the level of the moderately efficient.

The social situation of the school thus makes it extremely difficult to develop a system which would reward merit and invite continued efforts toward excellence, yet maintain a cooperative work group. Trump and his associates believe that a merit system can be brought into being by establishing "teacher teams" which would include teacher assistants (beginning teachers), instructors, teacher-lecturers, master teachers, and team leaders, thus providing a progression of responsibility based on differentiation in function and assessment of competence.[18] Teaching positions would then be graded and salary provided commensurate with competence and responsibility, plus experience and training. Only a very few places are trying such a plan.[19]

---

[17] Edward Gross, "Social Integration and the Control of Competition," *American Journal of Sociology*, LXVII, No. 3 (November 1961), 270-77.

[18] Trump and Baynham, *Guide to Better Schools*.

[19] A description of how this team concept might work is given by Myron Lieberman, *The Future of Public Education* (Chicago: University of Chicago Press [Phoenix Books], 1960), pp. 95-100.

Teachers, like other workers, want better pay, better working conditions, more recognition, and some control over what they are doing. As we have observed, the teaching profession is resisting merit pay proposals. How then, to get more money and more power? Organize!

The education profession today is caught between the professional organization of educators and the professional union of educators: the position and voice of the National Education Association and its affiliated groups, and the American Federation of Teachers, an affiliate of the AFL-CIO. Both organizations have been on the scene for some time. The NEA was founded in 1857 and the AFT in 1916. The NEA has grown steadily in numbers and influence. The AFT membership has always been small except in a few metropolitan areas, but its influence is growing.

The AFT is becoming a potent power on two counts: (1) its leadership successfully led a teacher strike in New York City in 1962, and (2) thereby won the right to hold an election which gave the union the power to represent the teachers of New York City in collective bargaining.

The success of this strike, and the power thus obtained for the union leadership, rocked the professional education world. The position of other educational organizations had been that teachers did not go out on strike. This coincided with the public's view that teachers, as public servants, could not strike against the government. Yet look what a small group of teachers had accomplished! They had actually made the New York City Board of Education move more rapidly towards a better salary scale and improved working conditions. As a consequence, membership in the AFT grew in several large cities. Talk of strikes has increased in several of these locations.

Teachers' strikes are not new, and whenever they occur a cry of anguish goes up. The strike is seen by nonunion educational leadership as destroying the professional image of the educator. As an opponent of teacher's strikes puts it:

> Teachers cannot have it both ways. They cannot expect professional status and the respect and security that goes with it, and at the same time demand the right to exercise the ultimate economic weapon of a labor union. Professional ethics are of a *higher order*, and the great majority of the nation's teachers . . . always have denied themselves the right to strike, however great the provocation.[20]

As can be noted from the above quote, the opposition to strikes arises partly out of an altruistic view of public service, but also from the lower status that comes from acting like a laborer. One might suspect that, had other *professional* groups at an early time in their history banded together into unions and used the strike as a way of forcing government as well as private enterprise to take heed of their demands, then educators would not mind being in the same company. The fact is, however, that

153

[20] Paul Woodring, "The New York Teachers' Strike," *Saturday Review*, XLV, No. 20 (May 19, 1962), 52. (Italics added.)

doctors and lawyers have achieved their policy control and economic eminence by using other organizational tactics.

It is important, however, to note a major difference between doctors and lawyers on the one hand, and teachers on the other. The former are typically self-employed; the latter are employed by an agency of the government. The loyalty of the physician or the attorney is first to himself and *then* to his profession. The teacher's loyalty is to himself, his profession, *and* to his employer, the school board. Thus the teacher can identify a target for his grievances; the doctor and lawyer cannot, but must use public pressure and private power to control policy. It is thus important that teachers be convinced that their condition is more like that of the self-employed professional than of the employed worker. If they are not so convinced, they will be tempted to use union tactics.

Teachers have a reputation for being antilabor. Certainly they are economically illiterate in the main, just like most of the college-educated public. Since many teachers are from the upper-lower or lower-middle class, they are not far from organized labor in origin. There is nothing like the *nouveau riche* for wanting to disclaim all associations with lesser forebears. Thus it is that many teachers, having moved into the middle class, are more conservative and less apt to identify with working class ambitions, than are average, educated middle-class adults.[21] However, even the average middle-class adult tends to side more with management than labor, and thus teachers think they are in good company if they are on the side of management. At least it is safer here than on the side of labor. Certainly their employers, school-board members, are not representative of nor sympathetic to union tactics. As was noted in Chapter 5, union members and working-class persons in general are woefully under-represented on school boards.

Another basis for the dislike teachers have for being associated with organized labor's tactics is suggested by Friedenberg:

> A teaching career provides security against the kinds of economic vicissitudes to which small businessmen and clerical employees are subject. The kind of security that people who are accustomed to think of themselves as working-class derive from a strong union, teachers obtain in some measure from a licentiate and tenure regulations. Public-school teaching therefore attracts a disproportionate number of persons to whom security is more important than real freedom in the conduct of their life or their professional activity.[22]

To behave, even within an organization, in an independent fashion, is to court insecurity and even trouble. Those who seek to teach are in a significant number of instances escaping childhoods threatened with economic or personal disruption or disaster. Having made the leap into respectability, often with great sacrifice and effort, the teacher is not likely to view with favor a call by organized labor that would jeopardize his job, or identify him with the lower-class elements of the community. The number of women in teaching, too, tends to work against the growth

[21] Robert E. Doherty, "Attitudes toward Labor: When Blue Collar Children Become Teachers," *School Review*, LXXI, No. 1 (Spring 1963), 87-96.
[22] Friedenberg, *The Vanishing Adolescent*, p. 79.

of teachers' unions. Women tend to be less interested in joining unions, less active when members, and far less militant. Since many women use teaching as a temporary job, pursued while catching a husband and starting a family, and returned to when the family needs more money, there is little incentive to be strong organization members.

It is probable that for the foreseeable future, wherever the AFT is successful, it will be within the anonymity of the big city, where not only is the struggle fiercer, but the ever-present face of poverty acts as a goad to the teacher, who sees the union as the most effective means available to escape the ever-present specter of the slum children he teaches daily.

There are striking differences between the NEA and the AFT policies. While the AFT favors collective bargaining, and strikes as a last resort, the NEA favors negotiations and sanctions. In collective bargaining, the teachers would come under the jurisdiction of labor legislation, which specifically excludes supervisors and other administrative personnel from participating in the discussions. The NEA, on the other hand, includes all professional personnel in its inclusive membership. It has been argued that in this way the bosses run the show, since school superintendents, principals, and supervisors might very well be able to dominate teachers. The NEA argues that it is right and proper for all to be in one organization since all have the same goal: the education of children. They claim that administrators do *not* dominate the organization. Sanctions, according to the NEA, would include publicizing school systems which indulged in unprofessional practices, and calling on all members to desist from accepting employment in such situations.

155

The NEA, it may be noted, has only reluctantly and recently come to enunciate even such a mild policy of action. But the gains of the AFT both in publicity and in membership have spurred the NEA. Teachers are getting restless. Not even high ideals and charitable views can make the working conditions seem good enough and the pay sufficient. The rewards of professional attainment are desired *now*.

The debate as to the proper role and function of organizations will continue for some time. As more money becomes available from federal sources it is possible that the pressure to unionize will diminish. But educators want real power, and they have glimpsed the power that organized action can bring.

SUMMARY

As education comes of age, moving into the realms of a true profession, many issues are opened to public debate. We lack clear-cut evidence from research, so unfortunately discussions of such things as teacher education, teacher selection, and merit pay are characterized more by rhetoric and dissention than by logic and analysis. Since it is impossible to define the good teacher to the satisfaction of all groups, it is impossible to pay good teachers more than others, yet salary inducements appear to be essential to the recruitment and retention of high-quality persons. The educational community is split, too, over the appropriate organizational means to obtain better pay and better working conditions, yet it is agreed that improvement will help attract and keep more and better teachers.

BIBLIOGRAPHY

BENNETT, MARGARET, "Teaching Is Better With!" *Saturday Review*, XLVI, No. 7 (February 16, 1963), 82-83. A teacher makes a good case for the value of professional education courses.

BENSON, CHARLES S., *The Economics of Public Education*. Boston: Houghton Mifflin Company, 1961. See especially Chapter 14 for a cogent analysis of the teacher salary dilemma.

"Collective Bargaining and STRIKES? or Professional Negotiations and SANCTIONS?" *Phi Delta Kappan*, XLIV, No. 1 (October 1962), 1-11. An editorial presenting a good summary of the key points of difference.

CONANT, JAMES B., *The Education of American Teachers*. New York: McGraw-Hill Book Company, 1963. This report has stirred much controversy among educators.

KERSHAW, JOSEPH A. AND ROLAND N. MCKEAN, *Teachers Shortages and Salary Schedules*. New York: McGraw-Hill Book Company, 1963. A Rand Corporation Research Study that provides a businessman's recommendations for rewarding merit and attracting persons in scarce teaching fields.

KOERNER, JAMES, *The Miseducation of Teachers*. Boston: Houghton Mifflin Company, 1963. A sweeping indictment of contemporary teacher education, with all biases showing.

KRUGMAN, MORRIS, ed., *Orthopsychiatry and the School*, pp. 170-203. New York: American Orthopsychiatric Association, Inc., 1958. In two chapters on "Teacher Education in Mental Health" an educator and a psychiatrist discuss the ways in which mental health concepts can be related to teacher recruitment, the analysis of the teaching task, and teacher education.

LIEBERMAN, MYRON, *Education as a Profession*. Englewood Cliffs, N. J.: Prentice-Hall, Inc., 1956. A vigorous advocacy of teachers' controlling their profession and its activities.

MCGRATH, EARL J. AND CHARLES H. RUSSELL, *Are School Teachers Illiberally Educated?* New York: Bureau of Publications, Teachers College, Columbia University, 1961. Comparisons are made among various professions to evaluate the extent of teachers' liberal education.

MORSE, WILLIAM C., "The Mental Hygiene Dilemma in Public Education," *American Journal of Orthopsychiatry*, XXXI, No. 2 (April 1961), 324-31. If there is a national mental health problem, what is the teacher's responsibility?

NATIONAL EDUCATION ASSOCIATION, RESEARCH DIVISION, *The American Public School Teacher, 1960-61*. Washington, D.C.: National Education Association, 1963. Reports on the personal and professional characteristics of teachers, their assignments and attitudes.

WARE, MARTHA, "Professional Negotiation," *NEA Journal*, 51, No. 8 (November 1962), 28-30. The position of the NEA regarding the essential characteristics of negotiation versus collective bargaining.

WILSON, CHARLES H., "The Case against Merit Pay," *Saturday Review*, XLV, No. 3 (January 20, 1962), 44. A well argued statement of what most educators consider to be the major reasons why merit pay will not do what its proponents claim.

WOODRING, PAUL AND JOHN SCANLON, eds., *American Education Today*, pp. 239-70. New York: McGraw-Hill Book Company, 1963. Part Six, "Educating Teachers and School Administrators," consists of reprints of articles on the subject, which originally appeared in the *Saturday Review*.

156

The modern school is a vast and intricate institution. Although the efforts of the total system are ultimately directed towards the individual student in the classroom with a teacher, there would be neither pupil, teacher nor classroom if it were not for the organized activities of many other individuals. The school, in this regard, appears to differ relatively little from any other organized group activity, be it producing breakfast food, publishing books, or selling insurance. The school system is, indeed, similar in some ways to other kinds of production organizations; it is also unique and peculiar in its organizational operations.

BUREAUCRACY IS HERE TO STAY

The continual grumblings about bureaucratic invasions of freedom reflect a normal suspicion of what is remote, complex and powerful; bureaucracies are all of these. They exist in government and in private enterprise. The bureaucracy of government is most resented because it affects us all, whether we wish it to or not: defense, public safety, taxation, etc. If private enterprise is riddled with bureaucracy, who cares?

THE
ORGANIZATION
SCHOOL

13

Bureaucracy in government is a covenient whipping boy for public discontent. It is not that legislators are venal, or legislation serves selfish interests, but that civil servants are incompetent left-overs from the business world.

The schools inevitably are tarred by the same brush, because, inevitably, the schools have spawned their own bureaucracy. It could hardly be otherwise. The job of the school is massive, and encompasses tasks far beyond classroom teaching.

THE SCHOOL SYSTEM AS A BUREAUCRACY

Bureaucracies develop because the numbers of persons involved in an enterprise are so great that face-to-face relationships with all of those involved is impossible. Bureaucracy also develops when the task is highly complex and covers large geographic areas. It is inconceivable that today's technical advances could have occurred without the social invention of bureaucracies.

So effective is this kind of organization that today's worker in American industry works fewer hours and makes more than at any time in history.

The students of social organizations hark back to the writings of Max Weber who attempted to describe the ideal bureaucratic structure. A summary of his model structure identifies the following as characteristic:

> . . . impersonal social relations, appointment and promotion on the basis of merit, authority and obligations which are specified a priori and adhere to the job rather than the individual . . . authority organized on a hierarchical basis, separation of policy and administrative positions, members of the bureaucracy being concerned with administrative decisions, general rules for governing all behavior not specified by the above, and, finally, specialization. If the organization is large and structured by these ideal conditions, it will be more efficient.[1]

The model suggested by Weber has been criticized and amended, but it still forms the basis for many theoretical discussions of bureaucracy. Most large institutions do not approximate Weber's construct, but the effort to rationalize operations continues. It seems helpful to be able to visualize an orderly hierarchy of relationships with policies, orders, ideas flowing in one direction, while reports, products and accounts flow in another. The ubiquitous organizational chart is an indispensable tool for administrative rationalization. No respectable system would be seen without one. It appears to provide a sense of position and stability.

What appears on paper may be far from the reality. In very few operations, even those with the most standard product, can the model on paper long remain in operation. Things are bound to change. A person dies, and though the position remains the same, a new personality may profoundly influence the ways in which others can or cannot do their work. A technical innovation may be adopted, which again will change working relations. Most bureaucracies are in a constant search for equilibrium, but

[1] Eugene Litwak, "Models of Bureaucracy Which Permit Conflict," *American Journal of Sociology*, LXVII, No. 2 (September 1961), 177.

few achieve it for more than a passing moment. This is particularly true of the schools, where organizational stability is not only difficult to achieve, but may actually be a major impediment to educational progress.[2]

The school as an organizational system can never approximate Weber's model because the very things that characterize his model are nonexistent in the school situation. Personnel in the school system are continually making new decisions about unique events (people); the school is staffed by persons with the same job title (teacher) but with greatly varying ability to develop a product which is never standard (learning), and there is a very unclear division between policy and implementation. To equate the organization of a school system with the organization of a government agency or a business enterprise is to attempt to compare potatoes with airplanes, or books with rifles.

Yet there are continual efforts to push the school organization into the same structural mold as that of industry or government. The resultant creakings and groanings of the system, the frustrations resulting from ambiguous roles and role relationships, reflect in part the lack of fit of the organizational model.

The position of the public school system is similar in some dimensions to that of the large university. In commenting on the institutional characteristics of the university, Presthus says that they show a good example of "organizational values applied to an inappropriate area." [3] Interestingly enough, Presthus ignores the large school system as a prime example of mass institutional organization, even though he concedes the presence of the university in this category. This is a clear and interesting case of sociological myopia.

Have sociologists and students of public administration forgotten that schools are part of the organized society? One who hasn't is William Whyte, author of a biting analysis of the schools of suburbia, in *The Organization Man*,[4] in which he points out the relationship between school values and social values. Similarly, *Crestwood Heights*, an analysis of the school in a Canadian suburb, shows how the school implements in practice the value orientations of the community.[5] In neither book, however, is the school as an organized institution related to the other organized forces which are products as well as creators of our modern society.

That organizational theory in general will not apply to the school system, despite valiant attempts by school administrators to capture the spirit of organizational stability in organizational charts, is due to other salient forces. The public school system is one of the few large bureaucracies that are not only nearby and visible to the public, but available for public manipulation.

[2] Lawrence W. Downey, "Organizational Theory as a Guide to Educational Change," *Educational Theory*, XI, No. 1 (January 1961), 38-44.

[3] Robert Presthus, *The Organizational Society* (New York: Alfred A. Knopf, Inc., 1962), p. 240.

[4] William H. Whyte, Jr., *The Organization Man* (Garden City, N. Y.: Doubleday & Company, Inc., 1957), 423-34.

[5] John R. Seeley, R. Alexander Sim, and Elizabeth W. Loosley, *Crestwood Heights: A Study of the Culture of Suburban Life* (New York: Basic Books, Inc., 1956).

For example, if people become disenchanted with the leadership of a school superintendent, they can make their feelings known to the school board, who, if sufficiently convinced, can fire him, sometimes, without any notice whatsoever.[6] It is impossible to imagine the same kind of action displacing, say, the director of a major government agency. To accomplish such a feat would take more than local irritation with some national policy—it would require mobilizing extraordinary pressure at the national level.

The board of directors of a corporation does not represent the stockholders in the way that a school board represents the public. Nor is the administrative director of a corporation in the same relationship to his board of directors as a superintendent is to the school board. The ways of operating are also significantly different. A corporation conducts much of its policy making in secret; to do otherwise might provide a competitive advantage to a rival. A school system is expected to conduct its business in public. The school board in many instances is legally required to hold a given number of open meetings a year, and there is usually a legal definition of those situations in which executive or private sessions may be held.

WHO IS BOSS?

The school is institutionally unique in the relationships existing among personnel in the school system.

There is continual confusion over who bosses whom in the school situation. If line and staff positions are identified, and placed on an organizational chart, does this really mean what the chart seems to indicate that it means? The school supervisor is often placed in a staff position; that is, he "serves" the individual teacher, and presumably has no administrative authority over him. The supervisor presumably cannot fire or hire or insist on compliance with supervisory requests.

Yet, teachers know very well that the supervisor, after a classroom visit, typically drops in for a chat with the principal. And if the supervisor is pleased, or displeased, don't you think the principal is going to hear about it? In a moderate sized system, most supervisors have more ready access to the superintendent than any teacher, who may not even know the superintendent by sight. If something is particularly amiss at a given school, it is a rare supervisor who will not tell the superintendent, and this includes reports on school principals.

The real power of the supervisor, as against that which is delimited on paper, can be inferred from the elaborate devices that schools utilize to warn teachers that a supervisor is in the building. In some schools a special bell is rung; in others a monitor goes from room to room with a specially coded message. Typically the elementary supervisor is treated with more deference than the secondary supervisor. The latter may be given short shrift by a principal who considers himself the undisputed head

[6] National Commission for the Defense of Democracy through Education, *Indianapolis, Indiana, A Study of the Sudden Forced Resignation of a Superintendent* (Washington, D.C.: National Education Association, May, 1960).

of a school of 2,000 students with 80 teachers, two vice-principals and a dozen other specialized personnel. Subject matter teachers in the high school may dread the supervisor's visit, but there is nothing in the rule book that says they have to do what the supervisor says. The supervisor is reduced to cajolery, the power of positive influence, or a slightly veiled show of force.

In effect, becoming a supervisor is a step upward in the status system, marked by increased salary and freedom, and it is understandable that supervisors, being human, expect to wield increased power, too. In the matter of ordering supplies, a supervisor may be charged with responsibility for approving purchase orders. This means, of course, that the teacher who desires material which is not approved by the supervisor might as well not ask. Who then is in charge of whom? Instead of making the relationship clear, the literature on school supervision almost without exception reiterates the need for supervisors who do *not* exercise line authority!

To the outsider, school supervision appears to be a case of supervisors who cannot supervise and of teachers who complain about the lack of help but resist what is at hand. The difficulty so often described in upgrading classroom practices springs in large part, we might suggest, from the virtual impasse described above. Supervisors can only rarely insist, and then only with great guilt, that teachers change their ways. Moreover, they cannot even hold out the incentive of a promotion or other reward that might be attained if practices were modified. In theory, supervision is not only necessary but crucial; in practice, supervisors are probably the least effective of school personnel, and the most stubbornly and idealistically dedicated to a doomed cause.

Despite the complaints of some lay critics that schools are too prone to jump on any new educational bandwagon, educational specialists working with teachers testify to the great difficulty encountered with very many in trying to induce change. Change, at least through the current supervisory mechanism, is slow and uncertain. Should supervisors have the authority to enforce their views, as do school inspectors in other countries? [7] Such a position is strongly resisted by leaders in the field of school supervision, and certainly it would be resisted by teachers as well. Upgrading, it is suggested, can proceed along the lines of in-service education advocated by Flanders whereby teachers are helped to see themselves in the act of teaching.[8] An alternative, proposed by Brickell, is to utilize the concept of the model farm or experiment station, so successful in introducing new techniques in agriculture. Demonstration centers in schools could be used to show teachers how new or different approaches work.[9]

Within the school building, the most potent influence on the teacher's classroom behavior is wielded by the principal. In theory, the principal is a master teacher who has risen from the ranks. In a bygone era, he taught

[7] Sylvia Ashton-Warner, *Spinster* (New York: Simon and Schuster, Inc., 1959), p. 10.
[8] Edmund J. Amidon and Ned Flanders, *The Role of the Teacher in the Classroom*.
[9] Henry M. Brickell, *Organizing New York State for Educational Change* (Albany: State Education Department, 1961).

as well as administered the school, and was considered a somewhat more competent peer. His opinions and supervision were respected.

Today the picture is quite changed. The principal in an elementary school may have taught one or two grades. If he is a man, he typically has had experience at the fifth or sixth grade, rarely lower. A well educated first grade teacher probably knows more than he does about the problems of instruction in her room. For example, he may not be an expert in the higher mysteries of introducing reading to first graders. How can he mediate between the phonics-only school, the sight-and-sound school, the grouping-for-instruction claque and the individualized-reading approach? He is lucky if he knows that such issues exist. His line relationship, then, is not superiority by virtue of knowledge, but superiority only in terms of *position*. The tradition of academic life, that colleagues are of equal merit in their field of specialty is obvious to anyone who is part of a school faculty, but it does not appear on the organization chart. Is the principal a leader or a boss? Is he the authority, or a consultant?

Because of the difficulties of defining the role precisely, life in a school is both frustrating and exciting. The personality of the principal will have more to do with how the school is run than his formal title. Teachers therefore are prone to use human wiles in influencing the principal. The principal in turn cannot depend on the authority of his office to maintain a well-run building. He must be fairly astute and subtle in his personal dealings with teachers.

Principals like to think that teachers prefer a well-organized, well-run school where the administrator's main function is to keep the machinery going smoothly, with short but businesslike faculty meetings. Many administrators enjoy the exercise of authority or have well-organized minds which find bookkeeping and schedule making satisfying. They may or may not have been master teachers themselves. Being a master teacher is not necessarily the best qualification for running so complex an enterprise as a modern school.

Teachers certainly like a well run school, but an even more profound and important preference is for a principal who recognizes them as persons, who appreciates their efforts, who rewards them with recognition.[10] Where there is no merit promotion system, such increments of personal recognition from the power and status figures become that much more crucial and important.

To what extent teachers really want principals to be "democratic" or to be authoritarian is open to question. Some teachers may prefer the principal who treats them with human warmth and is generous with personal recognition, while other teachers may prefer the strong father figure. As we noted in Chapter 8, teachers find it necessary to invoke the strong, omnipotent power of the principal to keep reluctant learners in line. Teachers tend, too, to speak with approval of the principal who "lets you know where he stands." They want a principal upon whom they can be

[10] Jean D. Grambs, Douglas Bevins, Angeline G. Boisen, and Harry Diehl, unpublished research, University of Maryland, 1963.

emotionally dependent, who will establish rules, set limits, and ask the faculty for help and advice only within somewhat restricted areas.[11]

Principals often feel, however, that teachers chafe at authoritative edicts, and complain about the principal who is "too bossy." In effect, teachers want it all ways. They want the firm father, the sympathetic counselor, the self-assured leader, and the accepting colleague. No wonder principals often declare that there is nothing more baffling than working with a school faculty. That schools are as well run as they are is no tribute to the organizational structure, but a tribute to the individuals who must operate within a basically incompatible system.

There may be value in organizational ambiguity. Certainly the schools offer a prime example of uncertainty which befogs all operations, and which requires a redefinition of relationships with every major personnel change. Such indefiniteness of function and responsibility could leave the way wide open for innovation and experiment. It is interesting that much lip service is given to research and trying out new procedures, but in practice most schools appear to be bound by conservative traditions. Despite organizational confusion and frustration there does not appear to be a major effort by educators to devise a more appropriate organizational model, or even to exploit the potential that lies in current organizational confusion.

The role of the school board in the school structure is one of the murkier areas of school administration. Tomes are written for administrators on how to help their school boards know what they ought to do in school affairs. When is the board really serving its proper function and when is it meddling? It is difficult for the public to identify who is actually responsible for school programs. Is it the school board or the professional administrator and his staff? When things appear wrong with the schools, the public blames the professional, and the professional blames the lay school board. One particularly interesting criticism of the schools which professional people currently find particularly galling is that coaches or other teachers are often found teaching academic courses for which they are not prepared. The professional educator for some reason or other becomes the whipping boy for this offense. No administrator *wants* to place an English teacher in a mathematics class, nor have a driver education instructor fill the extra period in United States History. The problem is one of money and of logistics. A school has to be quite large to provide a full schedule of physics classes, for instance, so it is cheaper to get one teacher to teach both physics and chemistry or mathematics. Yet clearly he cannot be completely competent in more than one such field. What school system would hire a full-time teacher for only a half-time load? The other problem is that the teacher scarcity in mathematics, science and languages means that someone from another field will just have to take over, or the courses cannot be offered. The board won't stand for the latter, but can't, or won't, face the consequences of having unprepared teachers assigned to "cover" the courses. Perhaps administrators *should* balk at such

163

[11] Jean D. Grambs, "Do Teachers Really Want Democratic Administrators?" *Nation's Schools,* 46 (November 1950), 40-41.

conditions, but in this instance the school board clearly has the power to insist that there be a teacher (even if unprepared) in each classroom. It is possible, of course, that administrators have been insufficiently imaginative in their utilization of teacher resources. Some experimentation among the very small high schools suggests that a sharing of scarce talent can be achieved. Administrators or school boards seem peculiarly loath to hiring part-time teachers for day schools, yet there are probably many married women in the community with adequate teacher preparation, who would be willing to fill the odd spots here and there although not to teach a full day. It is more expensive to have many part-time people than the equivalent full-time persons, so perhaps again it is bookkeeping limits rather than educational goals that determine policy.

Perhaps a more rational organization could be patterned after hospital administration. Here a specially trained administrator runs the machinery of the institution. But the actual professional operation is under a medical director who in turn is backstopped by a medical review board. Professional decisions rest with those who have to implement them, and the administrator in effect carries out those administrative functions which support what the professionals are trying to do.

Unfortunately, school organization was stabilized in its present form at a time when the only conceivable organizational pattern was that of the business or industry.

THE SCHOOL IS BIG "BUSINESS"

It is not accidental that schools have developed an hierarchical system which appears on the surface to be interchangeable with that of a government bureau or a business enterprise. Schools underwent their major growth spurt in the first quarter of this century at the same time the emphasis in business was on efficiency of organization. Since businessmen most often served on school boards of large systems the thinking of business-minded persons was easily embraced by school administrators. The appearance of the efficiency expert and the cost accountant, together with the interest in the development of a "science" of education, made the merger of these forces inevitable.[12]

The strong urge to fit the school system into the industrial system is typified by the reference to school buildings as school "plants." It is true that education is big. The temptation is to say that education is big "business." It is so usual to equate the educational system with the business system that one unconsciously falls into the error of referring to education in the same terms. While this may be considered merely a semantic quibble, it does point up one reason why it is difficult to discuss educational problems rationally, since actually education is *not* a business.

One of the reasons we think of the schools as a business is the large financial investment that is involved. Capital expenditures for school construction run into the millions in even the more modest school systems.

[12] Raymond E. Callahan, *Education and the Cult of Efficiency* (Chicago: University of Chicago Press, 1962).

Not only are current expenditures large, but they have increased at a great rate. Although enrollment in schools has increased 45 per cent since 1949-50 (while the total United States population increased 12 per cent), school expenditures other than for building have increased 154 per cent, capital investments have increased 221 per cent, and interest payments have increased 275.5 per cent since 1949.[13] It is understandable that school people become defensive when the public responds to such figures with an uneasy feeling that everything costs more than it used to, and probably therefore more than it should.

Not only are schools big in cost and cost increases, but they employ very large numbers of people. In 1959, one out of every 24 employed persons was engaged in public education. Of all employees who are *publicly* employed, over 30 per cent are in some kind of educational enterprise; national defense, the second largest public employer accounts for 16 per cent.

When Americans asked for free public education for all, they were asking for a larger operation than they could possibly predict. Free education means free books, free movies, free television, free transportation, free supplies, free equipment, free facilities. For each of the above "free" items, add a person, or (in a large system) a staff which must administer the program. Take books, for instance: obviously schools cannot operate without books. In a majority of schools, books are purchased directly by the school and lent to students or there is some modification of this system. Whatever the system, the schools order books. This involves a screening committee to choose the books. Then, there are purchase orders. A bookkeeper must record the orders, and note when the books have arrived. Replacements must be available when old books wear out. If the school provides one book per pupil per subject studied, figure out the volume of books that must be accounted for: 50,000 students, studying at least five subjects each, need at least 250,000 books.

Thus it is with the ever-increasing services of the schools. Several generations ago schools did not provide lunches. Now, with the federally supported hot-lunch program, (which helps ease the embarrassing farm surplus) schools must build and furnish cafeterias and lunch rooms, hire cafeteria workers, cafeteria supervisors, nutritionists, additional custodians, and so on.

Each additional increment of service adds to costs. Each addition is therefore open to question. Is it an unnecessary "frill" or is it worth the cost? Actually, however, while school costs have risen, most of the increase is in teachers' salaries, capital outlay, and interest charges. Costs for materials and supplies, when adjusted to equate dollar purchasing power, increased only $2.54 per pupil between 1941-42 and 1957-58.[14]

Continual efforts are made to keep costs down or reduce costs. One outcome of this effort to reduce costs has been the consolidation of school

165

[13] National Education Association, *Research Bulletin*, XXXVIII, No. 1 (February 1960), 21-22.
[14] Charles S. Benson, *The Emonomics of Public Education* (Boston: Houghton Mifflin Company, 1961), pp. 6-13.

districts. In 1931 there were 127,531 school administrative units, that is, individual school systems. In 1960 there were 40,605.[15]

The small school district and the small school are expensive to operate,[16] and Conant claims they cannot provide an adequate education. A school with a twelfth-grade enrollment of less than 100, Conant argues, cannot offer sufficient variety of subjects to meet the differing needs of students and society.[17] On the other hand, the research by Barker and associates raises some serious questions about the advantages claimed for school consolidation. Although larger size was supposed to mean greater variety of offerings, "schools differing in enrollment by 100%, had only 17% median differences in instructional variety. Increasing school size would appear to be a relatively ineffective means of achieving richness and variety." [18]

It is interesting to point out, too, that arguments for larger schools, which mention saving the cost of duplicate facilities, and offering the student a greater variety of courses, do not include any commentary upon the effect of school size on the teacher. It has been clearly documented by industrial research that larger units result in greater turnover, lower employee morale, and lower productivity. Given the peculiar demands made upon teachers by the constant interchange with volatile children, it is possible to predict that the schools with the highest morale are those with small faculties where the principal can provide more individual attention, and where group members can know and support each other. At the high-school level, it is true, teacher morale will be positively related to the opportunity to teach the subjects in which the teacher has competence; but, apart from this, large school size tends to produce all the symptoms of alienation found in industrial studies. It is probable that the large organized school has contributed an excessive share to the loss of many bright and able people from teaching.

An obsession with economy seems to pervade much of the policy thinking in school affairs. It is argued that reducing the number of school districts and enlarging the educational unit will decrease the costs of administering the schools. It would appear, for instance, that despite the addition of many new services to the schools the proportion of "administrators" to teachers has neither increased nor decreased materially.

One system, for example, employed 460 teachers and 48 administrators in 1940. In 1960, this system employed 3,317 teachers and 314 administrators. The ratio of teachers to administrators in 1940 was 9.6 to 1. In 1960 it was 10.6 to 1. In the classification of administrator were included superintendent, assistant superintendent, directors and assistant directors, administrative assistants, supervisors, and assistant supervisors, principals,

[15] Clayton D. Hutchins and Dolores A. Steinhilber, *Trends in Financing Public Education, 1929-30 to 1959-60* (Washington, D.C.: Department of Health, Education and Welfare, 1961), p. 78.

[16] Willard A. Wright and Wilfred H. Pine, *Costs of Rural High Schools in Central Kansas, 1956-57* (Manhattan: Kansas State University, February, 1961).

[17] James B. Conant, *The American High School Today* (New York: McGraw-Hill Book Company, 1959).

[18] Roger C. Barker, *Big School—Small School* (Lawrence: Midwest Psychological Field Station, University of Kansas, 1963), p. 233.

assistant principals, psychologists, and pupil personnel workers.[19] Were there too many administrators in 1940, or are there too few in 1960?

Unlike industry, schools do not provide additional supporting personnel as aids to more effective production. In 1900, for instance, it has been estimated that there were about 1.31 administrative or supervisory personnel for every 1,000 students. In 1958, there were 2.70. "This is an increase of less than two administrators or specialists per 1,000 pupils over a period of nearly sixty years." [20] It is hard to prove that schools are unduly burdened by administrative personnel. Perhaps, indeed, some of the travail of modern education can be laid to the fact that an increasingly costly and complex operation is being managed by relatively few more persons than ran the horse-and-buggy schools of half a century ago.

The question that seems uppermost is whether the school system can continue to expand without a proliferating variety of non-teaching personnel. It seems inevitable that the answer is "No." Yet this fact of life seems to the critical public to be an unnecessary demonstration of Parkinson's law regarding bureaucratic spawning.

The public tends to suspect that there are more administrators around than are needed. As we noted, within the private sanctums of business there may be incredible bureaucratic waste, but that is the problem of the business if it has any interest in making money and staying alive. A public bureaucracy has no problem of survival; it will outlast all of us. Since it operates publicly, the presence of many persons who do not seem to be "productive" makes the taxpayer uneasy.

What businessman running a million-dollar operation would stand for the understaffing of the clerical force which is standard in every school system and university? Obtaining additional secretaries in a school is considered a major administrative triumph. The public wants to protect its money, but refuses to admit that watching each dollar means mountains of bookkeeping. As a result, the business aspects of schools are apt to be several decades behind other enterprises with similar rates of expenditure. Teachers, for instance, have to play a major role in pupil accounting. This is like asking a front-line soldier to count the number of bullets he is firing. Yet this procedure is standard practice in schools. Similarly, teachers typically must type and duplicate their own tests and exercise material. This is like asking each individual soldier to run back to the supply depot every time he needed more ammunition. The failure of businessmen on school boards to see the clerical needs of teachers is one of the more agonizing problems of the professional educator, and one of the practical problems he faces in keeping good teachers in schools.

The public is convinced that the main business of the school is instruction. In school budgets, it is interesting to note, the costs for many of the non-teaching personnel and supporting services are included in the costs assigned to instruction. If "instruction" includes the salaries of clerks and principals and supervisors as well as those of teachers, why not include the salary of the bus driver who brought the students to

167

19 C. Taylor Whittier, "Summary of School Years, 1957-1961" (Rockville, Md.: Montgomery County Public Schools, June 12, 1962), p. 3.
20 Benson, The Economics of Public Education, p. 11.

school, without whom no instruction can take place? Or the custodian who cleans the room or the maintenance man who keeps it from falling apart? What are the costs of instruction, anyway? Benson allocates only 47.4 per cent of the total costs of schools to "salaries of instructional staff"; [21] yet the classification used above is that recommended by the United States Office of Education. The public can believe that 73 per cent of the school dollar is going for the direct instruction of the student, and if no one is quite clear just what kinds of expenses are part of the cost of instruction, is this important?

Actually, it makes a great deal of difference where the money goes, and how much is spent on what. While it can be proven that good education does cost more than poor education, it has also been shown that just spending more money on everything is not necessarily the way to improve school operations. In fact, it is argued on the basis of research that if more money were spent on relatively minor items, schools would improve more than the cost would suggest. "For example, while quality of teaching is improved by expenditure for supplies and equipment, it is still further improved by providing personnel who help the teacher make effective instructional use of these teaching aids." [22]

During the years between 1913 and 1930 business efficiency became the criterion of good school administration, and was equated with good education.[23] It was revealed during these crucial years, for instance, that a teacher was more efficient (that is, could teach better or more) with 30 students than with ten. *Ergo*, let the teacher have 30 (or as it turned out, usually more) students per class. A history teacher who could teach one group of 30 students, could easily repeat the lesson for any multiple of 30. Thus the secondary-school teacher was saddled with a teaching load of 180 students per day. Only in the name of efficiency could such a system of education have been foisted on the public, or on teachers.

The schools were ready objects of the thinking of the efficiency expert. After all, public money was being expended, no one wanted taxes to rise, and thus it was obligatory to get the most out of whatever money was available.[24] Interest in economy and efficiency in the period 1913-30 promoted the growth of the school survey by an expert. The surveyors were hired by school boards, and the major interest on both sides was measuring the amount of "education" per tax dollar. The school survey, in its early stages in the middle 1920's, and today, reports in utmost detail the financial and accounting aspects of the school enterprise.

But can one give an accountant's report on the educational product? Six years of schooling cannot be measured in the same way that one can measure the number of insurance policies sold per agent, or the number of ingots produced per furnace. The educational outcome will always evade measurement. It is understandable that to "practical" persons the

168

[21] Benson, *The Economics of Public Education*, p. 14.
[22] Committee on Tax Education and School Finance, *Does Better Education Cost More?* (Washington, D.C.: National Education Association, 1959), p. 31; William S. Vincent, "Quality Control: A Rationale for Analysis of a School System," *IAR Research Bulletin*, I, No. 2 (January 1961), 5.
[23] Callahan, *Education and the Cult of Efficiency*.
[24] *Ibid.*, p. 116.

problems of school finance should appear far more significant than the problems of what makes for a "true" education. The former can be added, subtracted and reported; the latter can only be debated.

Thus we see the conflict between efficiency and education. It is probable that this is a conflict which can never be resolved, since the ends sought are incompatible. Education can, by its very nature, never be efficient.

THE SUPERINTENDENT IS A LONELY MAN

The irritation that pervades many of the more or less querulous criticisms of school affairs often is expressed in derision of the school administrator. It is claimed that he knows more about bookkeeping and building costs than he does about English literature. It is further claimed that the culturally empty education that occurs in American classrooms is a direct result of this kind of business mentality in the leadership role in education.

Let us examine these arguments, since they help to illumine the organizational problem of public education. When queried, school superintendents indicate that the most important professional course they took was one in school finance.[25] Such a statement is enough to make liberal arts professors scream. To them it clearly indicates a lack of vision and lack of respect for the verities of education.

In actuality, what the superintendents report reflects a more accurate view of their role than does the wishful thinking of the lay critic. The administrator today is forced to be more concerned with costs than with program. As at least one study showed, boards in small districts tended to be more concerned with problems of personnel and finance, than with curriculum or relations with the community.[26] A wise superintendent does not want to distress his board, so he tends to bring to them questions to which there can be business answers.

It must be pointed out, too, that in the last two decades some of the most crucial problems facing local communities have been bookkeeping problems. During the depression years schools were either not built, or built sparely. The recovery period had just about reached the schools when World War II hit. During this period, construction only of vital buildings was permitted, which made it difficult for school systems to replace outworn buildings or provide new ones to keep up with population growth. When the war ended, with the astonishing baby crop to be educated, the school systems were caught in a spectacular shortage of space and personnel, one which is still to be solved in many communities.

There were too many children in areas where there were not enough schools. Populations were moving around at a fantastic rate, and settling in areas which were not used to having great population growth—and what

169

[25] *Professional Administrators for America's Schools*, Thirty-eighth Yearbook (Washington, D.C.: American Association of School Administrators, 1960), p. 47.
[26] Chester W. Harris, ed., *Review of Educational Research*, 3rd ed. (New York: The Macmillan Company, 1960), p. 152.

community was used to this phenomenon? Thus school personnel were engulfed in a whole series of major decisions that had to be made over and over again. Where do we need new schools? How many students will we have? What special facilities must the school house? Where can we get the land? What tax support must we have? How much will the school cost? How many more teachers, supervisors, supporting services will we need?

These are all difficult questions. When the postwar crisis hit the schools relatively few school administrators were ready. Current emphasis in the education of school administrators on the business aspects of school affairs recognizes the massive financial problems which school leaders must solve.

Despite the critics, school administrators want to have good school programs. Almost all of them have been teachers, and are aware of the problems of the front line. That they may soon forget how it feels to teach a class is no reflection on the administrators; it is the common problem of central office and field office; of generals and sergeants.

There is a suspicion abroad that the best way to rise in the educational hierarchy is to start as an athletic coach. If this were ever true, it is certainly not true today, although it may be useful to perpetuate this myth. Some critics claim that even if superintendents were not coaches, all they took in college were education courses. Again, the facts do not support this contention. A study of school superintendents shows the following distribution of undergraduate majors:

Behavioral sciences	18 per cent
Education	17
Physical and biological science	15
History and political science	15
Mathematics	11
English	9
Physical education and health	3
Industrial or vocational[27]	2

The figures indicate that less than 20 per cent majored in education, and most were what we might describe as typical liberal arts graduates with a specialty in a field outside of the applied field of education. However, to give some comfort to the critics, most superintendents of today come from relatively small communities. It has been noted that you can take the boy out of the corn, but you cannot take the corn out of the boy. Limitations in vision among school leaders may have less to do with the things they learned in college and university than with the things they learned in young boyhood back on the farm. Few American colleges make any impact on the value systems of students.[28] The school superintendent undoubtedly entered college or university with a firm system of values, studied, received a degree, and graduated with his values intact, just like most of his peers. As a graduate student, the neophyte superintendent

[27] American Association of School Administrators, *Professional Administrators*, p. 26.

[28] Phillip Jacob, *Changing Values in College* (New York: Harper & Row, Publishers, 1957).

has a more direct focus upon his final position. He tends to take course work and degree programs which make him an educational specialist. When he aspires to higher realms, he takes his doctorate in educational administration. As for the health of the American school system, should we be worried? Is there something wrong in having those who are to be expert in school affairs earn advanced degrees in that specialty?

The chief education officer in England usually has had experience at many educational levels, but there is no special program to prepare him for an administrative task. In most other European schools the local school administrator is either nonexistent or is quite subservient to the central bureaucratic control by the state.[29]

The American school administrator is a product of the scientific movement in education, which assumes that there is something about the educational process which can be studied independently of other variables, and to which the insights of administrators and experts from other fields can also have relevance, and which assumes that a person can be especially trained for a very complex and difficult position.

The school superintendent is accorded little respect by scholars in other fields. They would not have his job, no matter how well paid (the superintendents in the largest cities command the largest salaries given any public employee), because there is still an aura of the huckster in the role of the superintendent. This is quite so. He must be a public relations person who presents a good front for the schools. In addition, of course, he must be an expert in school fiscal affairs, school buildings, personnel arrangements. He is expected to know curriculum, administrative theory, and educational philosophy.

171

School leaders are attacked from time to time because they appear to spend more time talking about school financial problems than engaging in intellectual discussions. The average taxpayer is very lucky that this is so, since it is his money that the superintendent is keeping a close watch on. It would be interesting if the scholars who complain most loudly about the nonintellectual leaders of American schools were those whose pocketbooks were depleted because these persons made stupid decisions about school sites or allowed buildings to be put up by incompetent contractors.[30]

Whatever the superintendent does, however, he is wrong. If he works hard to raise salaries, he must often be particularly attentive to community interests and wary of community defenses. So much time may be spent on these community-directed activities that he is not readily available for staff visits. On the other hand, if he devotes most of his time to staff affairs, he will neglect community relations and salaries will not be raised. Whatever he does, there will be complaints.[31]

One can hope for utopia, of course. It would be nice if schools could

---

[29] Theodore L. Reller and Edgar L. Morphet, eds., *Comparative Educational Administration* (Englewood Cliffs, N. J.: Prentice-Hall, Inc., 1962), pp. 38, 62, 108ff.

[30] See Benson, *The Economics of Public Education*, p. 470.

[31] Melvin Seeman, "Administrative Leadership Is a Question of Style," *Nation's Schools*, LV, No. 1 (August 1957), 42-44.

be run by business experts who took care of all the sordid details of purchasing, site acquisition, and building planning and construction. Then the "real" school leaders could devote themselves to the true mission of the school: content and process of instruction. Why is this utopia not realized? Well, again, we have no one to blame but ourselves.

SCHOOL PUBLIC RELATIONS

A subtitle for this section might be: "How school administrators get the public to want what the school administrators want them to want." The schools are almost completely dependent on local good will for self-respecting survival. The schools will be there, even if the public is least interested in or unable to provide adequate support. The American public (except for one county in Virginia where the terrors of school integration were such that the schools were closed in 1959) wants education, and will keep its schools open, although they may allow them to continue poor or inadequate.

The goal of the professional person, therefore, is constantly to remind the public of the advantages of *good* education. School people are inevitably people with consciences. They are educated, hopefully, to know a good school system when they see one. They are made restless by conditions which are less than optimum. If this were not so, schools would soon be nonfunctional, and this our constantly changing society could not stand. The school administrator responds to both the demands of professional conscience and those of the larger society when he goes forth to "sell" the schools.

As soon as he embarks on his mission of "selling" the schools he is in trouble. For one thing, schools cannot be "sold." They are not a commodity, like toothpaste. Nor is there any competition in the marketplace. In most communities parents have only one choice of where to send their children. And they have practically no choice regarding who the children's teachers will be or even what subjects will be taught, or how. Thus the "selling" concept suggests a choice that is not there.

School administrators are those mainly responsible for "selling" the schools, but actually it is quite clear that everyone concerned with the operation of the schools is a public relations person. Every teacher appears as a topic of conversation at many dinner tables every night. To the degree that this appearance is favorable, will schools be supported. Teachers are thus admonished to act in such a way that the message the child brings home to dinner is a good one. Then the vote on the bond issue next year will be favorable, and teacher will get a raise, or a needed school will be built, or new facilities added. Bus drivers and school clerks are given advice regarding their public relations role. We must pat the hand that feeds us.

Unfortunately, this approach does not seem to work too well. Despite the superintendent's cozy bulletins home, the friendly principal, the cooperative teachers, the public is not always won to the cause of the school. At fault is the assumption that the schools can be "sold." To accept this viewpoint, straight from Madison Avenue, is to forget what schools mean to people. Selling the schools means, inevitably, that you tell about your successes, and hide your failures.

School people are told to give the press stories about those students who gained scholarships, those who won prizes, those who succeeded in some special activity. Nice pictures of cute kids having fun at school are continually fed to the press. Many of them are published. Kids *are* cute, and a school is fortunate that has a good photographer who can catch them in appropriate poses.

But it does not seem to work. We may suggest some hypotheses. In the first place, for every student who wins a Merit Scholarship, there are probably 5,000 who did not. So how impressed are the parents of the losing 5,000 with the knowledge that one succeeded? And in spite of all the appealing children studying happily, how many parents are struggling with Junior who has already failed first grade? In some school systems first-grade failure rates run as high as 20 per cent. These are discouraged, embittered, or resigned parents. They are not very likely to support schools. In their deepest hearts parents of the failing or nonsuccessful group are sure that a "good" school system could have done something for them.

The "selling" of the schools tells the parents that this is a good school system which just needs a bit more help—ready money—to be ever so much better. The hidden implication is that, given this additional support, all children will be really well educated and taken care of and no one will fail. After several generations of this message, which has not been realized in practice, the public becomes cynical. In actuality, in order to "save" every child, the investment in the schools and related welfare agencies would have to be about triple the current school investment. The public wants the end result, but is quite unwilling to risk the money involved, particularly since previous promises of school pay-off have not been kept.

It might be suggested that this promise of all good things be preceded by a realistic presentation of the current educational picture. For instance, most parents are quite unaware of the number of slow learners in a community. Schools do not tell them about the distribution of intelligence in their own area.

There is a peculiar folk notion that not only are most children equal, but a good school would be educating most of them more than the "average." This concept of course runs counter to the whole notion of test norms. When a school system announces that the students are achieving "above national norms" everyone is happy. For students in a system to be at the norm, is to suggest something is wrong. Yet by the very nature of a norm, only a minority of students can be above it! Just try to explain this to the public! In fact, so sensitive is the public to such information that test makers provide schools with instructions in how to arrive at local norms, so the schools can always be at the norm. It is interesting, too, that there are separate norms published for northern and southern schools, so the schools in the South will not look too bad or too different.

The problem of school dropouts, which is currently making headlines and upsetting public and school officials alike, has been an old headache to school people. But now the public is getting into the act. One can only wonder why it took so long. Perhaps it is because the schools did not want to admit, out loud, that schools were dull and unrewarding, and actually forced many students to quit at the legal age, long before they could be considered educated.

School people, imbued with the idea of "selling" schools, reject any counsel which suggests that washing their dirty linen in public is exactly the best procedure for getting it clean. This is completely counter to the advertising approach, of course. And to the degree that school personnel think that schools can be presented much as a commodity is presented for consumer acceptance, to that degree will there be confusion about what the schools are doing, and why they are not better.

It has been claimed that one of the problems of school-community relations is that educators do not talk English. Instead they talk something rather horrible called pedagese. It is possible to claim that too few educators talk pedagese; if they knew more of the specific language of their discipline they might be better able to tell the public something because they would have something to say. Most educators, when talking to the public, use commonplace language, and this tends to convince the public that what the educator is talking about is really nothing very special at all. If a layman can understand a specialist in testing, then anyone can be a specialist, so what is all the fuss about getting more specialists? Are they really specialists at all?

Despite the continued talk about close cooperation between school and community, in practice the cooperation almost always comes from the parents in the community. Again, public relations efforts are expended on encouraging parents to come to school to be told about the good programs schools are carrying out. Room mothers in elementary school help teachers and staff libraries. When it comes to the schools supporting community activities, however, the story is apt to be rather different. As Martin points out, the schools insist on fiscal independence, and are jealous guardians of their political independence.[32] The typical aloofness of school personnel from local governmental activities and political affairs is defended on the basis that schools must be nonpartisan. Thus the public relations programs of schools are bound to run into trouble. You cannot talk cooperation—meaning only that *those others* have to cooperate with *us*, according to *our* rules, and when *we* choose to play—and then expect to be taken seriously.

Basic, however, to the whole pattern of school public relations is that in too many instances neither the public nor the school leaders know really what they want. The major conflicts of values (discussed in Chapter 4) continually interfere with agreement or rational discussion. What Jules Henry refers to as "noise"[33] drowns out the real concerns of public and school. When reading the news stories about schools, or the articles by school personnel, or when hearing their informal discussions,

[32] Roscoe C. Martin, *Government and the Suburban School* (Syracuse: Syracuse University Press, 1962).

[33] Jules Henry, *Culture against Man* (New York: Random House, 1963), Chap. viii.

we are impressed with their lack of clarity regarding their own purposes and values, and with their lack of precision about what they do. Yet to blame the school personnel completely is wrong. The public also lacks clarity about its basic value and goals. And even trying to use the tools of the research scientist to study education, its process, and products, is to try to catch a rainbow and spend the pot of gold at its end.

SUMMARY

School administration is a no man's land of contradictory analyses and confusing practices. Although school organization has been modeled after business and government, schools are a unique kind of institution. This uniqueness, which lies in their function and in their relationship to the public, is not reflected in school organizational patterns. The result is ambiguity and uncertainty about roles and role relationships.

Seeing educational institutions in business terms has resulted in the growth of public relations procedures which are inappropriate to the school and which have not produced notable public support; yet, the effort continues to "sell" the schools to the public. Surely the schools are a significant enough institution to warrant a more searching analysis of its organizational structure and processes, so that in time both may become more appropriate to the function of education.

BIBLIOGRAPHY   175

ASSOCIATION FOR SUPERVISION AND CURRICULUM DEVELOPMENT, *Leadership for Improving Instruction*, 1960 Yearbook. Washington, D.C. Difficulties in achieving adequate supervisory relationships are analyzed.

BROOKOVER, WILLIAM B., *A Sociology of Education*. New York: American Book Company, 1955. The structure of the school is viewed by an educational sociologist.

ETZIONI, AMITAI, ed., *Complex Organizations: A Sociological Reader*. New York: Holt, Rinehart & Winston, Inc., 1962. Excellent selection of readings on a wide range of organizational processes, including Becker's classic on the teacher in the authority system of the schools.

FREEHILL, MAURICE F. AND J. ALAN ROSS, "The Elementary-School Principal—as Others See Him," *Elementary School Journal*, LXI (October 1960), 35-40. Teachers want a principal who provides recognition; parents want an efficient, but kindly, school manager.

GRIEDER, CALVIN, TRUMAN M. PIERCE, AND WILLIAM E. ROSENSTENGEL, *Public School Administration*, 2nd ed. New York: The Ronald Press Company, 1961. Typical of textbooks in this field.

GRIFFITHS, DANIEL E., *Administrative Theory*. New York: Appleton-Century-Crofts, 1959. Succinct summaries of major administrative theories in education, with a critique of the field.

GROSS, NEAL, WARD S. MASON, AND ALEX W. MCEACHERN, *Explorations in Role Analysis: Studies of the School Superintendency Role*. New York: John Wiley & Sons, Inc., 1958. Extensive research study of the school superintendent, with emphasis on the built-in role conflict of this position.

HALPIN, ANDREW W., ed., *Administrative Theory in Education*. Chicago: Midwest Administration Center, 1958. Basic statements on educational administrative theory, suggesting needed new understandings.

————, *The Leadership Behavior of School Superintendents*, Monograph Series, No. 4. Columbus: The Ohio State University, 1956. The superintendent is seen differently by the school board and his staff, and he acts differently toward each.

HARRIS, BEN M., *Supervisory Behavior in Education*. Englewood Cliffs, N. J.: Prentice-Hall, Inc., 1963. A textbook with readings in the area of school supervision.

KOOPMAN, G. ROBERT, ALICE MIEL, AND PAUL J. MISNER, *Democracy in School Administration*. New York: Appleton-Century-Crofts, 1943. An early description with examples, of what democratic school administration might be like. Interesting to read in light of today's school organizational patterns.

MC NASSOR, DONALD, "Barriers and Gateways in School-Community Relationships," *Journal of Educational Sociology*, XXVIII, No. 1 (September 1954), 1-10. Discusses why it is difficult for school and public to understand what the other is talking about, with some suggested remedies.

MERTON, ROBERT K., *Social Theory and Social Structure*, rev. ed., Chaps. 6 and 7. New York: Free Press of Glencoe, Inc., 1957. This discussion of bureaucracy and personality and of the intellectual in bureaucracy could be applied to the schools, although Merton limits his discussion to government and industry.

ROULEAU, JAMES P., *Staff Communication and the Superintendent of Schools*. Washington, D.C.: Washington Area School Study Council, 1963. (Mimeographed.) The difficulties the school superintendent faces in communicating within a large school system.

SEEMAN, MELVIN, *Social Status and Leadership: The Case of the School Executive*, Educational Research Monographs, No. 35. Columbus: The Ohio State University, 1960. The ambiguous position of the school administrator is shown by carefully done sociological research.

WILSON, CHARLES H., *A Teacher Is a Person*. New York: Holt, Rinehart & Winston, Inc., 1956. A school administrator's well written personal record, which provides illuminating insights into the school system.

INDEX

Publications by professors, 119
Public involvement, school problems, 39
Public schools, 61, 64, 69

RAFFERTY, MAX, 148
Reading programs, 79
"Reading" the teacher, 74-75
Record-keeping, high school, 100-101
Regional variations in schools, 58-60, 69
Research grants, 119, 121
Rickover, Admiral, 148
Rural areas
    class differences, 48
    farming, 47
    rural *vs.* city children, 48
Rural schools, 46-49
    curriculum, 48-49
    image of, 46-47

SCHOOL BOARDS, 35-38, 39-40, 55, 154,
    160 (*see also* Administration,
    school)
    board of regents, 122-23
    election of, 35-36, 37, 38
    legal powers of, 38
    policy-making, 37
    role of, 163-64
    rural, 48
    upper-class membership problem, 36-37
School public relations, 172-75
School system (*see* Administration, school)
Science fairs, 97
Science programs, 67, 79, 85, 109, 150-
    51, 164
Secondary school (*see* High school stu-
    dent)
Senior high school (*see* High school stu-
    dent)
Sexton, Patricia C., 37, 38
"Slow" *vs.* "fast" groups, 73
Slum children, 74
Small *vs.* large school, 166
Social studies, 32
Social valuation of children, 6-7, 137
Sociology of education, 80, 148
    defined, 2-3
Sociometric tests, 73
Southern states, education, 59, 60
    desegregation, 59
Speech habits, class influence on, 20-21
State aid, 65
Status system, 161
    college faculty, 118-19
    high school, 89-90, 91-92

Stendler, Celia B., 19
"Studying" the professor, 109-10
Suburban areas, 53, 54
    problems of inhabitants, 50
    segregation by income, 49-50
Suburban schools, 51-52
    curriculum, 51
Subversive teaching, 31-33
Superintendent, 43, 151, 160, 166
    budget-making procedure, 39-40
    education of, 170-71
    evaluation of, 169-72
    salary of, 171
    selection of, 38

TAXES, SCHOOL, 38-39
Teachers, 41, 127-56, 168
    and academic freedom, 30-31, 120, 124
    accreditation of colleges for, 146-47
    authority of, 131-35
    authority of, reorienting the, 133-35
    in big city schools, 55
    in Catholic schools, 63
    certification of, 147
    college, 109-10, 111-12, 115-20, 128,
        140, 151
    colonial times, 36, 150
    conferences with parents, 77-78
    and conforming students, 28
    and creative students, 28
    "democratic" type, 134-35
    demoralizing the, 135-36
    duties of, 128-30
    education of, 68, 134-35
    education of, evaluation, 143-48
    efficiency of, controversy, 148-50
    elementary school, 72-79, 128, 129, 137,
        138, 144, 145
    federal aid, 67
    guilt feelings of, 130
    high school, 85, 89, 92, 94-95, 99-100,
        101, 128, 129, 137, 144, 145
    hostility of parents toward, 132
    and innovation, 9-10
    low pay for, 39
    loyalty oaths for, 31-32
    male, 137, 139, 150
    multiple pressures on, 130
    opinions on training of, 145
    and pressure groups, 40-41
    in private schools, 61, 64
    public image of, 135-38, 140
    pupil counting, 167
    rating of, 151-52
    relations with parents, 132
    relations with principals, 161-63
    relations with students, 132

180